CRIME VICTIMS

University of Liverpool

Withdrawn from stock

Also by Basia Spalek:

ISLAM, CRIME AND CRIMINAL JUSTICE (Willan Publishing, 2002)

Crime Victims

Theory, Policy and Practice

Basia Spalek

Consultant Editor: Jo Campling

First published in 2006 by
PALGRAVE MACMILLAN
Houndmills, Basingstoke, Hampshire RG21 6XS and
175 Fifth Avenue, New York, N.Y. 10010
Companies and representatives throughout the world.

PALGRAVE MACMILLAN is the global academic imprint of the Palgrave Macmillan division of St. Martin's Press, LLC and of Palgrave Macmillan Ltd. Macmillan® is a registered trademark in the United States, United Kingdom and other countries. Palgrave is a registered trademark in the European Union and other countries.

ISBN-13: 978–1–4039–3542–7
ISBN-10: 1–4039–3542–4 paperback

This book is printed on paper suitable for recycling and made from fully managed and sustained forest sources.

A catalogue record for this book is available from the British Library.

A catalog record for this book is available from the Library of Congress.

Library of Congress Cataloging-in-Publication Data

10 9 8 7 6 5 4 3 2 1
15 14 13 12 11 10 09 08 07 06

Printed in China

For my family: Wiktoria and Wincenty Spalek, Marek and Neil

Contents

Acknowledgements

I would like to express my gratitude to David Stephenson, Ann Davis and Jo Campling, for their encouragement and for helping me to put emotions before analysis. Many thanks also to Mike Nellis for strategically placing books and articles in my path, to Bob Matthews for his technical and practical support, and to Salah El-Hassan for his role in helping to develop my research. Finally, I wish to say thank you to all those people who have fired my imagination: Andy Fiol, Andrzej Iwanowski, Mick Keenan, Andy Kowalski, H., Marek, Neil Whitehead and Natassja Smiljanic.

1

Introducing Victimology

Introduction

Within criminal justice sectors around the western world there is considerable, and rising, concern about individuals who are harmed by crime, so that policy makers have implemented a wide range of victim initiatives. For example, victim compensation schemes have been established in the United Kingdom, New Zealand, the United States as well as a wide range of other countries including Austria, Belgium and Canada, and victims' rights legislation has been enacted. These developments reflect broader cultural processes, whereby victimhood has become a topic of fascination amongst members of the general public, as demonstrated by the many books and articles that have been written by, and about, victims, and by the many television programmes that focus on portraying individuals' experiences of cruelty or their emotional or sexual problems.

Perhaps as never before, there is a need for a specific focus on the field of victimology which, according to the International Victimology Website, is:

> The scientific study of the extent, nature and causes of criminal victimisation, its consequences for the persons involved and the reactions thereto by society, in particular the police and the criminal justice system as well as voluntary workers and professional helpers.

This book looks at the theoretical, methodological, policy and practice issues to be found within victimology in order to help gain an in-depth understanding of the critical debates in relation to victimisation. A key argument developed throughout the book is that victimology as a subject area is rather limited, both conceptually and methodologically. Victimological work must become both broader in its scope and also more specific in documenting individuals' experiences, so that a wider range of victims are captured and a more nuanced approach to the study of victimisation is pursued, one that includes specificities of experience, which includes a focus upon the significant level of diversity to be found amongst

<u>victims.</u> First, brief summaries of the individual chapters are provided, and this is then followed by a discussion of key victimological terms.

Chapter summaries

Chapter 2 highlights the increasing concern with which victims' issues have been viewed by policy makers over the last forty years or so. The concern shown towards the victims of crime reflects wider cultural processes occurring in late modern society whereby people look to establish victim identities that can make them feel, at least briefly, that they are part of a wider 'community' of victims, due to the loss of a sense of 'belongingness' brought about by social and economic changes (Furedi, 1997; Howarth and Rock, 2000). Some writers view the increasing numbers of people claiming victim status as damaging, having the effect of encouraging people to view themselves in a passive way, as individuals against whom some harm has occurred (Sykes, 1992; Furedi, 1998). Nevertheless, this position does not differentiate between people's reactions as individualised responses to victimisation, victim identities as floating and ungrounded, and people's reactions as belonging to, and being expressed within, the broader, 'more solid', group collectivities that they may belong to. Whilst the former type of response might be viewed as disempowering victims, since reactions to crime are located firmly within the individual, and the 'we feeling' that people get from identifying themselves as victims is likely to be transitory and fleeting and easily discarded, the latter response might be viewed from a perspective of empowerment, since reactions to crime might be embedded within 'communities' sharing common identities based on race, faith, gender and so forth, and so might include an acknowledgement of, and be directed at, broader social systems of repression, so that victims might seek ways of challenging and changing these. Chapter 2 essentially situates developments in victim policy within a wider social, cultural and economic context.

Chapter 3 takes a detailed look at the sub-discipline victimology. The chapter highlights the many different victimological theoretical traditions that exist, including positivist, radical, feminist and critical victimologies. Debates emerging from these different perspectives include the extent to which victims should be held responsible for their plight, the scope of the label 'victim' and what types of harm should be considered to constitute a form of victimisation. When examining feminist perspectives on victimisation, it is argued that although feminist work has made a substantial contribution to documenting and understanding violence committed against women and children, a white, Eurocentric perspective has, however, underpinned much feminist work, so that Black[1] women's experiences have been overlooked. Indeed, a 'white perspective' has underpinned much victimological research, and so this is a core theme running throughout this book.

Chapter 4 examines the many different research approaches that have been used to document victimisation. It is argued that survey-based techniques are very popular tools, and that national crime surveys are now a commonplace feature of modern life. However, these have a number of important limitations, particularly in relation to diversity issues. Data produced by international and national crime surveys tend to group individuals from a diverse range of different communities together. The ethnic classifications that are used, for instance, and then the ways in which data is analysed and presented, means that significant differences between different communities are overlooked. Also, crime surveys tend to exclude white-collar victims, as well as child victims and disabled people who may be victims. Moreover, crime survey findings tend to be presented in a largely mathematical, detached manner, so that the data is presented in such a way as to appeal to reason rather than emotion. It would appear that the generic type of national and international crime survey belongs to a broader social scientific tradition that values 'objectivity' and 'rationality' over emotionality (Bendelow and Williams, 1998). It might be argued that generic crime surveys objectify research participants, resulting in work that fails to convey the sense of humanity and human suffering that is often at stake. Action groups, on the other hand, campaigning for the greater recognition of rights for gay, disabled or faith communities for example, tend to present the data obtained from the victim surveys that they undertake in such a way so as to evoke an emotional response in the wider audience. Emotionality is a concept that is developed throughout the book.

Chapter 5 presents the results of studies that have explored the process of victimisation. It appears that different types of crime, including rape, physical and sexual assault, robbery, burglary and incest, impact upon the victim in a multitude of ways – psychologically, emotionally, behaviourally, financially and physically. Whilst the differences between victims are often acknowledged, however, these have been insufficiently explored or addressed. By abstracting the categories of identity, research often fails to articulate what an experience of victimisation actually means to a person in terms of their race, gender, class (and so forth) subject positions, and so studies tend to homogenise victims and their reactions. Within the literature there seems to be an assumption that the experience of victimisation is generally the same for all people, regardless of significant differences in individuals' subject positions. This means that for individuals whose self-identities occupy positions that lie outside of the dominant norms around which the general experience of victimisation is understood, there is not much knowledge about, nor awareness of, their particular experiences nor how best to develop policy and practice around their specific needs. For instance, male victims have generally generated little interest from researchers, policy makers and agents of the criminal justice system. At the same time, apart from the significant work that has been undertaken in relation to the impacts of racist violence, research has not adequately looked at the experiences of minority ethnic communities for other forms of victimisation, thereby serving to marginalise minority voices from mainstream analyses of the process of being a victim. The argument that individuals' 'belief in a just world' is shattered as a result of becoming victimised may apply predominantly to people who have property, wealth or power (Furnham, 1991), and so marginalised communities may not necessarily experience victimisation in this way. When studying the victimising experiences of minority ethnic women, critical black feminists have introduced the concept of 'spirit injury' in order to explain and to try to understand the full impact of racism and sexism upon women's lives (Davis, 1997; Williams, 1997). An acknowledgement of spirit injury with respect to victimisation has some important implications when providing support to the victims of crime, since therapies aimed at a more spiritual level, such as the use of alternative forms of healing for example, might be more appropriate in some cases. Individuals' religious affiliations and beliefs should also be increasingly acknowledged when documenting experiences of victimisation, as religion can act as an important support mechanism.

Chapter 6 examines some of the main services developed to help meet victims' emotional, practical, financial, psychological and social needs. In Britain, these include the Criminal Injuries Compensation Scheme, Victim Support, and services linked to the Victims' Charters of 1990 and 1996, and the Victims' Code 2004. These initiatives form part of a broader official victims' movement, largely funded by the central government, which can be characterised as being underpinned by the notion of a 'deserving' victim, who is 'innocent' and distinct from the offender. As such, those victims who occupy 'non-ideal' victim status, either because of the type of crime that they have experienced or as a result of their socio-economic characteristics, do not necessarily receive adequate support. Mainstream victim services are also secular in nature, which means that people's religious and spiritual needs are not addressed. This is likely to have a profound impact upon uptake of service delivery by minority ethnic communities, since research shows that religious affiliation is a much more fundamental aspect of the self-identity of minority ethnic groups when compared to many White Christians (O'Beirne, 2004: 18). It is also important to note that within the general population, increasing numbers of people are seeking help from, and trying out, different forms of spirituality (McManus, 2001: 3).

Chapter 7 addresses the question of whether the harms and traumas suffered by victims can be improved via a greater emphasis upon the development of victims' rights. It is argued that enhancing victims' rights through existing legislative mechanisms will not necessarily lead to better and more appropriate responses to victims' needs. First, human rights legislation is somewhat idealistic, with there being a significant difference between the rights that new legislation is said to protect and the actual protection that it affords. As clearly demonstrated by the anti-terror legislation implemented in the United Kingdom in 2001, which involved suspending British obligations to the European Convention on Human Rights, human rights can be challenged and removed by political will, thereby illustrating their fragility (Smiljanic, 2002). At the same time, increasing victims' rights can have negative consequences for offenders because this may involve curtailing offenders' rights. The chapter also critically explores the ways in which victims' needs have been framed and used by government. It is argued that victims' emotional reactions to the harms that they have experienced have been translated into individual need using the discourses of consumerism and active citizenship. This is part of a broader movement towards the 'individualization of emotionality' that can be found in contemporary western societies (Karstedt, 2002: 304), whereby emotions are constructed as individual reactions, rather than as collective displays of group identity, to social and political events. This serves to disempower victims, so that victims' needs have been co-opted by government in order to pursue broader goals linked to the development and operation of more efficient systems of criminal justice, acting as disciplinary mechanisms on agencies of the criminal justice system.

Chapter 8 examines the unofficial victims' movement, which constitutes a powerful form of resistance against the ever-present movement towards the individualisation of victims' pain because this bears witness to injustices arising from wider social structures of oppression. Some of the action groups that belong to the unofficial victims' movement make up a broader social movement that is underpinned by identities in relation to race, gender, faith, disability and so forth, whose activities are aimed at achieving common political and social goals. This illustrates that people do not necessarily see themselves as individual victims, but rather, they can see themselves as being connected to others, as well as to broader social systems of inequality. The chapter examines white-collar victimisation, hate crime, and institutional violence, because these three areas comprise instances of victimisation that have traditionally been excluded from social and political debates about the 'crime problem'. Also, these areas clearly show how wider social structures can create, and/or impact upon, experiences of victimisation; and the cases used in this chapter also highlight the centrality of identity issues when conceptualising the developments within the unofficial victims' movement.

Chapter 9 sets out some new areas of research for victimological study. It is argued that the foci of enquiry within victimology are somewhat limited, due in part to the predominance of mainstream understandings of crime as the lens through which to view victimisation, and also due to an insufficient consideration of the level of diversity to be found between individual victims. This narrow focus has important implications, not only in terms of the development of the sub-discipline of victimology itself, but also in terms of policy developments and practice issues for individuals harmed by both criminal and non-criminal events. This chapter stresses that a particular focus upon non-traditional forms of victimisation should be pursued, as this may lead not only to the development of wide-ranging initiatives aimed at helping a broader range of victims, but also, this can lead to many important theoretical and methodological developments, developments that are directly relevant for victimology as a field of study. At the same time, identity issues are extremely relevant. The emergence of new social movements (e.g., the feminist movement) has led to demands for a recognition, or greater recognition, of victim status, as well as to the implementation of wide-ranging victim policies and initiatives. Also, the emergence of new identities has significant methodological implications. For instance, in light of the emergence of Muslim identities, as documented by social scientists, how can research strategies become more inclusive of these, so that Muslims' experiences and perspectives are adequately researched and understood, especially when both national and local crime surveys have traditionally used the variables of gender, ethnicity and age, and not religion, to inform the sampling process?

Social scientists need to explore more fully the sense of 'belongingness' that individuals gain from their identification with a particular victim action group, which may be a part of a broader group collectivity. By giving victims' identities a central position within work examining victimisation, this may be a good way of introducing greater diversity and specificity of experience within analyses of the process of victimisation for a broad range of crimes. Connected to this point, the notions of religiosity and spirituality need to increasingly feature in victimological work, since these may enhance a person's ability to cope with crime. Another area that requires greater focus is that of emotionality. Work with victims involves asking people to talk about their experiences of suffering, and emotions are very much a part of any study, and yet researchers have often insufficiently addressed this issue when writing up accounts of their work. A focus upon emotionality can lead to work that is more reflective and more open to the human meaning of victimisation, in a way that research participants are not objectified, but rather, their humanity comes through the work more powerfully. Importantly, being emotionally affected by research participants does not necessarily mean the work becomes 'biased'. The emotions that a researcher experiences whilst carrying out a piece of work can be used to reveal hidden decision-making processes which can be linked to power hierarchies inherent in research.

Chapter 10 comprises a conclusion. The key themes that have arisen from the discussions within the separate chapters are highlighted, and some policy and practice implications are discussed. It is argued that taking into consideration differences between victims is one of the most significant challenges facing social scientists.

Now that a summary of the book chapters has been presented, key victimological terms are introduced, in order to help acquaint the reader with the subject matter.

Victimology

There is some discrepancy over who first coined the term 'victimology'. According to Van Dijk (1997), victimology was first mentioned by Mendelsohn in 1947, when he presented a paper at a congress in Bucharest. However, according to Fattah (1992), 'victimology' was first phrased by an American psychiatrist, Frederick Wertham, in 1949, in relation to murder. Wertham (1949) argued that whilst the abnormal psychology of the murderer had been extensively discussed, the victim's vulnerability had largely been forgotten, yet to further an understanding of the murderer a greater focus upon the victim was needed, in terms of a science of victimology.

Victimology is often referred to as a 'sub-discipline' (Miers, 1989; Mawby and Walklate, 1994) because victim issues apply to a broad range of subjects, and researchers from a variety of backgrounds, such as psychiatry, psychology, law and social work, write about victimisation. But it can be argued that criminologists have had the greatest influence over victimology, since a significant proportion of the work that has focused on victim issues has been carried out by criminologists, while the development of national and local crime surveys has led to the burgeoning of research on criminal victimisation matters (Sparks *et al.*, 1977; Hough and Mayhew, 1983; Hanmer and Saunders, 1984; Hall, 1985; Jones *et al.*, 1986).

Every three years an International Symposium on Victimology is held, the first being organised in Israel in 1973, although whether the individuals attending these symposia would identify themselves as victimologists is a moot point. These symposia are closely related to the activities of the World Society of Victimology, which was founded in 1979 in Munster (Van Dijk, 1997). Some of the debates that have taken place at the symposia have been about the need for an independent discipline, and the issue of what the scope of victimology should be has been raised. One position, called penal victimology by Van Dijk (1997), is that victimology should focus upon criminal victimisation. Generally, this approach involves the utilisation of scientific methods of analysis, and has therefore been called scientific victimology by Cressey (1986). Other researchers, however, advocate the inclusion of a broader range of experiences of victimisation, such as the harms incurred by the victims of natural disasters or accidents. Indeed, the United Nations Declaration on the Basic Principles of Justice for Victims of Crime and Abuse of Power adopts a broad understanding of victimhood, since 'victim' is taken to mean a person who suffers physical, mental or emotional harm or injury, a person who experiences economic loss or the violation of their fundamental rights as a result of criminal activity and the criminal abuse of power. Van Dijk (1997) has labelled this latter approach as general victimology, however, it has also been categorised as humanistic victimology by Cressey (1986) when, at the fifth International Symposium in 1985, he argued that this victimological strand had been pursued by activists who had politicised the field of victimology, having provided no valid research to back up their claims. According to Cressey (1986), scientific victimologists must reclaim victimology, so that any assertions made are backed up by empirical research. More recently, Elias (1994) claimed that although much important victimological work has been carried out, victimology remains politically and conceptually restricted within a narrow focus. This is surprising when one considers the myriad meanings associated with the term 'victim', as discussed later, suggesting that a science of the victim should push through analytical boundaries and create novel ways of understanding victimisation.

Victim definitions

Originally, the word 'victim' was used within a specific context, in relation to the ritual practise of sacrifice as performed in ancient civilisations or cultures, when the life of a person or animal was taken in order to please a god (Karmen, 1990). Reflecting that women were frequently sacrificed (Walklate, 2002), the term 'victim' is female in many languages where nouns are gendered, for example, in Spanish the term is 'la victima' and in French it is 'la victime'. But the concept of 'victim as sacrifice' did not necessarily include notions of pain or suffering on behalf of the individual who was killed, and it wasn't until the nineteenth century that victimhood came to encapsulate a broader range of meanings, to include experiences of harm or injury (Furedi, 1997; Burnley *et al.*, 1998). Today, the word 'victim' is used in many different contexts, including disease, war, natural disasters and crime (Furedi, 1997; Burnley *et al.*, 1998), as the following Oxford English Dictionary definitions suggest:

A victim is:

a person injured or killed as a result of an event or circumstance.
a person or thing injured or destroyed in pursuit of an object or in gratification of a passion etc. (e.g. the victim of their ruthless ambition).
a prey, a dupe (e.g. fell victim to a confidence trick).
a living creature sacrificed to a deity or in a religious rite.

In everyday life, however, victim status is much more complicated than these descriptions would suggest, since it depends upon wider historical, social and cultural processes and their relationship to human action. At particular points in time, victimhood will become associated with particular types of characteristics, and these may be valued by wider society or they may be the basis around which persons labelled as victims are stigmatised. These factors will influence how individual victims perceive themselves, influencing the extent to which individuals accept the label 'victim', as well as affecting the kind of help they receive. It is also important to note that a criminal incident often affects more than one person, and so multiple victims are more commonly created rather than single victims (Young, 2000).

In some cases, individuals will be labelled 'victims' in the wider social arena even though they do not necessarily view themselves in that way. Indeed, people may actively oppose a label that they feel has been imposed upon them. If the stereotype of victim as 'passive' and 'helpless' is perpetuated in dominant representations of victimhood, during a time when individual strength is valued in society, then individuals may not situate themselves in terms of victimhood, despite the harms experienced, due to their distaste for the label 'victim' and the kinds of stereotypes that it elicits. The term may also help to stimulate the unpleasant feelings experienced in the process of being victimised, and so the victim label may be rejected (Lamb, 1999). At the same time, other aspects of individuals' identities, such as their gender, race or class, are likely to influence whether or not they embrace victimhood as an aspect of their self-identity. Men may particularly resist calling themselves victims, due to the threat that notions of passivity and helplessness may have for their masculinity, when the dominant representations of manliness valued in western society appear to include men as 'being able to look after themselves and their families', as men who are 'strong' and 'resilient'. This is not to suggest, however, that all men will reject the victim label, since some will be open to offers of help and support, and some will have aspects of their self-identity that might make them feel vulnerable, linked to their age, race or sexuality (Newburn and Stanko, 1994).

Victims may also not recognise that their experiences constitute victimisation. Lamb (1999) presents the case of a woman who, as a child, had been abused by her grandfather and did not consider this to be abuse until she entered therapy as an adult and was asked to recall what had happened. Pain and suffering may be seen as an integral part of life and so not identified as victimisation. This can be seen in some people who hold a strong religious belief, where this involves a perception that human trials are a part of life and so present opportunities for spiritual and emotional growth (Spalek, 2002). Furthermore, the 'victim' label may be rejected by some individuals because victimhood is not considered to be the defining lens through which to view their experiences. An abusive relationship may also include feelings of love and warmth between the abuser and the abused, and individuals may choose to interpret their experiences in light of these feelings, as a way of gaining a sense of control over the abuse (Lamb, 1999).

Alternatively, some individuals may strive for recognition of a specific victim status, believing that this may help them achieve justice or other financial or psychological goals. Examples of this include victimisation by white-collar deviance, since white-collar offences occupy an ambiguous status within society, so that they may not be viewed as criminal within broader social and political circles (Nelken, 1994). As a result, there are many instances where victims have grouped together to highlight the devastating consequences of white-collar deviance, and to campaign for more effective responses to their plight. Struggles to achieve victim status can also be seen in court cases, where an individual has been charged with committing a certain crime but maintains that the reason why s/he acted in this way is due to their victimisation. This can occur in trials involving women who have killed their husbands or partners, whose defence is that they were abused, the so-called 'battered women's syndrome'. This strategy can also be used by the defence counsel of cases where young people have killed their parents, by means of post-traumatic stress disorder to explain the reasons for the violence that took place (Burnley *et al.*, 1998). In Britain, during the trial of serial killer Rose West, both the defence and prosecution were involved in elaborate constructions of victimhood in order to help sway the jury. The defence unsuccessfully portrayed Rose West as a victim of a domineering, abusive husband, whilst the prosecution, in order to help secure a guilty verdict, portrayed West as an aggressive attacker who subjected the passive, innocent victims to sexual and physical violence (Winter, 2002). These kinds of court cases illustrate the flexibility of the categories 'victim' and 'offender' and the overlap between them, and yet little attention has been paid by researchers to this issue (Farrall and Maltby, 2003).

Victim passivity/victim agency

There is much debate about whether victimhood constitutes passivity, or whether human agency is also an important aspect of being a victim. Certainly, as discussed earlier, some individuals may be deterred from defining themselves as victims as a result of a perceived stigma attached to the notion of passivity. Some writers argue that the medicalisation of victims, particularly female victims, whereby a psychological or physical disorder is ascribed to explain their reactions, objectifies the body and sustains the notion of a helpless victim who has been overcome by an illness (Lamb, 1999). This is also problematic in terms of victims' responsibility. In other words, if victimisation is viewed as passivity, how can we encourage individual victims to take some responsibility over their subsequent actions, particularly when those actions involve violence and harms being committed against others?

Victims as survivors

A 'survivor' rather than 'victim' identity has been proposed, one which acknowledges active resistance on behalf of the victim, thereby challenging idealised notions of victim passivity (Williams, 1999a; Lamb, 1999; Walklate, 2002). This approach has been largely promoted by feminists, and so resistance against patriarchal oppression in general, and male aggression in particular, has been stressed. Also, women are viewed in literal terms as having survived the violence because they haven't been killed. A perceived benefit to this approach is that it is seen to be empowering victims, since victims' agency is highlighted. However, it can also be unhelpful, since individuals can be put under pressure to be a certain kind of victim, an idealised hero who has triumphed over adverse circumstances, when they may not feel that this has been their experience of victimisation so far. Moreover, the 'victim as survivor' stance may influence practitioners' perceptions, so that when working with victims this image of victimhood is idealised such that individual victims are encouraged to behave in a way consistent with survival, and penalised if they are perceived to remain as 'passive victims' for too long (Williams, 1999a). In effect, 'victim' 'survivor' is an artificial dichotomy. In situations of ongoing abuse, individuals are likely to be both victims and survivors, so that in some instances they behave in a way that suggests resistance, but in other instances they may ignore or accept the harms that are being committed against them (Lamb, 1999). Also, victims and survivors can be both active and passive (Walklate, 2002). In situations where a victim predominantly displays passivity and other 'weak' characteristics such as 'helplessness' or 'fragility', they may be doing so 'on purpose', with a specific intention in mind. A study of rape victims going to court by Konradi (1996), for example, shows that they were engaged in 'appearance management' so as to increase the likelihood of a conviction. This involved victims portraying themselves in culturally appropriate ways, as 'innocent' and 'polite', being overcome by tears when asked to talk about their experiences. Clearly, these women were consciously acting out a particular victim identity, even though the outward impression that was created was largely of a passive victim.

Secondary victimisation

The notion of 'secondary victimisation' has also been introduced in relation to crime victims. Secondary victimisation has been conceptualised as 'the inadequate treatment of victims by the criminal justice system' and may involve insensitive responses by the police or other criminal justice agencies (Maguire and Pointing, 1988: 11). Much research has been conducted looking at people's experiences of the criminal justice system, which may constitute their secondary victimisation, in terms of the police response to victims and the impact of court procedures on victimisation. Recognition amongst agencies of the criminal justice system that the reporting and prosecution of crime requires the victim has acted as a 'bargaining tool' (Zedner, 1994: 1230) in order to gain greater recognition of victims' needs.

Repeat victimisation

The idea of repeat victimisation has emerged from the collection of empirical evidence that shows that a good predictor of future victimisation is having already been a victim. For example, research has found that robbery victims stand a nine times greater chance of victimisation than individuals who have never been victimised, while sexual assault victims have a 35 times greater chance of being victimised than persons who have never been victimised. Households in Britain, once burgled, are re-burgled at four times the rate of unburgled houses (Forrester *et al.*, 1988: 22). Also the risk of revictimisation is greatest in the period soon after the victimisation for domestic violence, burglary, auto crimes and retail crimes (Farrell and Pease, 1993). Research and theories about repeat victimisation have practical implications for crime prevention strategies, compatible with reducing opportunities for crime.

Primary/secondary/tertiary victims

Further words used in relation to victimisation are that of 'direct' and 'indirect' victims, or primary, secondary and tertiary victims. Primary victims are those who experience the harm directly, whereas secondary victims can be considered to be those individuals who are indirectly harmed, as in the case of the significant others of murder or rape victims. Tertiary victims include a wider circle of people who may be affected by a particularly shocking event, such as the rescue and medical personnel involved in some kind of traumatic incident. Following the bombing of the Alfred P. Murrah Federal Building in Oklahoma City on 19 April 1995, killing 168 people, the US Department of Justice Office for Victims of Crime referred to tertiary victims as social service and mental health professionals, volunteers, emergency personnel, friends and colleagues, legal and medical personnel, victim advocates, clergy, schoolteachers and children whose world beliefs were shattered, jurors, bomb experts and construction workers.

Whilst the terms 'primary', 'secondary' and 'tertiary' suggest that there is some sort of hierarchy in the level of suffering experienced, it cannot be assumed that secondary and tertiary victims necessarily suffer less trauma than primary victims, since secondary and tertiary victims can also face significant physical, psychological and emotional pain. For example, during the Balkans conflict in the 1990s, thousands of women were raped in what was a weapon used in the war of ethnic cleansing. Many of the children born out of the rapes are orphans, having been rejected at birth, and experiencing severe physical, emotional and psychological deprivations. Clearly, the victimisation of one generation of people can be passed down to their direct descendants. The two World Wars of the twentieth century have involved the displacement, suffering and deaths of tens of millions of people. Trauma on such a large scale will be re-lived and re-experienced by many generations to come. Large-scale atrocities shape the psyche of an entire nation of people, and influence how they and their children relate to, and experience, the world around them. This is why, over sixty years since the end of the Second World War, people continue to remember and mark the pain and suffering that took place.

Conclusion

Clearly, victimology is a very broad research field, and the process of victimisation elicits many important issues. Chapter 2 provides a general overview of the main developments in victim policy that have taken place across the western world, situating them within a wider cultural, social and political context.

2

Victimhood, Late Modernity and Criminal Justice

Introduction

It has been argued that the cult of victimhood pervades contemporary western society (Furedi, 1997). Hundreds of books and articles have been written by, and about, the direct and indirect victims of events such as murder, rape, incest, kidnapping and war, with Dave Pelzer's best-selling novel, *A Child Called It*, which details a history of childhood abuse, perhaps epitomising our fascination with human suffering. Talk shows, such as Kilroy, Oprah, Trisha, Vanessa, the Jerry Springer show and Ricki Lake, constitute a form of victim entertainment, whereby the individuals taking part in these shows relay, in graphic detail, their experiences of cruelty or their emotional and sexual problems (Hume, 1998; Rock, 2002). Media careers have also either been launched on the basis of victimhood, or have been significantly enhanced by disclosures of victimisation. For example, media personality Ulrika Jonsson wrote her autobiography, *Honest*, which was released in 2003, and in this she revealed that she had been raped by an unnamed television presenter, thereby boosting the book's sales through the increased publicity that this allegation had generated. News stories are increasingly being organised around a media created 'televictim', whereby human-interest stories, which often involve experiences of suffering, are used as the vehicle through which major news events are covered and given meaning (Hume, 1998).

The predominance of victim issues in contemporary western society, and the increasing importance with which victims' experiences are viewed, can be clearly seen in the criminal justice arena, whereby the individuals harmed by crime have, over the last 30 years, become a central concern to policy makers, as evidenced by the wide range of victim initiatives in place and the large amount of victim legislation. Underpinning these developments are particular constructions of victimhood that can be linked to deeper societal processes. These processes create particular, 'idealised'

14

notions of victimhood which are then re-produced and mass marketed in media, social and criminal justice policy arenas, influencing the ways in which victims are represented, and creating norms around which victim behaviour and emotion is managed and morally judged.

This chapter aims to document the most significant developments in victim policy, particularly focussing upon Britain, the United States, Australia and Canada. Particular attention is paid to the construction of victim identities in contemporary western, or late modern society, as this will lead to a more nuanced understanding of the various victim-related initiatives being implemented. First of all, a brief historical account is given of the nature of the traditional role of the victim in criminal justice, as set out below.

Victims and criminal justice: an historical account

Historically, victims have played a central role in bringing offenders to justice. In the Middle Ages victims were responsible for gaining redress for the harms committed against them, which often involved some form of restitution by the offender (Doerner and Lab, 1995; Johnstone, 2002). Of course, this system was subject to biases according to how much power an individual held, so that the poor were substantially disadvantaged as both victims and offenders (Mawby and Walklate, 1994). This structure of justice slowly began to change as the Crown gained control of the compensation provided by offenders, which increasingly was given in the form of fines. Industrialisation also played a significant part, since the Industrial Revolution created larger, urbanised communities, so that the bonds between people became less personal, and so attention was rapidly focussed upon punishing the offender rather than restoring the victim (Doerner and Lab, 1995). At the same time, the development of the 'new' police in the nineteenth century in England and Wales led to the situation whereby police officers were increasingly responsible for gathering evidence against offenders (Mawby and Walklate, 1994). This preoccupation with offenders influenced the ways in which the criminal justice system developed, and as a consequence an adversarial system emerged. Throughout the nineteenth century, this was then imposed upon British colonies like Australia and America, and native forms of conflict resolution, involving notions of restorative justice, were repressed (Johnstone, 2002). The adversarial form of justice that developed led to the marginalisation of the victim, since their significance under this system was only as a witness to an alleged crime, a crime that was regarded as having been committed against the state. This meant that under the adversarial system of justice, the needs of the victim were largely forgotten, that is, until the rise of a 'victims' movement', the beginnings of which can be detected in the early 1960s, which involved the implementation of a myriad of victim initiatives.

State responses to victimisation

Victim policy has been rapidly instigated by governments across the western world, particularly in the last 30 years. A wide array of victim legislation has been implemented and financial, practical and emotional support has been provided to the victims of crime. It has been estimated that in the United States alone, several thousand pages of victim-related legislation have been enacted during this period (Sebba, 2001: 27). The first initiatives to be established dealt with the financial compensation of the victims of crime, with the world's first victim compensation legislation being passed in New Zealand in 1963. The world's first compensation scheme was established in England in 1964, called the Criminal Injuries Compensation Scheme, the first crime victim compensation programme in the United States was established in California in 1965, whilst the first Australian compensation scheme was set up in New South Wales in 1967 (Cook, David and Grant, 1999: 83). State compensation schemes are now in operation in a large number of countries, including Austria, Belgium, Canada, Denmark, Germany, Finland, France, Ireland, Luxembourg, the Netherlands, Northern Ireland, Norway, Poland, Sweden and the United States (Maguire and Shapland, 1997: 218).

National crime surveys have been implemented across the world, measuring (amongst other things) the extent and nature of victimisation. The very first survey was conducted in the United States following the urban riots that broke out in the 1960s across a wide range of cities. The threat that these riots posed to the stability of the American way of life led to the development of the President's Crime Commission in 1967, and studies carried out for this involved the very first crime surveys. The national crime survey then became a permanent feature of American public policy in 1972 (Rock, 2002). The principal victimisation survey in Canada is the personal risk survey contained in the General Social Survey (GSS). The data from this survey have added considerably to knowledge of crime patterns in Canada. In Australia, the Australian Bureau of Statistics conducts Crime and Safety Surveys at irregular intervals. These provide information on reported and unreported crime as well as the socio-economic characteristics of the victims (Cook *et al.*, 1999). In Britain the first British Crime Survey was carried out in 1981 and this is now done on a yearly basis. An International Crime Victim Survey (ICVS) is also implemented approximately every four years. This looks at respondents' experiences with crime, policing, crime prevention and feelings of unsafety. Surveys have been carried out in over fifty countries since 1989, including the developing world and countries in transition (Mayhew, 2000).

Recognition of victims' needs has further developed along an international footing, beginning with the Council of Europe, which in 1983, 1985 and 1987 put together a series of recommendations for victims, including state compensation and assistance (Maguire and Shapland, 1997). In 2002, the European Union's Council Framework Decision on the Standing of Victims in Criminal Proceedings came into force. This aims to ensure that all EU member countries provide certain minimum standards of help for the victims of crime (Victim Support, 2002: 5). The United Nations has also focussed upon victims, through the publication of the United Nations Declaration of Basic Principles of Justice for Victims of Crime and Abuse of Power in 1985, and then later with the publication of a United Nations Handbook on Justice for Victims in 1999. These developments have encouraged governments across the world to introduce initiatives aimed at relieving victims' plight. Criminal justice systems can lead to the 'secondary victimisation' of victims due to their inappropriate treatment and support. As a result, changes have been implemented in a wide variety of criminal justice agencies across a large number of countries, those following adversarial, as well as those countries adopting inquisitorial, systems of justice, significantly influencing victims' experiences of the police, the courts and their influence over the sentencing and punishment of offenders. For example, Victim Impact Statements have been introduced in many criminal justice jurisdictions, enabling victims to explain how the crime that has been committed has affected them personally. In some countries, like the United States, Victim Impact Statements can be made to the judge prior to sentencing and also at parole board hearings before the release of the offender (Garland, 2001).

Politicians have realised the political gain that can be achieved through claiming their support for victims by declaring the implementation of victims' rights. However, the extent to which these are legally enforceable, and the degree with which these signal a real benefit for victims, is questionable. In the United States, the first Federal victims' rights legislation was enacted via the Victim and Witness Protection Act of 1982. Other legislation soon followed, including the Victims of Crime Act 1984, the Victims Rights and Restitution Act 1990, the Violent Crime and Law Enforcement Act 1994 and the Victims Rights Clarification Act 1997 (US Department of Justice, 2000). The first Australian state to pass a victim's bill of rights was South Australia, when in 1985 the rights of victims of crime were listed in the Victims of Crime Bill (Cook et al., 1999). Other states have since followed suit, for example, New South Wales has a Charter of Victims Rights, established by the Victims Rights Act 1996. In Canada the Criminal Code sets out victims' rights, which include the rights to safety, security and privacy (Department of Justice Canada, 2003). In Britain the first Victim's Charter was published in 1990, however, this created no new rights for victims nor did it offer any mechanisms through which to enforce their existing rights (Williams, 1999a). A second Victim's Charter was issued in 1996 setting out twenty-seven standards of service that victims can expect to receive from the criminal justice system (Home Office Communication Directorate, 2001).

Many governmental and private, non-profit seeking agencies have developed, whose remit is to deal specifically with victim issues. In Australia, victim services have been formed on a state rather than national basis because crime has been viewed as being an issue for state governments rather than the Federal Government (Cook *et al.*, 1999). The state of Victoria was the site of the original Victims of Crime Assistance League (VOCAL) in 1980, which now operates across Australia (Cook *et al.*, 1999). Other Australian victim support services include the Victims of Crime Bureau, its objectives being to provide support and referral services to victims and to coordinate services to victims. Witness assistance services are also provided. In the United States, the Office for Victims of Crime is an agency of the US Department of Justice, administering federal funds for victim support services, as well as providing training to professionals who work with victims, and developing projects that enhance victims' rights. Within the Office for Victims of Crime there is a Terrorism and International Victims Unit, which is responsible for developing programmes and initiatives for assistance to victims of terrorism and to victims of trans-national crime like the trafficking of children. Another important victim agency in the United States is that of the National Organization for Victim Assistance (NOVA). This is a private, non-profit organisation of victim and witness assistance programmes and practitioners, criminal justice agencies and professionals. NOVA has helped to expand victim compensation programmes, and has helped to draft and ensure the passage of various laws to assist victims. In Canada, the Canadian Resource Centre for Victims of Crime was set up in 1993, this being a non-profit victim advocacy group. In Britain, the main national organisation campaigning on behalf of victims, as well as providing support to them, is Victim Support. This offers help to the victims of crime via a local network of victim support schemes; it also operates a Witness Service to provide support and information about court processes to witnesses, victims and their families, and operates a Victim Support telephone line. European and worldwide links are increasingly being made between the different victim organisations based in different countries, through which information can be shared and policies can be formulated. For example, in 1990, the European Forum for Victim Services was set up to promote the development of effective services for victims of crime throughout Europe, and to promote their rights in their involvement with the criminal justice process. This consisted of a coalition of national victim organisations such as the UK based Victim Support.

Late modernity and claims for victim status

The focus upon victim issues within criminal justice jurisdictions reflects wider social change. Contemporary western society is at a stage of late, or post modernity, where the human condition is increasingly characterised as being in a state of anxiety. Traditional social affiliations, based on family or social class, have been eroded, as evidenced by, for example, the reduction in union and party political membership (Bauman, 2004; Furedi, 1997). Rising divorce rates also mean that people are increasingly likely to live alone (James, 1997). At the same time, the reduction of the primary labour market and tenured secure employment, and the expansion of insecure employment, has led to an increasingly mobile labour force, thereby dislocating people from their local communities (Furedi, 1997; Young, 1999). At the heart of these social and economic transformations is the anxiety that comes with the loss of a sense of 'belongingness', so that people look to find or establish new identities, which can, at least for a brief moment, make them feel that they are part of a 'wider community', whilst continuing to be constantly 'on the move' (Bauman, 2004).

Whereas suffering has always been a part of human existence, what is so marked in today's society is that rising numbers of people are attaching the victim label to their own experiences (Furedi, 1997; Howarth and Rock, 2000). Some writers view the increase in the numbers of people claiming victim status as damaging, as being part of a 'culture of complaint', driven by claims for financial compensation, and having the effect of encouraging people to view themselves in a passive way, as individuals against whom some harm has been inflicted (Sykes, 1992; Furedi, 1998):

> The celebration of the victim identity represents an important statement about the human condition. It regards human action with suspicion. It presupposes that human beings can do very little to influence their destiny. They are the objects rather than the subjects of their destiny. Consequently the human experience is defined not by what people do but by what is done to them. The world of the victim is one where individuals exist in a continuous passive relationship to their experience (Furedi, 1998: 84).

Nevertheless, this position does not differentiate between people's reactions as individualised responses to victimisation, victim identities as floating and ungrounded, and people's reactions as belonging to, and being expressed within, the broader, 'more solid' group collectivities that they may belong to. Although the former type of response might be seen as disempowering victims, since reactions to crime are located firmly within the individual, and the 'we feeling' that people get from identifying themselves as victims is likely to be transitory and fleeting and easily discarded (Bauman, 2004), the latter response might be viewed from a perspective of empowerment, since reactions to crime might be embedded within 'communities' sharing common identities based on race, class, gender and others, and so might include an acknowledgement of, and be directed at, broader social systems of repression, so that victims might seek ways of challenging and changing these. Essentially, we need to differentiate between different types of victims' movements and locate victims' responses within these, as the following sections elucidate further.

Victims' movements

First, it is important to articulate what is meant by the phrase 'victims' movement'. The field of Social Policy can be used to help understand this concept, since much research has been generated exploring the dimensions and definitions of the phrase 'social movement'. Different writers here have defined social movements in different ways. However, Diani (1992: 7), reviewing the literature, explains that four characteristics appear to be present in most understandings of the concept, such that a social movement can be considered to consist of: networks of informal interaction; shared beliefs and solidarity; collective action on conflictual issues; and action which is displayed largely outside the institutional sphere and the routine procedures of social life. Specifically in relation to victim issues, Elias (1993) argues that many different victims' movements can be found, including the feminist victims' movement, the human rights movement, and what he refers to as an international victims' movement. Elias (1993) further argues that the different movements can be classified according to two basic types: the official victims' movement and the unofficial victims' movement.

The official victims' movement is conceptualised as being conservative, focussing mainly upon state definitions of victimisation, ignoring wider social and economic processes, with initiatives being funded largely by the government. The unofficial victims' movement, on the other hand, consists of victim support groups that follow a more 'radical' agenda in terms of situating individual victims' experiences within broader discourses that challenge racist, sexist and class-biased structures. For example, women's support groups or racial harassment projects might be classed as belonging to the unofficial victims' movement (Williams, 1999a). Researchers argue that these kinds of support groups are often marginalised by state officials when proposing new developments in victim policy, and they also often experience large shortages in funding, as governments tend to offer financial support predominantly to the official victims' movement. The official victims' movement is seen as less threatening precisely because it does not tend to contain radicalising strategies and does not tend to overtly criticise state agencies such as the police, or government policy (Elias, 1993; Williams, 1999a).

Perhaps another way of distinguishing between the official and unofficial victims' movements is according to the ways in which identities are formed, and emotions are reconstituted, within these movements. It might be argued that within the former movement, victims' reactions are constructed as individual responses to victimisation, and identity attachments are formed around a notion of an 'ideal' 'deserving' victim who is a consumer of the criminal justice system; whilst in the latter type of movement, victims' reactions are directed at wider social systems of inequality, and identities are fixed around broader group collectivities based on race, gender, class, religion and others.

Victim emotions and the social construction of victimhood

Social scientists have increasingly focussed upon emotionality as an aspect of social life. From this perspective, emotions are viewed as social constructions, in that how people feel and react to events are influenced by cultural, institutional and political processes. For example, according to Hochschild (1998: 11), emotions are not 'sealed biological events' but rather are managed, so that cultures have their own particular emotional dictionaries that shape and define how a person should feel within a particular context. Similarly, Karstedt (2002) suggests that reactions to crime are affected by 'emotional cultures' and 'their institutional settings'. Karstedt (2002) further argues that collective displays of emotion, based on group identity, are rare in contemporary western societies. Rather, emotions are experienced 'at a distance', when media portrayals of suffering encourage people to feel compassion and sympathy for the individual victims concerned; emotions are also experienced at a personal, individual level, as expressions and representations of the self.

Certainly, there is a healthy market for books written by, or on behalf of, victims and the constructions of victimhood arising from the mass marketisation of victims' experiences both constitute, and reflect, the wider social and cultural changes to reactions to crime that are evident in contemporary modern society. Thus, victims' stories are constructed so as to induce an emotional reaction in the reader, and they often stress the heroic and special qualities of the victim. To illustrate this point, the following phrases have been found on the back covers of victim biographies or autobiographies: 'Through her letters – the girls live again ... I found myself holding my breath, tears pricking my eyes' (Jurgensen, 1999); 'She survived a horrific rape and attempted murder. But her determination to recover and gain compensation brought her into surprising areas of resistance, into a system which could seem uncaring towards a victim' (Nuttall, 1997); 'However dreadful we imagine it was, the reality must have been far worse. Her survival, in my judgement, is entirely due to her own remarkable moral courage' (Slater, 1995).[1] Although these texts are produced in such a way so as to elicit an emotional reaction in the reader, they 'do not position the reader in a relation of equivalence or co-suffering' (Ahmed, 2004: 21). This means that these books encourage people to feel the process of victimisation 'at a distance', with the object of the feelings being the reader, who might experience a range of emotions, such as sympathy or anger at a personal level whilst reading the text.

'Ideal Victims', therapy culture and the individualisation of pain

In many ways, the mass marketisation of victims' experiences reflects the creation and perpetuation of an 'ideal victim', who is 'innocent', having played no part in his/her victimisation, and s/he has an ideal offender who is 'evil' (Henderson, 1992; McShane and Williams 1992). Factors such as the race, class and gender of victims will influence how closely they conform to the 'ideal' victim type. For instance, elderly people, children and women often receive a more sympathetic response to their victimization than working-class men (Elias, 1990). Police officers are often denied victim status if sustaining injuries during the course of their work. Following an incident, the media reportage tends to stress the bravery and commitment of police officers rather than their victimization. For example, following an incident in which four unarmed police officers were threatened at gunpoint in Manchester, the Assistant Chief Constable of Greater Manchester Police reportedly said, 'Their bravery is unquestionable' (The Guardian, 30 April 2002). In Britain, in 2003, a police detective was stabbed to death by a kitchen knife as he tried to restrain a suspect terrorist during a raid in Manchester. The Home Secretary is reported as saying, 'We rely on the bravery and commitment of officers in defending us against dangerous criminals and those who threaten the safety of our country.' Interestingly, when a former police officer was awarded £300,000 in compensation for the trauma that he had experienced on the day of the Hillsborough football stadium disaster in Sheffield, England, when 96 Liverpool football supporters were crushed to death in 1989, the Hillsborough Support Group challenged the award (Rock, 2002).

Ideal victims respond to their experiences of victimisation in socially accepted ways, and so for those individuals whose survival strategies are less socially acceptable, much controversy is generated about whether these people are 'real' victims and whether their responses to victimisation should be encouraged. For example, in 1999 in Norfolk, Britain, Tony Martin, a farmer, shot dead a burglar as he was trying to flee from his farmhouse. This case generated significant public debate about whether Tony Martin should be viewed as an offender, as someone who cold-bloodedly killed a burglar as he was trying to run away, or whether Martin should be viewed as a victim of a rural crime epidemic. The boundaries between victim and offender are therefore far from clear-cut, nonetheless, in the public's imagination the 'ideal' victim is clearly distinct from the offender.

Case study

In 2004, the Court of Appeal reduced Tony Martin's murder conviction for the shotgun killing of a teenage burglar to manslaughter, and so his life sentence was dropped and replaced by a five-year prison term. The Appeal Court judges accepted evidence that Martin had 'diminished responsibility' for the killing as a result of having a paranoid personality disorder, which had been made worse by previous burglary attempts at his farmhouse. In the original trial, the prosecution had argued that Martin was an angry man who had violent views about burglars. The defence team, on the other hand, had argued that Martin was genuinely terrified when he saw the burglars and that this was why he had fired at them.

Question

In what ways does this case study illustrate the inter-changeability of the categories 'offender' and 'victim'?

The 'ideal victim' largely conforms to the 'therapy culture' that pervades western society (Furedi, 2004), whereby reactions to crime are located firmly within individuals. The 'ideal victim' is also often linked to an 'ideal offender', who is 'evil' (Henderson, 1992; McShane and Williams 1992), and so can be linked to the process of the individualisation of blame that is evident in contemporary society. Within a therapy culture, the general public's emotional reactions to crime are directed at individual victims and offenders, so that in the aftermath of an event, both victims' and offenders' characteristics and behaviour are scrutinised and blame is directed at these agents rather than at any broader social and economic systems of injustice. These processes can also be linked to the emergence of an 'actuarial regime' in contemporary western society (O'Malley, 1992), which refers to a particular form of governance: that of governing populations through statistical analyses of risk (Simon, 1988; Ewald, 1991; O'Malley, 1992). Within this kind of regime, the pathological disposition of social systems is not examined, but rather, danger is conceptualised as a risk that individuals must manage (see Spalek, 2004). Risk is socially constructed, organised, worked and mass marketed through a range of institutions, procedures, analyses, reflections and tactics (Foucault, 1978; Beck, 1992). Insurance practices constitute a way of managing risk in an actuarial regime. Insurance practices occur in late modernity and reflect a society that is cutting its links with the past and with tradition, and opening itself up to a problematic future. Insurance is, in this way, a moral technology since individuals are no longer resigning themselves to Fortuna or to God but to statistical calculations (Ewald, 1991). Actuarial practices profoundly influence how individuals perceive themselves. People are understood in terms of occupying particular positions within a statistical distribution. These positions do not necessarily correspond to an individual's subject positions in terms of their class, ethnicity or gender, for example, and so fragment the social identity of a person, and reduce the possibility of group resistance. As Simon (1988: 774) argues, 'As people come to understand themselves through these actuarial representations they may be stripped of a certain quality of belongingness to others that has long played a role in our culture.'

The official victims' movement: victims as consumers of the criminal justice system

The movement towards the individualisation of pain can further be seen in the construction of the victim as a consumer of the criminal justice system. Many initiatives within the official victims' movement are aimed at increasing the efficiency of the criminal justice system through the increased involvement of victims. It is a well-documented phenomenon that the reporting and prosecution of most types of crime is heavily reliant upon victims because victims are often the most important witnesses to the case laid out by the prosecution (Winter, 2002). This means that a criminal justice system that is more 'user-friendly' to victims will lead to a more efficient detection and prosecution rate, since individuals will be more willing to give evidence in court. As a result, victims are viewed as being consumers of the criminal justice system, whose needs should be met by the provision of certain basic services. Although policy makers refer to the notion of victims' rights, these are largely translated into discourses of individual need, and not collective and social rights, and so victims are not encouraged to think of themselves in political ways, as belonging to wider collectivities whose experiences can be linked to broader racist, sexist structures, but rather are encouraged to think of themselves as customers of a criminal justice system.

Within an ethos of consumerism and individualism, victims are encouraged to think about their financial needs, so that people increasingly feel that they need monetary gain in order to feel better. According to Victim Support in Britain, financial compensation plays an important symbolic role by providing victims with formal recognition of their plight, so that a refusal of compensation from the state can 'lead people to feeling that they are not seen as worthy of society's sympathy' (NAVSS, 2003). This statement clearly links monetary compensation with the issue of personal worth, and is an example of how powerful the construct of victim as individual consumer is within the official victims' movement. This can serve to 'civilise' victims' reactions so that they focus upon demanding financial compensation rather than other, wider, societal changes.

Interestingly, the compensation paid to the victims of the terrorist attacks of 11 September 2001 has been a subject of controversy, since victims of other terrorist atrocities have raised concerns that the victims of 11 September have been granted a special status by the authorities due to the large sums of money involved, and the relative ease with which they have obtained compensation (Cullen, 2002).[2] For example, the survivors of the Oklahoma City bombing have reportedly been aggrieved because of the small amount of state compensation that they received as opposed to the compensation received by the victims of 11 September. As a result, action groups were set up to lobby for these victims to be included in the September 11 Victim Fund (Valenti, 2003).

'Ideal victims', official responses to victimisation and existential anxiety

The 'ideal victim' type that features in official responses to victimisation is so influential in today's society because it is the basis around which members from the general public form identity attachments. This means that when people who represent the 'ideal victim' in the public's imagination speak about their experiences, and when politicians, and other significant actors such as the police, make claims on behalf of these people, the general public feels that these claims also apply to them. This is because the 'ideal' victim type performs the symbolic role of reassuring the wider audience that although a terrible, inexplicable event has occurred, nonetheless meaning can be ascribed through emphasising the specialness of the victims, as pure, blameless (hence passive) people against whom an evil act was committed by a depraved individual.

Philosophers, psychotherapists, sociologists and social psychologists have written about 'existential anxiety' that is part of the human condition (Janoff-Bulman, 1983; Giddens, 1990; Bauman, 2004). In late modernity, existential anxiety is heightened, not only because of the increasingly fragmented lives that people lead (as explained earlier), but also because individuals no longer necessarily lead lives that are structured around notions of a divinely constructed world to help give them a sense of meaning, and safety, in an uncertain world (Bauman, 2004). A victimising experience can cause a great deal of distress not only to the people directly involved, but also to the wider audience who become aware of the terrible event, as this brings into the open the vulnerability of human beings and the disorder that can engulf their lives.[3] Hence the contemporary fascination with 'ideal victims' operates as a way of establishing order over an insecure and unstable world.

Nevertheless, bearing in mind the fluidity of identity attachments in late modernity, the public's attachment to the 'ideal victim' is likely to be short-lived, as it is not grounded in any shared histories or shared experiences based on more 'solid' forms of 'togetherness' that were more common in the modern era. 'Ideal victim identities' are also likely to be transient and fleeting, since in conditions of late modernity, being 'fixed' to an unmoving identity is unpopular and undesirable (Bauman, 2004). 'Ideal victims' may therefore go on to claim 'survivor' status. Underpinning the 'victim as survivor' identity is the theme of individual victim as an agent who has resisted their abuse to become emotionally and psychologically stronger. Simon Weston and the late Princess Diana provide good examples of this 'victim type'. Simon Weston, a survivor of a ship attack during the Falklands War in 1982, who suffered extensive burns and had to endure as many as seventy operations, has featured in six BBC documentaries and has written a book, *Moving On* described as being part autobiography, part self-help, about his battles with depression and post-traumatic stress disorder. When Princess Diana was interviewed on British television in 1995, and she spoke about her depression, bulimia, suicide attempts, and being married to a cold, uncaring husband who loved somebody else, she nonetheless tried to present herself as a strong woman, as a person who had experienced trauma but had nonetheless survived to be able to now help other people and to claim the title of 'queen of hearts' (James, 1997; Hume, 1998).

Case study

Between 1 September and 3 September 2004, 1200 teachers, parents and children were held hostage by terrorists in a school in Beslan, southern Russia. By the end of the siege, more than 300 hostages died when bombs exploded from inside the school buildings. In the aftermath of this tragedy, bitter divisions have opened up in the small Beslan community, and many teachers have become the focus of blame, with parents accusing the teachers of moral failings. There are also stories of men making vows of vengeance over the graves of their wives or children.

Source: David James Smith Beslan: the Aftermath *The Sunday Times* magazine 12 December 2004, pp. 31–38.

Question

Rather than becoming 'better', 'stronger', people, in what detrimental ways might victims react to their experiences?

Ideal victims and punitive responses to offenders

The 'ideal' victim is a mechanism through which more punitive responses to crime and disorder are implemented (Garland, 2001). Politicians pay particular attention to 'ideal victims' (particularly in a climate of high crime rates), since the articulation of their experiences acts as a way of pushing through a 'law and order' agenda that metes out severe punishment to offenders. Thus, politicians will hold press conferences to announce new legislation, often being accompanied by crime victims. Laws can also be named after victims (Garland, 2001). This can clearly be seen in the case of Megan Kanka of New Jersey, a seven year-old who was murdered in 1994 by a neighbour who was a twice-convicted sex offender. Following campaigns instigated by Megan's family to give public access to information about the whereabouts of sex offenders, legislation dubbed 'Megan's Law' was passed by Congress by 1996, which requires states to release relevant information to protect the public from sex offenders (Office of the Attorney General State of California Department of Justice, 2003). Access to information via the Worldwide Web sparks further controversy here. A significant number of states offer sex offender databases on websites, many of which are freely available to the public regardless of area of residence. Some databases provide photographs as well as physical descriptions, dates of birth and details about the offence, others provide home and work addresses (The Virtual Chase, 2005).

The pursuit of a 'law-and-order' approach to crime has led to increasing rates of incarceration across many countries, amid a declining concern for offenders' rights (Williams, 1999a). The lure of public popularity through appearing to be 'tough on crime' has led to many politicians highlighting victims' experiences and tapping into citizens' anxiety and concerns about their personal security. Repressive laws have been passed, leading to the rise in the number of people incarcerated. For example, under Bill Clinton's administration in the 1990s, the 'Three Strikes and You're Out' sentencing policy was implemented, whereby offenders who have committed three serious offences receive a mandatory 25-year prison sentence, without the possibility of parole. California is the state with the most individuals incarcerated as a result of this legislation, since a third offence here does not have to be serious or violent in order for the offender to be given a life sentence (Burt *et al.*, 2000).

Incarceration rates in Britain, Australia, Canada and the United States America have relentlessly risen over the last two decades. On 31 December 2002 there were 2,033,331 adults in state or federal prison in the United States up from 1,319,000 in 2001 and up from 216,000 in 1974 (US Department of Justice, 2002: 1; Bonczar, 2003: 1). In Canada, the federal penitentiary population grew by 22 per cent between 1989 and 1995, twice the historic average rate of growth, and despite the fact that crime rates started to drop in 1991 (Boe *et al.*, 1998: 1). In Australia, between 1984 and 2003, the overall imprisonment rate increased from 86 to 153 per 100,000 adult population. In 2002, there were 22,492 prisoners, compared to 15,559 prisoners in 1992, an increase of 45 per cent (Australian Institute of Criminology, 2005: 1). In England and Wales, the prison population stood at 75,740 in November 2004 (Home Office, 2004a: 1).

Incarceration rates have risen despite the existence of a social movement advocating the use of community, restorative-based notions of justice that might lead to a reduction in the number of people imprisoned. Supporters of restorative justice argue that this can provide an opportunity for offenders to repair the psychological and material harms caused to victims, reducing their fear and feelings of powerlessness. At the same time, in contrast to retributive forms of justice, restorative justice can encourage offenders to accept responsibility for their actions and can help prevent their stigmatisation through, where applicable, diverting offenders away from custody (Johnstone, 2002). Western governments have certainly revived their interest in restorative justice methods, particularly with respect to offending youth, and many programmes are being implemented across the world. There is also some evidence that victims generally do not hold particularly punitive views on offending (Maguire, 1982; Shapland *et al.*, 1985; Elias, 1994) and they are interested in pursuing restorative justice approaches and may find them to be beneficial (Masters, 2002). However, it seems that single-issue victim groups, pressurising for more repressive responses to crime, have dominated contemporary debates about justice. Single-issue victim groups that contain individuals whose characteristics resemble the 'ideal victim' type can engage in vociferous campaigns and can use the general public's emotional attachment to the 'ideal victim' to pressurise politicians to implement new, repressive laws. It is also interesting to note that in punishing offenders, this serves to detract attention away from the more complex questions relating to human frailty that an experience of victimisation elicits. Thus, in contemporary western society, whilst there is little impetus to engage with the larger issue of existential anxiety, the punishment of offenders constitutes the focus upon 'smaller tasks which humans can handle' (Bauman, 2004: 73).

The increasingly repressive tactics used against offenders are not necessarily beneficial to victims. Williams (2003) argues that an increasing emphasis upon punishment and retribution can undermine rehabilitative efforts and ideals. Resources are inevitably switched from treatment into control. In Britain, whereas extra funding has been allocated to deal with the expanding prison population and to increase the number of police officers, state funding for organisations helping victims has either been frozen or cut (Williams, 1999a). It is also questionable how much satisfaction victims achieve through the utilisation of repressive responses to crime. In Texas, victims can witness the execution of 'their' offender. However, it is not clear that in doing so, victims will subsequently experience closure.[4] Indeed, the death of the offender can mean that victims no longer have anyone that they can focus their blame on. This issue was clearly demonstrated in Britain, in the case of serial killer Harold Shipman. In 2000 Shipman, a family doctor, was jailed for life for the murders of 15 women. A later inquiry into his crimes decided that at least 215 of his patients were killed.[5] When Shipman committed suicide in 2004, some of the relatives of those murdered by Shipman were angry that he was able to kill himself whilst imprisoned, and they were angry that this denied them ever finding out answers in relation to why Shipman committed the acts that he had.

The unofficial victims' movement: 'non-ideal victims', group identities and attachments

Within the unofficial victims' movement, victim action and support groups are formed to campaign for a number of different issues. One of these might involve claiming victim status, since within state discourses, individuals' experiences may not necessarily be viewed as victimisation by crime. For example, in Britain, following the financial scandals of Maxwell, BCCI, Barings and Lloyd's, victims came together and campaigned for greater recognition of their needs. Financial compensation was just one part of campaigning activities, individuals also strived for changes to the ways in which the financial system is policed, as they saw themselves as the victims of a deregulated market.

Embedded within the kinds of campaigns that action groups engage in here, there can be a collective group identity, linked to individuals' race, class or gender (and so forth) positions. As such, action groups may seek to challenge what are seen to be the oppressive social conditions that have contributed to members' victimisation. For example, the work carried out by individuals and groups that can be located as belonging to the 'feminist movement' has played a vital role in raising awareness of the victimisation of women and children, placing this squarely onto policy makers' agendas. Previously, the violence committed against women and children was largely hidden, because victims rarely reported their experiences to the police due to the (often valid) belief that police officers would not treat their complaints seriously, also, due to a fear of retaliation by the offender. National crime surveys also have not been able to measure the full extent, and true nature, of the violence committed against women and children as a result of the ways in which questions are structured and how the surveys are actually carried out. In the 1970s and 1980s feminist research documented the crimes that occur in the home, in the private as opposed to the public arena. In an important study on battered women, for example, Dobash and Dobash (1979) highlighted the severity of the violence perpetrated against women, which included broken noses, serious wounding, fractured bones and disfigurement. Within the feminist movement there is a belief that the crimes committed against women and children can only be understood, and reduced, if the broader context of patriarchy is acknowledged, this being male economic, political and legal power, underpinned by male violence (Radford, 1992).

Another pertinent example that can be provided here is the work carried out by the Islamic Human Rights Commission (IHRC) and the Forum Against Islamophobia and Racism (FAIR). Underpinning and driving forward the campaigns run by these organisations is a sense of the wider Muslim faith community that activists, and their friends, families and peers, belong to. The justifications used by some of the terrorists post-11 September have unhelpfully linked Muslim communities to the terror atrocities that have been committed around the world, making them 'non-ideal victims'. Terrorists, like the men found guilty of the Bali bombings in 2002,[6] may claim that their actions are in revenge for the worldwide suffering of Muslims at the hands of the United States and Israel, and so Muslim communities have had great difficulty in separating themselves from the extremists in the public's imagination. As a result, negative stereotypes of Muslim and Arab communities continue to pervade western perceptions of Islam, where Islam is interpreted as 'the other', as the antithesis of western society, as inhumane and evil (Said, 1978). This is perhaps why UK talk-show host, Robert Kilroy-Silk, appears to have received so much public support for his anti-Arab comments, which portrayed Arabs as suicide bombers, in a Sunday newspaper. This is also why anti-Muslim sentiment and Islamophobia, long-standing features of western societies, have heightened in the wake of the terror attacks. According to an IHRC report, The Hidden Victims of September 11 (2002), Muslims have experienced malicious phone calls, death threats, and women and children in particular experienced physical and verbal abuse. These experiences have had a significant impact upon Muslims' sense of well-being and the negotiation of their personal safety, with many women in particular changing their daily routines, avoiding places that previously would not have been regarded as being dangerous, like town centres for example (Spalek, 2002). Women have not, however, been the only targets of hate crime. Some Muslim men have also been physically and verbally abused and mosques have been vandalised, even firebombed, leading to many Muslim communities investing in closed circuit television or requesting an increased police presence. Campaigns run by Muslim groups have also included attempts at dismantling Islamophobia, or 'unfounded hostility towards Islam' and 'unfair discrimination against Muslims' (Conway, 1997: 10). Campaigns have therefore also featured attempts at changing inappropriate stereotypes and misrepresentations of Muslim communities.

The examples overleaf illustrate that a significant feature of some of the victim action and support groups that can be classified as belonging to the broader unofficial victims' movement is a sense of a wider collectivity that individual group members belong to, and identify with. As such, individuals' actions may be directed at wider social systems of inequality. These responses represent a powerful oppositional force to the increasing dominance and pervasiveness of the 'ideal victim' as an identity around which emotional and psychological attachments are formed in late modernity, and the increasing individualisation of victims' reactions. Indeed, from this perspective, individuals may also actively reject the label 'victim', since suffering may be interpreted as belonging to a wider political or social 'cause' or struggle. In Northern Ireland, for example, Gibson (1998: 23) refers to the case of a ten year-old boy who was admitted to hospital as a result of sustaining horrific burns injuries when unsuccessfully trying to throw a petrol bomb. His mother allegedly said, 'Isn't he a wee hero to the cause?'.

The examples above also illustrate that victim identity is a contested space. The 'victim' label is contingent and complex, shifting frequently according to social practices, race, class and gender relations (Lamb, 1999; Walklate, 2002). Howarth and Rock (2000) argue that additions to the label 'victim' can be useful in increasing our understanding of crime, since the different groups of people who come forward to claim victim status and the wide variety of experiences featured here can open up new areas of analysis.

Conclusion

Victimisation, as an aspect of social experience, generates much media, political and social interest in contemporary western society. Within the criminal justice policy arena, victim legislation has been passed and numerous initiatives aimed at the victims of crime have been implemented. In this chapter it has been suggested that processes occurring within, and the initiatives developing from, the official victims' movement might be considered to individualise victims' pain, thereby disempowering their reactions to harmful events. Nonetheless, developments arising within the unofficial victims' movement might be considered to be more empowering of victims, since victim identities may be based on more 'solid' forms of belongingness, based on race, class, gender, religion and other factors and so victims' reactions may involve an acknowledgement of, and be directed at, wider social systems of oppression. Victimhood is therefore a complex concept, being contingent upon intricate psychological and social processes, its construction helping to determine what forms of victimisation and what kinds of people are helped. This means that we need to take a closer look at the label 'victim' and try to locate it within a broader theoretical framework of understanding. Chapter 3 therefore explores the (sub)discipline of victimology and examines the relevance of theoretical, victimological debates in furthering our understanding of contemporary responses to crime and victimisation.

Questions

1 What factors have helped to place the victims of crime firmly onto criminal justice policy agendas?
2 Can anybody legitimately claim victim status?
3 In what ways might victimhood be viewed as a social construct?

3

Victimology: Theoretical Perspectives

Introduction

A plethora of research studies have been carried out surveying the general
area of victimisation. These can be linked to broader theoretical traditions,
such as positivist, radical, feminist and critical victimologies. This chapter
aims to examine each of these victimological perspectives in order to illustrate how a focus upon theory can enhance our understanding of victimisation, by making the values and assumptions that underpin victimological
work visible. This chapter demonstrates the diverse ways in which victimhood can be understood, and the theoretical traditions discussed here are
also found in criminology, which illustrates the intimate connections
between victimology and criminology, and the way in which researchers
make contributions to both areas. It is clear that underpinning each theoretical position are different notions of, and emphases upon, socio-structural
processes and human action, which influence the ways in which victimisation is understood and analysed, skewing our understanding of how criminal
and non-criminal events impact the lives of individuals.

Positivist victimology

Although Wertham is believed to be the person who first defined the word
'victimology' (Fattah, 1989), the founder of the (sub)-discipline victimology
is regarded as being Von Hentig (1948) (Zedner, 1994; Mawby and Walklate,
1994). Von Hentig (1948) argued that researchers were focusing too much
attention upon the perpetrators of crime, and not enough attention was being
paid to victims. Von Hentig adopted what has been called a positivist perspective, which has also been labelled conservative victimology (Karmen,
1990), conventional victimology (Walklate, 1989), penal victimology and
interactionist victimology (Van Dijk, 1997). The defining characteristics of

positivist victimology are considered to be the discovery of factors that influence a non-random pattern of victimisation, the examination of how victims contribute to their victimisation and a focus upon interpersonal crimes of violence (Miers, 1989). Von Hentig was first to identify a number of factors which were considered to contribute to the likelihood of being victimised. He created a victim typology which consisted of several general classes of victim, including the young, the old, female, the mentally defective and immigrants, minorities and dull normals. Von Hentig also presented 'psychological types of victim' which involved the depressed, the acquisitive, and the wanton. These psychological attributes could be inherited or acquired. However, Von Hentig's typology can be criticised for being based on anecdotal observation rather than empirical evidence. His book '*The Criminal & His Victim*' was not written on the basis of any empirical analysis conducted by Von Hentig himself, but rather involves a series of observations made by him. As a result, there is little sense of how he formulated these categories. A lack of an empirical foundation is also a criticism of Mendelsohn's (1956) work. Mendelsohn (1956) created six categories of victims, consisting of the 'completely innocent' to the 'most guilty' (Mawby and Walklate, 1994). Again, this work consists of anecdotal, impressionistic evidence (Miers, 1989). Early victimological work thereby involved placing scrutiny directly upon victims and examining their attributes. Later work in the positivist tradition, including the work of Wolfgang (1958) and Amir (1971) (Wolfgang's PhD student) continued to do this, through developing the notion of 'victim precipitation', whereby it was argued that the victim precipitated the victimising event. For example, Wolfgang studied homicide cases in Philadelphia, and concluded that 26 per cent of those were cases where the homicide was due to victim precipitation. Amir examined police reports on forcible rape in Philadelphia, and categorised 19 per cent of his sample of 646 rapes as cases where the victim precipitated the event (Amir, 1971: 259). Amir devised a typology of victim behaviour from the 'accidental victim' to the 'consciously' or 'unconsciously seductive' victim (260). Amir argued that once the victim and offender are drawn together, a process is set in motion whereby victim behaviour and the situation which surrounds the meeting between victim and offender will determine the course of events which leads to the crime. Moreover, Amir (1971: 335) further suggested that his study refutes the belief that victims are not responsible for their victimisation, since he found that either consciously or by default some victims of rape precipitate the crimes committed against them.

Feminist researchers have criticised the above approaches, suggesting that examining victims' behaviour for its role in the perpetration of a crime may constitute blaming the victim, thereby holding them responsible for their plight (Mawby and Walklate, 1994). In particular, this work has been criticised for the way that these studies naturalise men's sexual violence: women and girls are held responsible for sexual and non-sexual crimes committed against them. As discussed later on in this chapter, feminist research views victims' actions not in terms of their culpability, but in terms of the strategies that individuals engage in in order to mitigate any harm which might be incurred through any violence, or potential violence which may be committed against them (Kelly, 1988; Stanko, 1990). However, countering the feminist critique, Fattah (1989) maintains that research which focuses upon the role that victims play in their victimisation is not to be understood as directly blaming them, but rather can be understood as trying to find the factors which may account for why particular individuals come to be victimised. Nonetheless, there seems to be a thin line between blame and account, especially within discourses that emphasise the duty of citizens to avoid victimisation.

John avoid victimisation → Secondary victimisation

It has been suggested that examining the role of victims in the victimising event has led to a greater understanding of criminal behaviour, as patterns of victimisation and offending are not necessarily separate entities. As discussed earlier, the roles of 'victim' and 'offender' may in some instances be interchangeable. For instance, in the case of an argument between two people which escalates into a fight, the person first attacked may kill his/her attacker (Fattah, 1993). Other studies have confirmed that victims and offenders are not necessarily distinct (Sparks *et al.*, 1977; Chambers *et al.*, 1984; Fagan *et al.*, 1987; Singer, 1981). Fattah (1989) therefore argues that through examining the demographic and behavioural characteristics of victimisation, criminology can be transformed, from being a static one-sided study of the offender, to being a dynamic, situational approach which views criminal behaviour as the outcome of processes of interaction.

Case study

In 2002 in Britain a famous snooker player was accused of raping a young woman. This woman went back to a hotel room with him and she claimed that despite telling him that she did not want to have intercourse due to her having a boyfriend, she was subsequently raped. The QC defending the snooker player argued that 'Sometimes, in the heat of passion, when a woman says "no" she doesn't necessarily mean no. You can say "no" a thousand times, but you show by your actions you don't mean it, it doesn't mean consent is withdrawn'. He was found to be not guilty.

Question

Should a victim's behaviour be examined to see how they contributed to their victimisation, and is this the same as blaming the victim?

Lifestyle and routine activities

The lifestyle approach (Hindelang, *et al.*, 1978) and routine activities theory (Cohen and Felson, 1979) are also part of the positivist tradition. These approaches do not directly address the motive of offending, rather they focus on the convergence in time and space between the offender and victim and how this influences crime (Gottfredson, 1981). 'Lifestyle' is defined as being 'the way in which individuals allocate their time to vocational activities and leisure activities' (Garofalo, 1986: 720). It is argued that differences in lifestyle affect the risk of victimisation because lifestyle affects the probability of being in a particular location at a particular time, coming into contact with a potential offender (Gottfredson, 1981). For example, according to a study by Lasley and Rosenbaum (1988), victims' work schedules, the number of weekend evenings spent away from home and the level of alcohol consumption correlated positively to the chances of being a repeat victim of crime. A study by Smith (1982) revealed that victims were more likely than non-victims to engage in unstructured activities that were more likely to bring them into contact with strangers. But the lifestyle model also considers the influence of structural constraints upon human action, so that things like tax policies (which may encourage or discourage marriage, influencing the number of people living alone) or the availability of public transport (which may influence the number of occasions that people leave their houses) are factors that are also taken into account when studying victimisation (Garofalo, 1986).

The routine activities model is very similar to the lifestyle approach. Crime rates are portrayed as being affected by the convergence in time and space of the three minimal elements necessary: motivated offenders, suitable targets and the presence of capable guardians against the violation (Cohen and Felson, 1979). This approach predominantly tries to explain victimisation by direct contact predatory violations. 'Direct contact predatory violations' have been defined as 'involving direct physical contact between at least one offender and at least one person or object which that offender attempts to take or damage' (Cohen and Felson, 1979: 589). 'Routine activity' is taken to mean any recurrent and prevalent activities, for example, work, leisure, social interaction, which provide for general population and individual needs. According to Cohen and Felson, from the end of the Second World War, certain socio-economic processes have led to a dispersion of activities away from households, which has increased the amount of exposure to crime, and thus has increased the amount of crime taking place.

The lifestyle and routine activities models have been criticised, as they provide only a partial analysis of the role of human action and structural constraints in victimisation (Mawby and Walklate, 1994). It seems that the models define 'lifestyle' and 'routine activities' according to those aspects of life that can be articulated and measured through a victimisation survey. This means that those parts of our lives which may not be articulated or uncovered via a victimisation survey, for example, racial or sexual violence, are omitted (Genn, 1988). Furthermore, the lifestyle and routine activities models base risk of victimisation according to public and not private space, since researchers using these models examine the probability of victimisation in relation to the amount of time spent in public places. This means that the private domain is excluded from assessment of the risk of victimisation (Walklate, 1992), yet cases like domestic violence and incest typically occur within the home (Dobash and Dobash, 1979). Individuals within the lifestyle and routine activities models are also viewed in a passive way, as living within their structural constraints rather than actively opposing them. Also, the models implicitly blame the victim for their plight, since victimisation is viewed as a result of a person's lifestyle or routine activity, which can be changed (Walklate, 1992). The structural processes that contribute to risk of victimisation, whilst being acknowledged, are left unquestioned, being viewed predominantly as matters of public policy rather than as issues stemming from racist or sexist structures (Walklate, 1992). Finally, both the lifestyle and routine activities models focus very narrowly upon conventional understandings of crime, so that street crime and burglary are the focus of attention, thereby neglecting a wide range of other illegal activities such as corporate crime.

Despite these criticisms above, the notion of lifestyle and routine activities has been used by researchers working within a perspective labelled as 'administrative criminology' in order to help explain variables which have been found to influence risk of victimisation as uncovered through the administration of local and national crime surveys, like the British Crime Survey for example (Laub, 1990; Mawby and Walklate, 1994). Administrative criminology has sought to reduce the opportunities of committing crime, and so crime prevention strategies and victim initiatives have been pursued, which involve reducing the risks of victimisation through a range of preventative measures (Clarke, 1992). The British Crime Survey has been analysed in order to identify those groups of people most at risk from crime in order to target crime prevention strategies effectively (Mayhew and Hough, 1988). This is discussed in more detail in Chapter 4.

The notion of repeat victimisation can be linked to the lifestyle and routine activities models, since crime is viewed in terms of the convergence of an offender, a victim and the absence of a capable guardian (Farrell and Pease, 1993). Resources have been targeted at those who have already been victimised in order to prevent their repeat victimisation (Forrester *et al.*, 1988; Farrell and Pease, 1993; Pease *et al.*, 1994; Pease, 1998). For example, houses which have been burgled can be placed within a neighbourhood watch scheme, and have their security upgraded so as to reduce the likelihood of a future burglary. Similarly, individuals whose lifestyles increase their likelihood of victimisation can be monitored and suggestions can be given on how to reduce their likelihood of falling victims to crime (Farrell and Pease, 1993). Critics have argued that crime prevention strategies emerging out of the notion of repeat victimisation do not address the wider structural processes that influence victimisation, holding victims responsible for their plight (Walklate, 1992). However, Farrell and Pease (1993) argue that the method advocated does not blame the victim but rather attempts to induce lifestyle changes so as to reduce the likelihood of being victimised. Similar to heart attack victims being encouraged to stop smoking or to lose weight, crime victims can be encouraged to reduce their risks of being re-victimised (Farrell and Pease, 1993).

Summary

Positivist victimology uncovers patterns of victimisation, and so research results can be used to effectively implement crime prevention strategies as well as other victim-focussed policy initiatives. However, this approach fails to adequately address the structural processes that influence victimisation, processes that can be linked to gender, race, and class power relations. Violent and property crime has also tended to be the focus of analysis, thereby excluding other forms of victimisation.

Radical perspectives seek to broaden the terms 'crime' and 'victim' so as to include a wider range of experiences, as the following section discusses.

Radical victimology

Radical perspectives became prominent in both criminology and victimology in the 1970s and 1980s. While there is disagreement on whether radical victimology had an influence on radical criminology (Friedrichs, 1983; Jones *et al.*, 1986), it appears that the two emerged at around the same time. Radical criminological and victimological perspectives emerged as a response to radicalising events in the larger world, like the war in Vietnam, also a result of a paradigm crisis within sociology and related disciplines (Friedrichs, 1983).

Researchers adopting a radical perspective have focussed their attention upon oppressive structural conditions that victimise large amounts of people, these having been overlooked by researchers taking positivist approaches. For example, Schwendinger and Schwendinger (1975) argued that through focusing upon events which are defined as criminal by the state, mainstream criminologists omitted the damaging practices carried out by people in positions of power, practices which are highly injurious but which are not defined as crime by the state or the wider society. Similarly, Quinney (1980) has criticised the predominant focus of an emerging field of victimology on victims of traditional, conventional crimes. This, he argued, had the effect of portraying a view of reality which was promoted by a capitalist system, thereby limiting the concept of victimisation.

The research studies labelled as taking a 'positivist' victimological/ criminological stance do not question the 'victim' label, but rather take this as given and analyse victimisation through the personal characteristics and lifestyles of those who have been labelled 'victims' (Miers, 1989). In contrast to this, researchers working from a radical perspective question the social construction of victimhood, asking who is afforded the label victim most easily, and who has the power to label (Mawby and Walklate, 1994). Radical perspectives challenge ideologies that work to present the law as being partial and just, rather, legal processes that can be linked to the perpetuation of power hierarchies. Marxist radical perspectives focus attention upon the interests of the capitalist enterprise, analysing how capitalist practices create victims. Some writers have argued, for example, that within a capitalist system, 'workers' are victims, since they are exploited by those individuals who own the means of production. The deaths and injuries which occur at work due to unsafe work practices and conditions constitutes criminal victimisation (Friedrichs, 1983). Some researchers adopting a radical perspective have viewed criminal offenders as being the victims of an economic system which instils aspirations for material wealth but which deprives them of the means to achieve that wealth (Gordon, 1973; Greenberg, 1981). According to Quinney (1980), street crimes are the actions of people who have been brutalised by the conditions of capitalism. The offender is thus responding to a capitalist system, but when caught within the net of the criminal justice system will be punished (Reiman, 1979).

Radical perspectives also include a focus upon human rights when accounting for crime and victimisation (Schwendinger and Schwendinger, 1975; Elias, 1986). Any infringement of a human right is regarded as being a crime, and the person whose right is impinged constitutes the victim. Every person should have the right to racial, sexual and economic equality, and that any social system which causes the abrogation of these rights is immoral and illegal. Within this perspective, victimisation is broadly conceived, thereby including a much wider range of victims than traditional, or positivist, approaches would consider. Thus, individuals brutalised by state oppression, war, and corporate crime are victims whose experiences need to be documented and whose oppression needs to be brought to an end (Quinney, 1980; Mawby and Walklate, 1994).

The analyses above illustrate how radical perspectives on victimisation have extended the notion of victimisation to include that of victimisation by social systems. In this way, radical perspectives have attempted to challenge societal structures which impact upon, and influence, victimisation. It can be argued that this approach is quite distinct from the approach labelled as 'positivist victimology'. However, radical perspectives have been criticised for adopting an overly simplistic view of structure and its impact on individuals. Structure is largely viewed in terms of a class system, which is based around the means of production, with the ruling class seen a consisting of those individuals who own the means to production. Such a viewpoint obscures the more complex structural processes which impact upon individuals, processes such as race, religion and gender, so that it has been suggested that a more sophisticated analysis of structure and its relationship to human behaviour is required (Mawby and Walklate, 1994). More recently, Elias (1994) has suggested the adoption of a 'peacemaking ideology' that places blame upon social institutions for the harms that people experience. This approach is seen to move away from simplistic analyses of the role of capitalism in victimisation by emphasising the cultures of violence that predominate in society, which can be linked to broad social problems like poverty, injustice and state abuses.

Case study

In May 2002, in Potters Bar Hertfordshire England, a train derailed killing seven people and injuring a further seventy-six. The rail maintenance company responsible for the section of track where the train derailed argued that sabotage of the points could not be ruled out. Nonetheless, it seems that this was an attempt to deflect scrutiny away from them, since in a report issued by the Health and Safety Executive (HSE) the points involved in the crash were described as being poorly maintained. Moreover, the HSE also argued that there appeared to be no guidance or instructions for setting up, inspecting or maintaining these particular points.

Question

Do you think that those killed or injured in this rail disaster are 'victims' of a 'crime'?

Left realism

Radical perspectives that view crime as a rational behaviour under a capitalist system have also been criticised for losing sight of the victim, since they have tended to romanticise street crime without taking into account the full impact of this upon victims and the wider society (Friedrichs, 1983). National crime surveys reveal the intra-class and intra-racial nature of much crime, so that the victimisation of people living in poor and deprived areas should be taken seriously. As a result, radical left realism emerged, which is associated most strongly with the work of Jock Young, Roger Matthews, John Lea, Richard Kinsey in Britain, and constitutes a theoretical and political development within British criminology, offering a programme of research and reform in the 1980s and 1990s (Walklate, 2001). Strands of a left realist approach can also be found in the United States and Australia. For example, Currie's (1985) work, *Confronting Crime*, may not have been called left realism by the author but radical arguments about the nature of American criminal justice policy are made here (in Brown and Hogg, 1992). Left realism approaches crime from a perspective that includes a focus upon the offender, the state, informal control and the victim. A significant aspect of radical left realism thereby consists of a focus upon victimisation, and the development of an 'accurate victimology', as other radical criminologies have overlooked the reality of crime for individuals living in high crime areas (Young, 1986). Left realists have developed and implemented locally, geographically based surveys that take into account the variables of age, race, sex and class. This constitutes an approach that tries to convey the lived experiences of those people living in communities where the threat of criminal victimisation is considerable (Matthews and Young, 1992). Local crime surveys have been carried out in areas such as Merseyside, Islington (see Jones *et al.*, 1986), North London, Hilldrop, West Kensington, Hammersmith and Fulham, and many of these have been funded by local councils. These surveys have uncovered higher rates of victimisation than the British Crime Survey, and are discussed in detail in Chapter 4.

Criticisms have been levelled at left realism. Mawby and Walklate (1994) argue that while left realists have offered a much more detailed portrayal of victimisation at a local level, they have nonetheless focused predominantly upon the relationship of class to victimisation, to the detriment of race, gender and age. Thus, for example, left realists' understanding of race issues is seen to be partial and incomplete (Sim, *et al.*, 1987), and the extent to which their research methods capture women's experiences of victimisation is questionable, since women may not wish to relate their experiences through a local crime survey (Walklate, 1992). At the same time, left realists have been criticised for failing to perceive men as victims, and for omitting to document the overlap between the categories of 'offender' and 'victim' (Farrall and Maltby, 2003). Left realists' assertion that it is important to take seriously those issues that people define as being serious, as a way of responding effectively to people's needs (Matthews and Young, 1992), has also been questioned. Walklate (1992) argues that there may be situations that people do not define as being serious and yet those might still have a detrimental effect on their lives. For example, people may not always be aware of the serious consequences that environmental pollution has on their health. However, in response to this criticism, left realists maintain that hidden processes can be included in local crime surveys. For instance, it may be possible to add questions relating to the prevalence of illness caused by chemical pollution to a criminal victimisation survey (Matthews, and Young 1992). Indeed, the Second Islington Crime Survey included questions about commercial crime, health and safety and pollution (Pearce and Tombs, 1992). However, these attempts might be viewed as being mere gestures, since left realism has focussed mainly upon conventional crime, that is, street crime, so that a truly radical approach that might widen the boundaries of the 'crime' category is missing (Walklate, 1992).

Feminist perspectives

Feminist perspectives have made many important contributions to developing an understanding of victimisation. Feminist work has highlighted forms of abuse experienced by women that have been largely hidden, since women may not report the violence committed against them to police, and both national and local crime surveys have failed to detect the true level of crimes committed against women, such as rape, wife battering and sexual assault (Hanmer and Saunders, 1984; Hall, 1985). An element of feminist work, seen crucial to improving women's lives, has thus been the articulation of women's experiences of male violence. Women's lives are framed by the social structure of patriarchy, which consists of male economic and social power, underpinned by the use of, or threat of, violence (Radford, 1992). By utilising research methods that are sensitive to women's needs and experiences, feminist work has thus uncovered previously hidden forms of victimisation, and men's power to define abuse has been challenged. For example, an important study carried out by Dobash and Dobash (1979: 52) documented the shocking violence endured by battered women, including broken noses, serious wounding, fractured bones and disfigurement, whilst Russell's (1982: 35) study of women revealed that in a random sample of 930 women, 24 per cent had experienced at least one rape in her lifetime and another 31 per cent an attempted rape.

Another distinctive element of feminist work has been a focus upon women's agency, in other words, how women resist and manage their lives around violence. Women are viewed as not just 'victims' who have violence committed against them, rather, women are viewed as actively struggling against their material conditions, attempting to mitigate the harms caused by physical and sexual danger. For example, Dobash and Dobash (1979) suggest that battered women strive to improve their relationship with the abuser, particularly in the beginning of a violent relationship. Women also argue and defend themselves. Indeed, the avoidance of danger is an integral part of the everyday lives of most women, as illustrated by Stanko (1985). The notion that women resist and manage their lives around violence is thus a common theme in feminist research. This is why many feminist researchers have questioned the term 'victim', as this carries connotations of passivity. Although some women are killed by men, and some feel that certain aspects of their lives have been completely ruined by violence, many women nonetheless manage to reconstruct their lives, emotionally, psychologically and physically, and this kind of reconstruction should be acknowledged through use of the word 'survivor' rather than 'victim' (Kelly, 1988; Lamb, 1999).

A white, Eurocentric perspective has, however, underpinned much feminist work, such that Black women have been overlooked through 'gender essentialism', the view that there is a monolithic women's experience (Harris, 1997: 11). The interconnected sources of black women's oppression, relating to structures of race, gender and class, have thereby been unexamined by white feminism (Carby, 1997). Black women writers and researchers have, particularly since the 1980s, produced a large volume of work about their lives, suggesting that feminism must increasingly contend with the heterogeneity of women. However, many argue that this has had little impact upon mainstream academic disciplines, with Black women remaining invisible and silenced (Collins, 1998; Bolles, 2001; McClaurin, 2001). Certainly, within the broader victimological field, differences between people in relation to their ethnicities and cultures have tended to be omitted. It appears that a 'white perspective' has underpinned research, so that what appears to be 'normal', 'neutral' or 'common-sense' is in fact a particular lens through which the world has been viewed. Researchers have rarely acknowledged differences between themselves and their research participants, and so white people's lives and the norms that govern those lives have tended to occupy a central position. Mama (2000) cogently argues that cultural analysis is largely missing from work on domestic violence, yet the dynamics of race, class and culture frame women's experiences. Researchers working within the victimological arena must fully take on board issues of ethnicity and cultural diversity. Little is known about the specificities of experiences of victimisation for specific groups of individuals, particularly those who occupy different cultural, religious and racial heritages from those whose experiences constitute the 'norm'. According to Walklate (2001), a post-modern feminist position on women's lives avoids making any claims or statements on women in general. Rather, the specificity and diversity of experiences is recorded, whilst acknowledging that there may be certain similarities between different groups of women (Walklate, 2001).

Critical victimology ⌐key theory

Critical victimology arose as a response to what were perceived to be the problems and deficiencies with positivist and radical victimologies. As highlighted in this chapter, neither conventional, nor realist nor radical victimologies have incorporated an adequate understanding of 'agency' and 'structure' into their theoretical frameworks. Conventional victimology either views the victim as passive or as responsible for the crime committed against them, and does not tend to include an analysis of how structural processes impact on victimisation. Although the lifestyle and routine activity models mention how political and social processes may influence people's daily lives, these perspectives do not constitute a critical analysis of the structures of race, gender, class and age and the relationship of these to victimisation. The work of the left realists, while arguing that the victim is aware of their victimisation and needs to be taken seriously, including a race, age, class and gender perspective, has been criticised for not fully articulating the relationship between agency and structure. For instance, left realism does not fully express the problem of how structural conditions may have an impact on people's lives even though people are not necessarily aware of those conditions. Nor does it document how people actively resist the structures that they live within (Walklate, 1992). The radical perspectives of writers such as Gordon (1973), Quinney (1980) and Greenberg (1981) can be criticised for providing an overly simplistic view of the state and law. This is because the state and law are viewed predominantly in relation to a class structure based around the means of production, and yet many more structural processes matter. Although feminist research has involved quite a detailed analysis of the structure of patriarchy, and how women act in and resist this, it can be argued that through taking a gendered perspective, the structures of race and class have been neglected, as well as how individuals act within and upon these structures.

Advocates of a critical victimological perspective are keen to propose that this perspective involves the pursuit of a sophisticated theoretical analysis of the relationship between agency and structure, that is, how individual action is constructed and reconstructed within material conditions (Walklate, 1992). Empirical work is important, but any empirical investigation must take account of individuals' conscious and unconscious activity, the structural processes which form the background to this activity, and the intended and unintended consequences of action which may change the conditions in which people act, to examine the 'processes that go on behind our backs, which contribute to the crime and victims that we see as opposed to that which we do not see' (Mawby and Walklate, 1994: 19). Critical victimology is thus concerned with documenting how individuals act within and resist the structural conditions within which they live (Mawby and Walklate, 1994). A critical victimology also sets out a framework which problematises the state and charts the many connections between political, economic and social processes and victimisation. One criticism that has been made against critical victimology is that it has not paid much attention to empirical findings that suggest that the categories 'offender' and 'victim' are interchangeable, and that there is a connection between being victimised and having offended (Farrall and Maltby, 2003). Another criticism relates to the issue of documenting processes that victimise individuals even though people may not be aware of those processes. It seems to be problematic to document individuals as experiencing oppression when they may not view themselves as being oppressed. Is it possible to document individuals' own perspectives and yet at the same time to claim positions for them that they do not claim for themselves and is this ethically defensible? (Andrews, 2002). Can a researcher claim a source of knowledge beyond that held by the participants in a study? In doing so, is this perpetuating a form of elitism? Advocates of critical victimology must contend with these sorts of issues and give greater clarity on how to go about carrying out a piece of empirical research within this theoretical tradition, making visible the dilemmas and ethical considerations that a researcher may be faced with.

Conclusion

This chapter has taken a close look at victimology and the many theoretical perspectives that can be found here. Each one of the perspectives featured in this chapter furthers our understanding of victimisation. For example, positivistic victimology allows us to think of victimisation as a risk that varies according to the socio-demographic spaces individuals occupy and the lifestyles that they lead, in order that crime prevention strategies can be effectively targeted. Radical and critical victimologies broaden the lens through which crime and victimhood are viewed, and consider the vital role that socio-structural processes play in victimisation, whilst feminist work stresses the violence carried out against women within a patriarchal society, and highlights the survival strategies that women engage in when managing their lives around male aggression. At the same time, however, these theoretical perspectives can also be criticised. For example, positivist victimology has involved examining victims' behaviour for their role in the perpetration of a crime, and this might be viewed as victim blaming. Radical victimologies have tended to adopt an overly simplistic view of structure and its impact on individuals, with structure here being viewed in terms of a class system, thereby obscuring the more complex structural processes relating to race, religion and gender, that may impact upon individuals' lives. Feminist perspectives have tended to ignore ethnic and religious differences between women, so that Black women have remained largely invisible and silenced, despite the important work carried out by Black feminist researchers.

Reflecting the different theoretical positions described in this chapter, many different methodological approaches have been adopted when researching victimisation, since the particular theoretical standpoint taken by a researcher significantly influences the choice of research methods used. The various strategies utilised when attempting to document victimisation is examined in the following chapter, Chapter 4.

Questions

1 How does a positivist victimological perspective differ from a feminist perspective when examining victims' actions?
2 In what ways do radical perspectives broaden our understanding of victimhood?
3 Which theoretical victimological position do you think offers the best approach to understanding the impacts of the following types of crime:

   (a) burglary
   (b) environmental pollution
   (c) domestic violence

4

Researching Victimisation: Contesting Victimhood

Introduction

The contested nature of victimhood is perhaps most apparent when we look at the different research approaches that have been used to document victimisation. Research is inextricably bound to theory, this means that political and ideological notions of victimhood have underpinned the work carried out on victimisation. In addition to influencing the choice of research method used, ideologies surrounding victimisation have impacted upon the actual application of the chosen method, and have influenced how research findings have been presented to the wider audience.

Survey-based techniques are very popular tools in documenting the process of victimisation, and have been used to explore the experiences of a wide range of victims from a variety of different theoretical perspectives. Another common approach has been the use of interviewing, whether through structured, semi-structured or unstructured interviews. This chapter highlights the main approaches that have been taken to researching victim-related issues, illustrating how these constitute part of the wider struggle over understandings of victimhood.

National crime surveys

National crime surveys are now a commonplace feature of modern life in western democratic society, and play an important role in gathering information about a wide range of crime-related issues for national governments. But whilst survey research is a long-established social science technique, the application of survey-based methods to help measure and explain perceptions and experiences of crime has a relatively recent history, taking shape within a particular political and social context. The rapid escalation in officially recorded crime rates since the end of the Second World War has helped to focus government attention on victim surveys, due to the well-recognised shortcomings of officially recorded offences as a way of gauging the true extent, and nature of crime (Chambers *et al.,* 1984). But the actual origins of the victim survey can be traced back to 1960s America, when public opinion polls first asked citizens to pick out the social problems they paid most attention to and juvenile delinquency emerged as being a concern shared by many people (President's Commission on Law Enforcement and Administration of Justice, 1967: 50). Soon after, in 1967, the President's Commission on Law Enforcement designed and implemented a victim survey. The Los Angeles riots of 1965, which killed 34 people, injured 1032 and destroyed property to the sum of approximately $40million (President's Commission on Law Enforcement and Administration of Justice, 1967: 32) acted as a catalyst for focussing the state's attention on a wide range of crime-related issues. In 1972 the first round of the National Crime Survey was conducted, which involved a national sample of 72,000 households (Mayhew, 2000). The National Crime Survey was later re-named the National Crime Victim Survey (NCVS) (Koffman, 1996: 44).

In Europe, the first large-scale victim survey was conducted in Finland in 1970 (Mayhew, 2000: 92). In Britain, victim questions first appeared in a 1966 survey on moral attitudes, and the General Household Survey has also included questions on burglary since 1973. The first National Crime Survey in Britain was carried out in 1981, and was called the British Crime Survey (Hough and Mayhew, 1983). Interestingly, the first British Crime Survey was conducted at a time of urban disorder in the United Kingdom, paralleling the American experience 15 years earlier. In April 1981 there was serious disorder in Brixton, London, and this was followed by a series of serious disturbances in July 1981 across a wide range of cities, including Liverpool, Manchester, Birmingham, Sheffield, Nottingham and Leicester. The British Crime Survey was shortly followed by a national survey in Scotland in 1984 (Chambers *et al.*, 1984), and Northern Ireland now has its own survey as well.

National crime surveys are considered to have a number of important functions. First, they are seen to provide an alternative, more accurate, measure of crime than that recorded by the police. There are many reasons why the police figures are not an accurate reflection of the nature of crime in a society, and why the police statistics undercount the level of crime. A person must first recognise what has happened to them as being a crime and they must then decide to report the incident to the police. However, many individuals choose not to inform the police. This may be due to a number of reasons, for example, the event may be considered to be too trivial, or perhaps the victim believes that the police won't be able to do anything anyway, or perhaps simply they are too fearful of the offender.

A police officer once notified must also then record a reported event as a crime, and, due to there being insufficient evidence, or due to technical reasons, an officer may simply 'no-crime' a reported incident. This means that a change in the willingness or ability of the public to report crimes to the police, or a change in police recording procedures, can have a significant impact upon official crime statistics, even though the real level of crime has remained the same (Koffman, 1996). It has been estimated that compared to police statistics, the British Crime Survey counts almost four times more incidents (Koffman, 1996: 65).

National crime surveys include questions about a wide range of offences and also focus on a large number of crime-related issues, and this is why they have also been referred to as 'generic surveys' (Mayhill and Allen, 2002). Generic surveys allow policy makers to examine a broad range of issues. For instance, researchers are able to explore the levels of crime reported to the police, why people don't always report incidents, and what types of incidents tend to be unreported. National crime surveys also include a focus upon attitudes to the police, attitudes towards the criminal justice system, towards sentencing, and also towards individuals' fear of crime (Mayhew, 2000). Indeed, the study of crime-related anxiety has gained increasing government attention, due to the detrimental impact that high levels of fear of crime can have upon community life (Hale, 1992). The wider context to crime can also be explored via the generic victim survey, and so national crime surveys also include questions examining the psychological, financial or physical effects of the crime upon the victim, the methods used by the offender, and whether the offender was under the influence of alcohol or other types of drugs and so forth (Mayhew, 2000). Generic victim surveys are also used to identify and help explain the variables that influence risk of victimisation (Mawby and Walklate, 1994; Mayhew, 2000). For example, national crime surveys reveal that people aged over 60 are least likely to become crime victims, whilst people aged between 16 and 29 have the highest rates of victimisation for personal crimes of violence and theft (Mirrlees-Black *et al.*, 1997: 32). Crime surveys also show that although sexual and domestic offences are committed mostly against women, men are more likely to be victimised by street crime (Mirrlees-Black *et al.*, 1997). Married people report less victimisation than single or divorced people, whereas unemployed people are over-represented in victimisation statistics (The Canadian Urban Victimisation survey, 1984; Garofalo, 1986: 141; Mayhew *et al.*, 1993; Mirrlees-Black *et al.*, 1998). Surveys also suggest that people belonging to minority ethnic groups experience high levels of victimisation. For example, findings from the British Crime Survey show that Pakistanis and Bangladeshis are significantly more likely than white people to be the victims of household crime. They are also significantly more likely to be the victims of racially motivated attacks than Indians, Blacks or Whites (Clancy *et al.*, 2001: 2). However, it has also been argued that when factors such as sex, age, the occupation of the head of the household, unemployment, marital status, educational level, household income are taken into account, these help to explain the higher victimisation levels (Smith, 1997; Mayhew, 2000). Findings from the British Crime Survey also indicate that more than one-third of assaults directed against Asians and blacks are considered to be racially motivated by respondents (Bowling and Phillips, 2003). Crime surveys also suggest that lower income groups are more likely than others to suffer personal violent victimisation, including sexual assault, robbery or physical assault. The characteristics that are associated with high risks of victimisation are thus similar to those associated with offenders: offenders and victims are disproportionately male, young, single, and urban residents of lower socio-economic status (Fattah, 1989).

Although adopting a similar format, the different national crime surveys that are carried out in different countries vary according to how regularly they are implemented, the samples that are used, and the sorts of questions that are utilised. In the United States, the National Crime Victim Survey collects victimisation information twice a year, with US Census Bureau personnel interviewing household members in a nationally representative sample of approximately 42,000 households, involving about 76,000 participants. Households stay in the sample for three years and new households are rotated into the sample on an ongoing basis (Department of Justice, 2003). The British Crime Survey moved to an annual cycle from 2001/02, with 40,000 interviews of people aged 16 or over, now taking place each year. Previous sweeps were held in 1982, 1984, 1988, 1992, 1994, 1996, 1998 and 2001. Ethnic minority booster samples have also been used in order to specifically document the crime and policing issues faced by minority ethnic groups, since a sample of the general population will not contain a sufficiently large number of individuals of minority ethnic identities. British Crime Survey samples originally were taken using the electoral register. However, due to the under-representation of young people, the unemployed, those living in rented accommodation and minority ethnic groups, the Small Users Postcode Address File (PAF) is used, which has a better coverage of household addresses. A drawback with this sampling procedure is that unlike the Electoral Register, the PAF does not list occupants' names (Mayhew, 2000). In Australia, a national survey is carried out as a supplement to the ABS Monthly Population Survey. Information about personal crime and safety issues is sought from the residents of private dwellings aged 15 and over. The survey was first conducted in 1975 with a 12 month reference period and conducted over 3 months. It was repeated in 1983, 1993, 1998 and 2002. Statistics generated by this work can be found at the Australian Bureau of Statistics.

National crime surveys tend to be divided into three core sections. The first section gathers demographic data about the respondent. Screening questions are also used here in order to ascertain whether s/he or other members of their household have been victims of a crime. The second part of the survey is then administered to those individuals who have been identified as victims or whose household has been the victim of a household offence. This victim form is used to gather information about the nature of the offence, its impact and costs, whether it was reported to the police, the police response and details about the offender. The final part of the survey consists of a follow-up section, which is given to all victims and also to a proportion of non-victims, this being used to collect information on respondents' lifestyles, also their fears and attitudes towards crime, their own experiences of the police, and their own law-breaking activities.

An International Crime Victim Survey (ICVS) has also been developed. This was first carried out in 1989 in order to compare the rates of victimisation across different countries. Since the independent national surveys use different sampling techniques and questions, they cannot be used to make accurate comparisons between different countries. Therefore the ICVS has been introduced – this being a fully standardised survey using similar methods of sampling, survey procedures and data analysis and being implemented across a wide range of countries, including both the western and developing worlds. The ICVS examines householders' experiences with crime, the police, their crime prevention strategies and their fear of crime. Social and demographic information is also collected in order to assess individuals' risk from crime. So far, three rounds of the international survey have been implemented in 1989, 1992 and 1996 and researchers have found that this type of survey is expensive and logistically difficult to carry out. There can also be problems relating to the ownership of the research findings and the release of data, since countries with high crime rates will be especially sensitive to this kind of information being presented to the wider public (Mayhew, 2000).

Despite their popularity, and their extensive use by government agencies, national crime surveys can be criticised on a number of theoretical, political and empirical levels. Originally, the National Crime Survey in the United States was promoted by an American Democrat Party that was committed to pursuing social justice through reducing levels of deprivation, poverty and a lack of opportunity that framed both victims' and offenders' lives. This was shortlived, however, since the rise of a new administrative criminology heralded a movement to the right of the political spectrum and the victim survey then came to be used as a tool for mapping out crime so as to increase the social control of problem areas (Jones *et al.*, 1986). In the 1980s, under the governments of President Reagan in the United States and Prime Minister Thatcher in the United Kingdom,

national crime surveys became the political tools of a New Right movement. Under both the Reagan and Thatcher regimes, free market policies
were pursued, whereby the notion of individualism within the context of a
reduced public sector was promoted under the banner of active citizenship
(King, 1987; Hayes, 1994). This entailed the belief that citizens not only
have rights but also have certain responsibilities (O'Malley, 1992; Mawby
and Walklate, 1994).

National crime surveys have been used as a way of identifying those
groups of people most at risk from crime in order to achieve crime prevention strategies as effectively as possible (Mayhew and Hough, 1988). It has
been argued that in this way the overall level of crime might decrease, since
offenders will have less opportunity to engage in criminal activity. This
means that national crime surveys belong to a tradition which holds the individual citizen responsible for reducing their risk of victimisation through
engaging in crime prevention strategies (O'Malley, 1992; Mawby and
Walklate, 1994). Yet discourses that emphasise the duty of citizens to avoid
victimisation can be regarded as implicitly blaming victims for the crimes
that are committed against them, a position that is morally and ethically
questionable. Another problem with the notion of individual responsibility is
that it does not take into consideration the structural processes that impact
upon, and constrain, human action. Poverty and social deprivation may mean
that individuals simply do not have the resources to successfully engage in
crime prevention strategies, which casts doubt on the idea that individuals
have a responsibility to protect themselves from crime (Mawby and
Walklate, 1994). When the British Crime Survey was first implemented during the 1980s, amid large-scale urban disorder, the patterns of victimisation
that it revealed were not used by the government in order to try to examine
the underlying structural reasons for those patterns in order to alleviate social
injustice, but rather, the survey's findings were used as a way of applying
resources in an endless war against crime (Young, 1986). This is despite the
fact that the Scarman Inquiry into the urban riots in the 1980s concluded that
they arose out of social and economic disadvantage, high levels of
unemployment, poor housing and widespread racial discrimination (Benyon
and Solomos, 1987).

Although measuring a higher amount of crime than official police statistics, national crime surveys do not document all crime. Surveys often omit
victimless crimes, such as drug possession. Crimes that the National Crime
Victim Survey excludes are homicide and arson (Kinderman *et al.*, 1997),
whilst the British Crime Survey excludes fraud, drug dealing and murder.
The surveys largely focus upon conventional types of crime, such that
white-collar offences tend to be ignored. Tombs (2000) argues that these
surveys could include questions about health and safety issues at work
or about other types of corporate deviance. However, amongst those

responsible for administering the national crime surveys there may be an implicit assumption that victims of white-collar crime are unaware of their victimisation, and so white-collar offences have been omitted from analysis. This, however, is an inaccurate over-generalisation about the nature of white-collar deviance, since in many cases of white-collar crimes individual victims do become aware of the crimes that have been committed against them. High profile cases of financial crime, such as BCCI, Maxwell and Lloyd's reveal that victims know that they have lost money as a result of the deviant activities of white-collar offenders (Spalek, 1999), and so national crime surveys could in fact be used to measure the extent of this type of victimisation. However, there is little political incentive to include white-collar offences in a national crime survey, as their inclusion would mean an increase in the overall level of victimisation recorded, and thus politicians would have to tackle this large area of social injustice, an area that has traditionally attracted minimal state regulation since this has been viewed as imposing too many costs on business (Snider, 2000).

Another limitation of the national crime survey relates to sampling. No sample can ever represent the population adequately, and by targeting households, national crime surveys tend to exclude many potential victims, those who are at high risk from crime, including homeless people or those in non-household accommodation. Crime surveys exclude people who are in institutional care settings, and so offences against people with disabilities are not recorded (see Williams, 1999a for further discussion about victimisation in relation to disability). Some respondents are impossible for interviewers to locate at home, others are too busy, or simply refuse to take part, yet victimisation rates may be higher for non-respondents than for respondents. These surveys also ask people to recall experiences of victimisation in a particular time period, and so are subject to memory errors (Mayhew, 2000). Household surveys also predominantly focus on people aged 16 or over, and so this excludes children's victimisation, yet studies have found that criminal victimisation is a common feature of many young people's lives (Anderson *et al.*, 1994). As a result, some surveys have included samples of children, and indeed the NCVS interviews people aged 12 or over. However, this does mean that children under the age of 12 are excluded (Department of Justice, 2003).

National crime surveys are theoretically underpinned by the lifestyle model of victimisation, which means that only those aspects of lifestyle that can be articulated and documented are focussed upon. Some experiences may be so common that they will not be relayed to the interviewer, as the individual being interviewed may view them as being just an ordinary part of their everyday lives and not 'crime'. For example, in relation to violent racism, racist assaults may be such an integral part of individuals' everyday experiences that they do not come to the respondent's mind in an interview. At the same time, victim surveys do not provide details about the relationship between the offender and the victim, the geographical, historical and social context to crime, and 'non-traditional' responses to victimisation such as retaliation or forgiveness (Bowling, 1999). Victim surveys also focus on public space, yet when we consider women's victimisation in particular, this often takes place in private, inside the home (Walklate, 1992). In a national crime survey, crime tends to be viewed as a series of discrete events rather than as an ongoing process between individuals. This approach assumes that people mainly lead crime free lives and that once in a while they may be so affected. The British Crime Survey imposes a limit to the number of incidents that an individual can say happened to them, which means that crimes outside of this figure are not included in the research (Genn, 1988), yet according to Bowling (1999), experiences of racial harassment may take place over a number of years. The 1998 British Crime Survey, for example, has imposed a limit of six crime events (Mirrlees-Black *et al.*, 1998: 70), and so the level of multiple victimisation is underestimated by surveys, and may indeed not be included at all (Genn, 1988).

Sensitive topics such as sexual victimisation, domestic violence, racist violence and other forms of hate crimes are considered to be significantly under-counted by national crime surveys. Victims may be unwilling to disclose details of very traumatic incidents to interviewers, especially when other people (the perpetrator even) may be present in the same room. Studies have found that women are much more likely to disclose sensitive information when the interviewer is female and specially trained, yet it is often too expensive to gender-match interviewers with interviewees when conducting national crime surveys (Myhill and Allen, 2002). Due to these sorts of difficulties, some large-scale surveys specifically focussing on women's victimisation have been carried out. These have been utilised particularly in Canada with the adoption of the 'Violence Against Women Survey'. Australia and the United States, together with other countries in Europe, have followed suit. An International Violence Against Women Survey is being proposed, which would use a standard set of questions across a wide range of countries (Myhill and Allen, 2002).

National crime surveys have been redesigned in order to try to increase the level of crime reported to interviewers, especially the level of sexual victimisation. In 1993 the National Crime Victim Survey was redesigned and a new methodology was adopted (Department of Justice, 2003). It was decided that an enhanced screening section was needed that would better stimulate respondents' recall of victimisation, and that additional questions on the nature and consequences of victimisation were also needed. The issue of specifically improving the measurement of crimes against women was raised and questions on rape, sexual assault and domestic violence were enhanced. Researchers argue that the redesigned procedures have led to an increased number of victimisations being counted. For example, 44 per cent more personal crimes, 49 per cent more crimes of violence and 157 per cent more rapes have been counted (Kindermann *et al.*, 1997: 2). Researchers have found that cueing respondents for non-stereotypical crimes, such as those involving offenders who are known to the victim, increases respondents' affirmative answers.

The British Crime Survey has also tried to tackle the issue of the under-counting of sexual victimisation and domestic violence. In 1992 a self-completion component was introduced into the survey, which dealt specifically with sensitive topics. Screener questions were shown on a card and the respondent was asked to reveal their answers by writing them down on a piece of paper and placing their answers in a sealed envelope, known as the pen-and-paper format (PAPI). In 1994 computer laptops were used to fill in questionnaires and this opened up the possibility of using Computer Assisted Self-Interviewing (CASI) for the self-completion modules, which involved respondents operating the laptops themselves. This new methodology led to an increased count. For example, when the system changed from PAPI to CASI, the percentage of 16–29 year olds who admitted to taking drugs rose from 12 to 20. It was also found that whereas only 0.7 per cent of women answered positively to the 1994 main screener question on sexual victimisation, in contrast, 7.5 per cent of women responded positively using the self-completion module screener questions on sexual victimisation (Myhill and Allen, 2002: 8). Other topics included in the British Crime Survey self-completion modules include domestic violence and stalking. This technique also appears to mitigate against the effects of the interviewer's gender, since women are no less likely to report sexual victimisation when the interviewer is male, as when the interviewer is female, using this new technique. The British Crime Survey excludes child abuse as this is considered to be too sensitive an area for a generic survey, and furthermore, self-completion modules on sexual victimisation and domestic violence are restricted to those aged under 60. This is because it is thought that people over 60 may be referring to different dynamics of violence, such as their abuse in care settings rather than domestic violence (Myhill and Allen, 2002). The increased rates of victimisation uncovered by CASI may be due to a number of reasons. The use of a computer might boost the professional appearance of the interviewer, who may also appear to be more neutral to the research participant. Participants may also feel a greater degree of privacy when typing answers directly into a computer (Mayhew, 2000). Certainly, the use of new technology and its impact upon victims' responses is an area that needs to be explored further.

Case study

The British Crime Survey is a large household survey in England and Wales asking about people's experience of crime in the last 12 months and their attitudes to crime-related topics. In 2001/02 and 2002/03, as in some previous sweeps of the survey, an extra sample of people from black and minority ethnic backgrounds were interviewed. The findings here indicate that people from black and minority ethnic backgrounds were more likely to have high levels of worry about burglary, car crime and violence than white people.

Source: H.Salisbury and A.Upson (2004: 1) 'Ethnicity, victimization and worry about crime: findings from the 2001/02 and 2002/03 British Crime Surveys' Home Office Research Findings 237, pp.1–6.

Question

What factors might account for the high levels of fear of crime amongst black and minority ethnic people?

Local crime surveys

Another problem associated with national crime surveys is their lack of providing precise local knowledge, despite the fact that crime is both geographically and socially focussed (Jones *et al.*, 1986; Garwood *et al.*, 2000). This shortcoming has been acknowledged by the Home Office in Britain and so in the mid 1980s it encouraged and helped finance two local crime surveys, one in Nottinghamshire (Farrington and Dowds, 1985) and the other in Merseyside (Kinsey, 1984). Previously, Sparks *et al.*, (1977) carried out a local crime survey in London, however, the study's aims were more methodological as the authors were interested in how well the newly developed survey techniques worked when documenting victims' experiences. The Merseyside Crime Survey involved a sample of 3500 people who were interviewed in the Merseyside area. The report highlighted that individuals living in poor, socially marginalised communities were at high risk of victimisation, an issue that the British Crime Survey tended to overlook through its focus upon statistical averages (Kinsey, 1984).

In the 1980s a new criminological body of work emerged, which was labelled as 'radical left realism'. This movement was a response to the inadequacies of the national crime survey as an instrument to uncover differential crime risk, particularly the high risks that women, minority ethnic groups and socially disadvantaged people faced. Radical left realism was an attempt to provide policies that would specifically help these categories of people, policies derived from the left of the political spectrum, thereby providing a better alternative to the draconian law-and-order policies developed by the New Right politics of the government at that time. Radical left realism introduces the concept of the 'square of crime', in that crime consists of the dynamics of the offender, victim, informal social control and state (policing). Studying victimisation is thus a central tenet of left realism. Local victim surveys developed by left realists are said to be explanatory rather than descriptive or exploratory (Jones *et al.*, 1986). They build on existing knowledge regarding the distribution of risk from crime, and the variables of gender, ethnicity and age are used to inform the sampling process (Walklate, 2001). In this way, the intra-class and intra-racial aspects of crime are acknowledged and lie at the core of left realism.

In 1985 the London Borough of Islington commissioned the Middlesex Polytechnic Centre for Criminology to undertake a crime survey of the area, this being an impoverished part of London. The researchers carried out 2000 interviews with individuals over the age of 16 drawn from a representative sample of households that were selected from enumeration districts. A second sampling exercise was also carried out, involving the generation of an Ethnic Minority Booster sample of Afro-Caribbean and Asian people aged over 16. The researchers also asked respondents whether any other member of the household had experienced any of the crimes included in the survey. The survey itself consisted of two core components. The first part measured a wide range of crime-related issues, including attitudes to the community, to crime, to the police, and experiences with crime as victim, as a witness, and also experiences with the police and with other agencies that deal with crime. The second part of the survey covered the details related to the offence, the offender, and the impact of the crime on the victim. Questions that the Islington Crime Survey (ICS) contained that had not, up to that time, been used in any other victim survey included a focus on non-criminal forms of harassment, such as being shouted at or being followed, and a look at interracial victimisation and also questions about heroin use were included (Jones *et al.*, 1986). At the same time, racist violence was also explored. A later local crime survey, the Second Islington Crime Survey, included questions about commercial crime, injury at work and pollution (Pearce and Tombs, 1992). The findings here included that of those respondents giving definite answers about their experiences of buying goods and services, 11 per cent had been given misleading information about a product that they had bought, 21 per cent believed that they had been deliberately overcharged, and 24 per cent had paid for what turned out to be defective goods or services (Pearce and Tombs, 1992: 71).

The approach taken by radical left realists is considered to more accurately reflect the victimisation experiences of women and minority ethnic people than the national crime surveys administered by central governments (Walklate, 2001). Thus, for example, the ICS uncovered a larger number of sexual assault victimisations than the British Crime Survey. Nonetheless, the extent to which feminist concerns have been adopted by left realism is questionable, with many arguing that the survey method cannot capture women's everyday lives in relation to men (Stanko, 1988; Brown and Hogg, 1992; Walklate, 2001). The concept of a continuum of violence has been introduced by feminist researchers, whereby women's experiences of violence are perceived as consisting of a series of events that pass into one another in a way that each separate event is not distinguishable from the other (Kelly, 1988). This includes the wide range of abuse, intimidation, coercion, intrusion, threat and force that frames many women's lives, thereby highlighting the difficulty of approaching women's victimisation through a survey-based approach that tries to measure discrete events. Indeed, according to Walklate (2001), both national and local crime surveys incorporate a middle-class, male-based perspective in viewing crime as a clear, distinct event. As a result, both local and national victim surveys insufficiently capture the intricate nature of women's victimisation and the negotiation of their personal safety. For this reason, feminist researchers have carried out their own work on women's victimisation, using methods that have been underpinned by feminist research principles, and these are discussed later in the chapter.

Specificity in victim research

All types of generic crime survey, whether carried out at international, national or local levels, are underpinned by a largely conventional view of crime, such that street and property offences are mainly focussed upon, and so other types of victimisation are either undercounted or missed out altogether. Generic crime surveys, in their broad scope, also do not provide an in-depth analysis of the experience of victimisation. This means that researchers interested in exploring non-conventional crimes, or in examining a particular type of victimisation in greater detail, have carried out their own studies, using quantitative and qualitative approaches, and obtaining their samples of victims in a number of different, innovative, ways. Unlike the generic crime surveys, which use household sampling techniques, researchers have contacted specific groups of victims via the police, hospitals or court records (Burgess and Holmstrom, 1974; Maguire, 1982; Levi and Pithouse, 1992; Stanko and Hobdell, 1993; Indermaur, 1995), or via victim support agencies such as Victim Support schemes, Rape Crisis or local Women's Aid refuges (Sales *et al.*, 1984; Corbett and Maguire, 1988; Kelly, 1988; Stanko and Hobdell, 1993). Samples of victims have also been taken from local communities, and publicity in national and local media has also been used as a way of obtaining research participants (Sales *et al.*, 1984; Kelly, 1988). Gaining access to victims can be problematic, particularly with respect to sensitive areas of research. In some cases, access has been negotiated via victim campaign groups, which may be following a particular political agenda, and so the researcher here may unwittingly become part of that agenda.

White-collar victimisation

One area that traditionally has been under-researched is that relating to white-collar victimisation. An assumption that victims of white-collar violations often do not consciously know that they have been victimised has helped to marginalise victims' experiences and so the individual impact of white-collar violations has seldomnly been addressed (Box, 1983; Fattah, 1986; Nelken, 1994). Nonetheless, since the late 1980s and early 1990s, more studies have focussed directly upon the victims of white-collar crime. These studies have involved the in-depth interviewing of victims (Spalek, 1999, 2001), and case studies of large-scale incidents such as Agent Orange, the Bhopal Disaster and the Dalkon Shield have also been undertaken, highlighting the physical damage that white-collar violations wreak, illustrating that such incidents are as harmful as, if not more harmful than, the damage caused by conventional crime (Mokhiber, 1988; Grabosky and Sutton, 1993).

Only a small number of victim surveys relating specifically to white collar crime have been carried out. These surveys suggest that unlike street crime, white-collar crime does not necessarily disproportionately victimise the poor and marginalised (Titus, Heinzelmann and Boyle, 1995). A study by Titus *et al.* (1995) found that the variables associated with victimisation by street crime – area of residence, class or status, marital status, race or gender – did not appear to be very relevant to victimisation by personal fraud. The only two demographic factors significantly associated with victimisation were that of age and education. Age was negatively associated with likelihood of victimisation, meaning that older people were less likely to be victimised. This reflects findings from victim surveys that reveal that older persons are less likely to be victimised by street and property crime than young people (National Crime Survey Data, 1994: 24). A suggested reason why this may be the case is that young people may be more receptive to promises of monetary gain in cases of fraud than older people (Titus *et al.*, 1995). Looking at education, those with a better education were victimised more often. The reasons for this are unclear, although Titus *et al.*

suggest that a reason why education does not seem to protect a person from being defrauded is that an individual may mistakenly believe that their education may give them a greater ability to cope with con artists, thereby actually making them think that the investments that they undertake are genuine (when in fact they may not be). Variables such as area of residence, class, race or gender may not be significant when analysing risk from white-collar victimisation because the location and distribution of white-collar violations may be quite different from that of street and property offences. Variables influencing risk of victimisation from street and property crime are generally associated with individuals' lifestyles and routine activities (Mawby and Walklate, 1994). However, the applicability to white-collar violations of those aspects of lifestyle and routine activities currently identified within the literature is questionable. For example, alcohol consumption has been linked to increased risk of victimisation by street crime (Lasley and Rosenbaum, 1988). However, this may have little significance when looking at risk from white-collar crime. Increased risk from victimisation by street and property crime has also been associated with the time spent outside the home (Hindelang *et al.*, 1978), however, this may also be irrelevant to white-collar violations, as activities which are carried out inside the home (e.g., answering the telephone, using the Internet) may lead to a person being victimised. Poor council estates and multiracial urban areas contain the highest rates of victimisation by street and property crime (Jones *et al.*, 1986; Crawford *et al.*, Jones, 1990). This relationship may not be relevant for instances of white-collar deviance, since white-collar violations can straddle many different geographical locations as offenders can make use of communications media. This means that a white-collar violation can be committed outside of the geographical location of the victims, and can be carried out simultaneously on persons from a variety of geographical and social locations (Titus *et al.*, 1995). Multinational companies market their goods and services at a wide variety of different countries, so that in the case of a dangerous product this may harm large numbers of people across the world. For example, in the case of thalidomide, information which revealed that the chemical was dangerous was suppressed by the company producing this medication, causing thousands of children around the world to be born with disabilities (Walklate, 1989). Unsafe products can also be dumped in poor countries whose regulations are less stringent than in those of the industrialised countries, resulting in large-scale victimisation. The Dalkon Shield continued to be marketed in less developed countries, despite there being overwhelming evidence in the United States that it had dangerous side effects upon those women who used it. Similarly, birth control pills with high levels of oestrogen were sold to poor countries, even though the bad publicity which these contraceptives received made them unsaleable in the western world (Coleman, 1994).

Crimes against businesses

Commercial victim surveys have also been designed and implemented, since crimes against business have traditionally received less attention from policy makers and researchers than crimes against individuals or domestic properties (Douglass *et al.*, 2003). Surveys here have examined non-household targets such as banks, building societies, post offices and industrial estates, although the surveys tend to be small in scale (Mayhew, 2000). In the last ten years, a number of research studies have also examined the level of retail crime, particularly in the United States and Britain. In Britain, the first national survey of 3000 retailing and manufacturing premises was carried out by the Home Office in 1993. This study found that almost 80 per cent of retail premises and 63 per cent of manufacturers had experienced one or more incidents of crime in 1993. For retailers, customer theft was the most common form of crime, whereas a particularly common form of crime experienced by the manufacturers was vehicle crime (Mirrlees-Black and Ross, 1995: vii–ix). In 1998, the Scottish Executive Central Research Unit carried out the first research enquiry into the extent, nature and costs of crime as it affects businesses in Scotland. This survey revealed that roughly six out of ten businesses experienced crime in the year 1998, with many of them being repeat victims since on average, businesses reported nine incidents in that time period (Burrows *et al.*, 1999: 1). In 2001, Bamfield carried out the first retail crime survey to measure differences in retail crime costs across 16 Western European countries, including Austria, Belgium, Spain, Sweden, Denmark and Finland. The survey looked at theft by customers, staff and suppliers rather than other types of crime such as robbery, arson or terrorism. A self-report questionnaire was sent to the head offices of major retailers. On the basis of this, in the year 2000/01 retail crime in Europe is estimated to have cost 29.599 billion euros. This figure also includes the costs involved in implementing security measures, since retailers spend significantly larger amounts of money on this when compared to private households or other types of business (Bamfield, 2003: 130). In 1999, the Australian Institute of Criminology carried out a survey of crimes committed against small businesses. The findings here reveal that of the 3834 small retail businesses in the sample, almost half reported having experienced some type of crime during the previous year. The most common crimes experienced were burglary (experienced by 27% of retailers), shoplifting (experienced by 21%), vandalism (18%), and cheque/credit card fraud (10%) (Australian Institute of Criminology, 2003).

Rural crime

Rural crime surveys have also been implemented. These have been commissioned by local councils and local community safety partnerships and have looked at a wide range of issues, including: burglary and vehicle theft in rural areas; the victimisation of local minority ethnic communities; crimes against business organisations; and people's experiences and views of policing. In August 1999, the case of farmer Tony Martin highlighted the plight of Britain's rural communities, many of which have lost confidence in the police. Tony Martin claimed that he had shot at the burglars in self-defence. The jury however, at his trial found him guilty of murder and he was originally given a life sentence. This provoked much controversy and many members of the public were outraged at his murder conviction, and so police chiefs vowed to do more to combat rural crime. Eventually, Tony Martin successfully appealed against his murder conviction and the Court of Appeal reduced this to manslaughter, which led to a significant reduction in his prison sentence. This case focussed central government concern upon the plight of rural communities, and so Home Office researchers have looked at the crime experiences, as well as the fear of crimes of individuals living in rural areas, using the British Crime Survey. This is possible since the British Crime Survey uses the ACORN classification of 54 neighbourhood types, based on the social and housing characteristics of the immediate area. Researchers argue that ten of these areas can be defined as being rural, and, on the basis of this, estimate that one quarter of the British Crime Survey sample of households are those located in a rural area. Findings from the British Crime Survey suggest that the levels of burglary, vehicle-related thefts and violence in rural areas has been consistently lower than in non-rural areas over the last two decades, and yet in the public's perception the rural community is no longer the crime-free idyll that it was once imagined to be (Aust and Simmons, 2002). The Australian Institute of Criminology has carried out national annual surveys, which look at farm crime. Results from the second National Farm Survey, which was conducted during 2001 and 2002, and which included a sample of 1309 farms, reveal that over 13 per cent of farms experienced crime. The most common type of farm crime was found to be livestock theft (6% of all farms), followed by theft (5%) and vandalism/damage (3%). Moreover, large and remote farms more commonly experienced higher levels of livestock theft, whereas smaller and highly accessible farms more commonly experienced higher levels of damage/vandalism (Australian Institute of Criminology, 2003).

Hate crimes

Specialist victim surveys are carried out by, and on behalf of, a wide range of action groups, which campaign for greater equality for individuals according to their ethnic, and religious identities, their sexual orientation and their disability. Many campaign groups have their own websites and a myriad of victim surveys can be found here. These surveys provide statistical information about the extent and nature of victimisations that are being experienced by particular communities. However, sample sizes tend to be small and so the generalisability of the findings is questionable. For example, Muslim organisations have been monitoring Muslims' experiences of Islamophobia. In Britain, the Islamic Human Rights Commission (IHRC) documented the rise in aggression against Muslims following the September 11th attacks in the United States. Information was collected from a wide range of Muslim organisations; also victims were directly reporting incidents to the IHRC. According to the report, *The Hidden Victims of September 11th* (2002), the IHRC documented 188 cases of verbal and written abuse, 20 cases of discrimination, 108 cases of psychological pressure and harassment and 344 serious crimes of violence. Bowling and Phillips (2003) also argue that although this type of work is often richer than academic sources of information, it might be considered to be partisan in nature.

Action groups tend to present the data obtained from victim surveys in such a way so as to evoke an emotional reaction in the wider audience. This means that qualitative information about specific incidents of victimisation, which can include the brutal and harrowing details of a particular event using graphic language to illustrate the abuses endured by individuals, tends to be presented. For example, Stonewall, a UK based gay rights organisation, presents the results of a study that was carried out in 1996, which looked at hate crimes committed against lesbians and gay men. The fact that individuals were beaten up, or hit, punched or kicked is stressed. The common names that survey respondents were called is also highlighted, names such as 'queer', 'lesbo', 'faggot' and 'dyke' (Mason and Palmer, 1996). This is in stark contrast to the ways in which data is presented within the generic type of international, national and local crime survey discussed earlier in this chapter, whereby findings tend to be presented in a largely mathematical and detached manner, so that although victims' reactions to a criminal event are documented, an emotional response in the person reading the survey's findings is not sought. It seems that the way in which the generic crime surveys present data is underpinned by a particular view of the reader: as an unemotional being, whose body is separated from his/her mind. Data is thus presented in such a way as to appeal to reason rather than emotion. It would appear that the generic type of crime survey belongs to a broader social scientific tradition that values 'objectivity' and 'rationality' over emotionality (Bendelow and Williams, 1998). It might be argued that generic crime surveys objectify research participants, resulting in work that fails to convey the sense of humanity and human suffering that is often at stake.

Data produced by the generic type of international and national crime surveys also tend to group individuals from a diverse range of different communities together. The ethnic classifications that are used and the ways in which data is analysed and presented, means that significant differences between different communities are overlooked. For example, the British Crime

Survey uses the following ethnic classifications: White (British, Irish, Other White background), Mixed (White and Black Caribbean, White and Black African, White and Asian, Any Other Mixed background), Asian or Asian British (Indian, Pakistani, Bangladeshi, Other Asian background), Black or Black British (Caribbean, African). However, there is little consistency in the research reports that arise from the British Crime Survey in terms of the kind of ethnic classifications that are used. In some instances, statistics are presented according to the general categories of Asian, Mixed Background, Chinese/Other, Black and White.[1] Where Pakistanis and Bangladeshis are grouped together with Indians within a broader Asian or South Asian category, this can serve to obscure the particular difficulties faced by Pakistani and Bangladeshi communities, because these groups experience more socio-economic deprivation, and higher offending and incarceration rates, than Indian groups. In other reports, greater disagregation can be found, so that Pakistanis' and Bangladeshis' experiences will specifically be referred to rather than the broader Asian or South Asian category. Researchers designing and implementing the British Crime Survey argue that greater disaggregation of minority ethnic groups is desirable. However, on the grounds of cost-effectiveness, given the size and geographical distributions of the diverse communities, this has not happened. Researchers also argue that they would like to differentiate between Pakistani and Bangladeshi groups. However, due to the numbers being too small to support reliable statistical analysis, the two groups are combined (Clancy *et al.*, 2001). By grouping different communities together within very broad categories, it means that we do not have data in relation to specific groups of people, such as Afghans, Iranians, Turks, Kurds, Somalis, Nigerians and Kosovans, and so policies cannot be set to target these specific communities. At the same time, the religious identity of individuals is bypassed, and so the documentation of the experiences of crime that religious communities have is omitted. Muslim men, women and children, as well as places of worship, in particular have become the targets of hate crime. Sikh and Jewish communities have also been victimised, with synagogues being vandalised and individuals being attacked. This discussion highlights the urgent need for generic international, national and local crime surveys to consider including religious identity when documenting individuals' experiences. Events that take place in the global political arena can have a significant impact on individuals' safety and their sense of well-being, and the long-term nature of the 'war on terrorism' means that religious communities are likely to continue experiencing violence, harassment and abuse from the general public.

Feminist research on women's victimisation

Another area that the generic crime survey fails to capture in any detail is one regarding women's experiences of crime, and so feminist work has been crucial in documenting women's experiences of victimisation. Illuminating women's experiences of sexual and physical violence, abuse and harassment has been part of a wider feminist struggle to make visible women's experiences within social scientific discourses which have traditionally been gender-blind (Cain, 1990; Kelly *et al.*, 1994). As discussed earlier, violence committed against women may not be reported to the police, nor relayed in generic national and local victimisation surveys. In an interview situation, women may not reveal the full extent of the violence committed against them because of the presence of children or the abusive partner at the time, or it may be too distressing to talk about it to the interviewer, particularly when the interviewer is male (Hall, 1985). Thus, feminist writers have argued that both national and local crime surveys fail to detect the true level of crimes such as rape, wife battering and sexual assault (Hanmer and Saunders, 1984; Hall, 1985).

Feminists have used both quantitative and qualitative research methods in order to uncover previously hidden forms of victimisation. This means that a wide range of research strategies can be found in feminist work, including the use of in-depth interviewing, participant-observation, the use of personal journals and the implementation of questionnaires. An approach common to much feminist work is that of involving research participants in the design and analysis of a study, so that the participants are active collaborators in the research process and outcomes. In terms of exploring women's victimisation, this approach means that researchers have invited participants to read and provide feedback on reports, and research tools have been explained to participants. At the same time, the individuals taking part in a particular study may be asked to help develop the categories and questions that are used (Hoff, 1990). In feminist research, a non-hierarchical relationship between the researcher and the researched is pursued through an openness when interviewing, so that a less-structured approach is sought whereby the interviewer is willing to answer any questions that the interviewee poses, since interviewees may want to place the researcher in terms of her being a woman with whom they have shared, common experiences (Oakley, 1981). There is also a concern about the possible consequences that taking part in a research study may have for the participants. Carrying out work on victims of domestic violence may place women in a dangerous situation, whereby the presence of a researcher may antagonise the perpetrator and lead to future violence being committed against the victim. Concerns for women's safety are therefore built into the research strategies that are adopted (see Hoyle, 1998). In contrast to most generic crime surveys, feminist work also often involves the measurement of violence over a lifetime, since violence taking place over a number of years may have a cumulative impact upon the individual concerned (Kelly, 1988).

Pursuing a feminist methodology when documenting women's experiences has led to a greater sensitivity to, and understanding of, women's issues. By pursuing a non-hierarchical relationship between the researcher and the researched this can lead to the research participants being more open with the researcher, so that particularly sensitive or traumatic incidents might be revealed. At the same time, by including research participants in the actual design and data analysis of a study, this can result in research that uses and reflects the participants' own language, experiences and understandings. Also, it can mean that it is less likely that participants will feel exploited, and more likely that the research has been carried out for them rather than on them. However, it may be the case that not all research participants are treated in the same way by the researcher, so that not all participants are given full subject status and allowed to fully engage in the research process. Those participants whose standpoint the researcher shares in terms of political choice and sympathy are more likely to engage in the process of interpretation and theory generation (Cain, 1986). At the same time, black women researchers and activists have criticised feminism for rarely acknowledging differences between themselves and the women that they research. White feminists often assume that there is no power differential between themselves and black women, and that their experiences as women are sufficient to establish trust and rapport. As an oppressed group, white women have therefore not viewed themselves as also being likely oppressors (Hooks, 1982), even though black feminist researchers have accused them of adopting theoretical positions and research strategies that adopt a racist perspective and reasoning (Amos and Parmar, 1997; Collins, 2000). Mainstream feminist analyses must therefore engage much more fundamentally with differences between women. Tackling diversity amongst women raises many important theoretical and empirical issues for western feminism. For further discussion see Edwards and Ribbens (1998), Afshar and Maynard (2000), and Spalek (2005b).

Case study

Using feminist principles of research, Spalek (2005b) interviewed ten Muslim minority ethnic women who wear the Hijab in order to document their experiences of victimisation. Spalek (2005b) argues that her subject positions of being a 'woman', being 'white' and being a 'western academic' influenced the data collection and analysis phases of the research.

Question

How, and in what ways, do you think that the gender, race and western outlooks of the researcher influenced this study?

Conclusion

Victimisation can be explored from a wide variety of perspectives, using a broad range of different research strategies. The survey technique has perhaps dominated victim research, illustrating the remarkable flexibility of this research method, which has been utilised by researchers adopting different theoretical traditions. Clearly, generic international, national and local crime surveys have many limitations, despite their popularity amongst state officials. The victimisation of religious communities, women and children are rarely documented, and victimisation by white-collar crime is almost completely ignored. As a result, information about these areas of human experience must be found elsewhere, via the work of feminist or radical researchers, or via the work of victim or community action groups. Research here offers the most important glimpses into hidden forms of victimisation, and the often harrowing and brutal experiences of victims are presented to the wider audience. An experience of victimisation can include a plethora of emotional, psychological, behavioural, physical and emotional impacts, and these are discussed in detail in Chapter 5.

Questions

1 What are the advantages and disadvantages of national crime surveys?
2 What are the main characteristics of feminist research?
3 In what ways can national and local crime surveys obscure the experiences of particular minority ethnic communities?

5

Understanding Victimisation: Exploring Harms

Introduction

Since the 1970s much research has been generated exploring the consequences of a broad range of victimisations upon those individuals either directly or indirectly involved.[1] Researchers from many different subject disciplines have contributed to this vast area of work, and for the purposes of this chapter, we shall be focussing mainly upon the research that has been carried out by social scientists, particularly from those involved in the fields of criminology, criminal justice, victimology and social psychology.

The research here suggests that the process of victimisation is often severe and multi-faceted. Different types of crime, including rape, physical and sexual assault, robbery, burglary and incest, impact upon the victim in a multitude of ways, psychologically, emotionally, behaviourally, financially and physically. This includes immediate effects, as well as those lingering over weeks, months and years. Research also suggests that the severity of the experience of victimisation, and the long-term impact on victims, is likely to vary according to the nature of the event that the victim encounters, the demographic characteristics of the victim and the kind of support mechanisms that the victim has access to.

Whilst the differences between victims are often acknowledged, however, these have been insufficiently explored or addressed. By abstracting the categories of identity, research often fails to articulate what an experience of victimisation actually means to a person in terms of their race, gender, class (and so forth) subject positions, and hence studies tend to homogenise victims and their reactions. This chapter, therefore, not only seeks to present the existing literature that explores the experience of victimisation, but also seeks to suggest areas that require an enhanced focus, if the issue of diversity amongst victims is to be pursued. If agencies of the criminal justice system, as well as organisations from the voluntary and welfare sectors, are seeking to develop effective ways of supporting and helping victims, then greater attention must be paid to differences between victims, and the implications that these differences have for service delivery. This chapter stresses that victim belief systems are of crucial significance when understanding the process of victimisation.

Victimisation: the psychological impact

The shattering of cognitive meanings

According to social psychologists, individuals lead their daily lives around cognitive meanings relating to themselves and the world around them. These cognitive meanings consist of a belief in personal invulnerability; a belief that the world is meaningful and comprehensible; and a positive view of one's self (Janoff-Bulman, 1985). These meanings provide individuals with expectations about themselves and their environment. A victimising experience can fundamentally alter these assumptions, such that the victimised person feels a sense of helplessness and vulnerability, a sense of incomprehension at what has occurred, and a negative view of him/herself and wider society. Victimisation simply does not 'make sense' as its meaning does not fit with the social laws of invulnerability, a meaningful world, and a positive view of one's self that the person previously held about the world (Janoff-Bulman, 1985). For instance, a consequence of being burgled is that individuals might experience a general disillusionment with humanity, and a complete loss of faith in people (Maguire, 1982). Moreover, as the majority of burglaries remain unsolved, many victims may also spend many hours wondering about the identity of the offender, leading them to be suspicious of their neighbours, any trades people operating in the area or any other individuals with whom they come into contact with on a regular basis (Mawby, 2001). Individuals experiencing violent property crime also report becoming more suspicious of people in general (Indermaur, 1995). In Kelly's (1988: 202) study of women with experiences of rape, incest or domestic violence, over 90 per cent felt that their attitudes to men had been affected by the assaults. By far the most common response was distrust of all men or certain groups of men. This reflects other findings in relation to women who have been raped, which indicate that many women report negative feelings towards men and a reduced trust (Katz and Mazur, 1979). Hence following victimisation, individuals' perceptions may be marked variously by feelings of danger, insecurity, and self-questioning of one's own behaviour (Janoff-Bulman, 1985).

The loss of a sense of control

Many studies of victimisation document how such experiences can lead to a loss of a sense of control, and a feeling of vulnerability for the individuals concerned (Taylor *et al.*, 1983; Kelly, 1988; Brown *et al.*, 1990; Indermaur, 1995). For instance, a study examining the impact of violent property crime on individuals found that it was a loss of control and power that disturbed victims for a long time afterwards (Indermaur, 1995). Similarly, families of murder victims often experience a loss of control and a sense of powerlessness, intensified by factors which lie outside of their control such as, for example, having to arrange a funeral (Brown *et al.*, 1990). Women who have lived through sexual violence also often report a loss of a sense of control over their lives (Kelly, 1988). This can in turn lead to a loss of self-confidence (Taylor *et al.*, 1983; Kelly, 1988; Indermaur, 1995).

Self-blame

Some individuals find ways of restoring a sense of control, thereby increasing their self-confidence. One way is through the process of self-blame. Researchers have documented that there are two types of self-blame: attributing blame for the victimisation to one's behaviour; or attributing blame to one's personal characteristics. It is argued that the former is adaptive to a victimised individual's survival, whilst the latter is detrimental. This is because by holding his/her own behaviour as in some way being responsible for the victimising experience, the individual is restoring a sense of control over her/his life since they believe that they can change their behaviour in order to prevent a future victimisation. Holding one's character as responsible, on the other hand, does not restore control, since personality characteristics cannot be so easily changed (Janoff-Bulman, 1985). According to Kelly (1988), women who have experienced sexual violence review their own behaviour in terms of provocation, risk-taking and avoiding assault. Through examining their own behaviour, women hope to discover what they could have done differently in order to avoid further victimisation. This may have the positive effect of placing the individual back in control (Kelly, 1988). Similarly, a study examining the impact of rape found that where the woman attributed the rape to her own 'irresponsibility' she was able to regain some sense of control over her fate and to re-establish the world as a safe and predictable place (Mezey, 1988: 76). In these instances, women are blaming themselves not in terms of preventing the assailant's actions, but rather, for being victims, and so their attacker's actions are not necessarily exonerated (Miller and Porter, 1983). On the other hand, when blame is placed upon personal characteristics, this may lead to depression (Janoff-Bulman, 1985).

Women abused by their husbands or partners face the task of attributing blame not only to one episode of violence, but to a series of episodes. Thus, victims of domestic violence look for reasons to explain the actions of their partners (Miller and Porter, 1983). Research about battered women commonly shows that women often blame their own personalities for continuing to live with the abuser and being subjected to repeat assaults. This is further compounded by the abusers often trying to justify their actions through blaming the victim. Inadequate institutional responses, and a cultural norm which stresses that women are largely responsible for the success or failure of human relationships may also influence women's tendency for self-blame. Battered women may therefore feel shame, through their perceived failure (Dobash and Dobash, 1979; Hoff, 1990). Other factors have also been found to influence battered women's self-blame and self-confidence. In Miller and Porter's (1983) study of women abused by their partners, the more extreme the women perceived the violence to be, the more certain they were that it was their partner's and not their own, fault. A battered woman's self-esteem may also not be affected where the woman blames a part of her personality that she respects, for instance, her independence. Indeed, this may lead to the woman being more optimistic about her future. Self-confidence may also not be affected where the battered woman blames a characteristic of hers that she no longer believes she has (Miller and Porter, 1983). In the case of violence carried out against lesbians and gay men, this may lead to the victimised individual blaming their own sexuality for the violence that they have experienced (Curry and Stanko, 1997). This may have a severe impact upon how well these individuals cope with their victimisation (Bard and Sangrey, 1979).

Comparing one's experiences with that of others'; hypothetical worlds

Following a victimising experience, individuals may also favourably compare their experiences with those of other people's, as a way of coping with their trauma. For instance, in the case of a huge fire which broke out in Los Angeles, which damaged many properties, in the newspaper the *Los Angeles Times* (April 21st 1982), a young father was quoted as saying 'We were luckier than the retired ones', whilst a 78-year-old woman was quoted as saying 'I'm worrying about the younger people' (Taylor *et al.*, 1983: 30). Individuals who have been victimised also often create hypothetical worlds in which the victimising experience is even more devastating. Individuals may be repeating the fears that they had during the traumatic episode. For example, rape victims report more terror around the possibility of being murdered than the rape itself at the time of the event (Taylor *et al.*, 1983). Rape victims also frequently note that they could have been killed, or subjected to greater violence (Burgess and Holmstrom, 1974). Constructing 'worst case' scenarios can have a positive effect, as individuals then come to believe that they have been lucky, because the outcome of the event may have been much worse.

A search for meaning

A further psychological way of mitigating the detrimental effects of victimisation is through finding meaning in the victimisation experience itself. If the victimisation can be seen to be serving 'a purpose', then the victimised individual can to some degree restore the belief in a just, ordered world (Janoff-Bulman, 1985). Taylor *et al.*, (1983: 32) highlight the case of a woman who had been savagely beaten, shot in the head and left to die, but who had survived. She was later quoted as saying that the event had led to a reconciliation with her mother. In a study looking at victims of father–daughter incest, women's search for meaning was found to be very important. Thus, although sexual abuse had terminated an average of 20 years ago, over 80 per cent of the sample of women still reported searching for some reason regarding why the abuse occurred (Silver *et al.*, 1983: 86). For those who did find reasons, they did so through examining the situation in their homes at the time of the abuse, together with the character, motives and behaviour of their fathers. The longer the abuse continued during childhood the longer the search for meaning in adulthood. Where women found some understanding of the events that occurred in their lives, it helped them to cope with their victimisation (Silver *et al.*, 1983). Similarly, in a different study of women who had been abused as children by their fathers, it was found that those women who were able to understand why this had happened, were less psychologically distressed than those who could not make any kind of sense out of the experience (Janoff-Bulman, 1985). However, a substantial proportion of incest victims do not find a reason which explains why the abuse occurred, and in Silver *et al*'s (1983: 7) study, over 50 per cent of the women could not understand why they had been sexually violated.

Attitudes towards perpetrators

Attitudes towards perpetrators have also been examined and the results here are rather mixed, illustrating the heterogeneity that can be found amongst crime victims and their reactions. Some authors suggest that where the victimisation is particularly severe, such as in the case of the death of a partner or child, individuals may be more likely to exhibit hatred towards the offender. Strong retributive attitudes towards offenders may also be experienced. This involves the belief that the person who caused the death of their partner or child should receive punishment commensurate with the heinous crime that was committed (Brown *et al.*, 1990). In these cases, the bereaved are especially distressed if the perpetrator fails to show remorse for what has happened. In the case of burglary, retributive feelings may be comparatively rare. In Maguire's (1982: 140) classic study of burglary victims, for example, fewer than 30 per cent thought that their burglar should receive a custodial sentence. It seems that these individuals believed that prison is an inadequate response to criminality and that the offender should repay his/her debt in a useful way by working for the community. However, those who had been most seriously upset by the burglary were the most likely to display vindictive feelings towards the offender. This included a desire for personal revenge or corporal punishment. Those who believed the burglar to be a professional were more likely to want severe punishment than those who thought that the crime was committed by 'amateurs', such as young people (Maguire, 1982: 140). In Shapland *et al*'s. (1985) study of victims of violent crime, it was found that individuals were not particularly punitive in the sentence that they believed the offender should receive.

Victimisation: the emotional impact

The emotional reactions commonly documented by researchers include shock, confusion, helplessness, anxiety, fear and depression (Gittleson *et al.*, 1978; Dobash and Dobash, 1979; Katz and Mazur, 1979; Janoff-Bulman and Frieze, 1983; Shapland *et al.*, 1985; Brown *et al.*, 1990; Ehrlich, 1992; Stanko and Hobdell, 1993; Indermaur, 1995). For example, Indermaur's (1995) study of victims of violent property crime shows that the individuals experienced feelings of shock, surprise, fear or horror when initially confronted by the offender. Maguire's (1982) study of burglary victims illustrates the severe emotional consequences that this crime has for victims. When asked to indicate what had been the worst thing about the incident from a checklist, 44 per cent of victims indicated this to be emotional turmoil which might include anger, shock, upset/tears/confusion or fear.

Fear

Some researchers argue that in many instances, the fear that people feel relates to a fear of death at the time of the victimisation. For example, a study carried out by Stanko and Hobdell (1993) exploring the impact of physical assault upon male victims, indicates that for some of the men here the fear they felt was related to the terror that they might be killed during the time of the assault. Women who have been raped commonly fear death at the time of the violence (MacDonald, 1971; Burgess and Holmstrom, 1974; Russell, 1975; Katz and Mazur, 1979). After the rape, many women will then fear being raped again, they may also have a fear of all men in general, there may also be a subsequent fear of sexual intercourse, a fear of pregnancy, a fear of venereal disease or of contracting AIDS (Burgess and Holmstrom, 1974; Katz and Mazur, 1979). Domestic violence also elicits a high level of fear in victims, with women reporting fearing their husbands and the likelihood of experiencing violence in the future. Women thus become nervous and expect future incidents (Dobash and Dobash, 1979). Less serious male crimes against women can also elicit significant levels of fear. For example, in cases where men genitally expose themselves to women ('flashing'), women here may report high levels of fear, due to them being frightened of the possibility of sexual assault or even death at the time of the offence. McNeill (1987) argues that the main influence upon how each individual woman reacts to 'flashing' is often related to a realistic personal assessment of the possible danger in that particular situation (McNeill, 1987). A common emotional response to burglary is fear, particularly amongst women. In Maguire's (1982) study of burglary victims, 15 per cent of the individuals indicated a general reaction of insecurity, resulting in fear when entering the house or some of its rooms, or feeling fearful when alone in the house during hours of darkness.

Anger

Anger is also a common response to crime, particularly amongst male victims. For example, Maguire's (1982) study of individuals victimised by burglary found that while almost 50 per cent of female victims reported shock or some form of emotional distress, the most common initial reaction by men was one of anger. These reactions included a wide range of severity – anger ranged from 'indignation' to 'blind fury' (Maguire, 1982: 124). With respect to the issue of sexual violence against women, some research studies suggest that women who have been raped often express little overt anger towards the rapist (Katz and Mazur, 1979; Mezey, 1988). Some argue that this may be because women are conditioned to repress their feelings of anger (Katz and Mazur, 1979), on the other hand, Mezey (1988) argues that this may be because during the rape itself many women have to suppress their anger in order not to provoke a greater level of violence from the attacker. Thus, anger towards the rapist rarely emerges, and the woman often then tends to blame herself (Mezey, 1988). Women who are violently beaten by their husbands or partners may feel intense anger. Sometimes the anger is directed at behaviour other than the physical abuse itself: for instance, if the partner spoils a special occasion such as a child's birthday (Dobash and Dobash, 1979).

Post traumatic stress

Severe reactions that may result from a victimising experience have been described as 'post-traumatic stress disorder' (PTSD), which is presented in the American Psychiatric Association's DSM III (1980). PTSD includes the victimised individual re-experiencing the trauma via memories, intrusive thoughts, dreams and a numbing of responsiveness. Post-traumatic stress disorder can also often involve feelings of detachment from others, a diminished interest in significant activities, an exaggerated startle response, sleep disturbances, trouble in concentrating, and the development of phobias (Janoff-Bulman and Frieze, 1983). Male victims of assault commonly display phobias, a disruption to routine sleep and social patterns, hyper vigilance and exaggerated startle responses (Stanko and Hobdell, 1993). Individuals victimised by burglary may experience a difficulty in sleeping, and in at least three cases in Maguire's (1982) study, paranoid symptoms were displayed where the victims believed that somebody held a grudge against them and was 'watching' them. A disturbing long-term effect almost exclusively experienced by women was that of a 'violation or a presence in the house' (Maguire, 1982). In cases of sexual assault, when the attacked person fears for his/her life during the assault, this is likely to lead to post-traumatic stress disorder (Sales *et al.*, 1984). Families of murder victims experience sleep disturbance, including nightmares, acute stress and isolation (Brown *et al.*, 1990).

Internalising or hiding emotions

Some researchers suggest that emotions might be repressed by some victims and that this might be detrimental to them due to the physiological changes that this might induce, for example, by raising blood pressure levels. However, Wortman (1983) suggests that expressing emotions may not always have a beneficial effect, especially when other people may respond to the victimised individual in a negative way. Emotions such as anger and bitterness may evoke a less sympathetic response from others than fear or guilt. Negative responses from other people may have a negative effect upon how well the victim survives the event (Wortman, 1983).

Victimisation: the behavioural impact

In many instances of victimisation, individuals report a change in their behaviour. These changes can be quite specific, although more pervasive lifestyle changes are also common. Researchers have highlighted how, following a victimising event, many individuals will avoid particular situations or locations where they feel unsafe as a consequence of the act that has been perpetrated against them. These locations may be the actual places in which the criminal event occurred, but there may also be other locations which contain similar characteristics to the place in which the crime originally took place. For example, Stanko (1990) highlights the case of one man who was often beaten in the toilet by his school peers. As a result, this man never uses public toilets:

> I've been terrified of men's rooms. Especially in places where men are apt to congregate, just because that was the place where I used to get beat up the most. (Stanko, 1990: 47)

In a study of rape victims (Scheppele and Bart, 1983: 69–71), while 12 per cent responded that the rape had caused a minimal change to their behaviour, 33 per cent were more likely to see situations similar to the ones in which their assaults took place as dangerous. These women would avoid the places where they were attacked, as well as the times that they were attacked (i.e. day or night).

Often, a more general, pervasive lifestyle change is brought about as a result of an experience of victimisation. For example, McNeill (1987) highlights the case of a woman who was flashed at whilst she played tennis at the age of fifteen with a friend in the early evening. This woman stopped playing tennis altogether. Other women in McNeill's (1987) study reported no longer going out at night as a result of their experiences (McNeill, 1987). Verbal abuse against lesbians and gay men can restrict their everyday behaviours through the fear of physical attack. Some of these individuals may withdraw from public space altogether (Herek, 1992). Rape often has a significant impact upon women's behaviour. Scheppele and Bart's (1983) work, for example, illustrates that 32 per cent of the rape victims who took part in the study exhibited a 'diffuse reaction', whereby women perceived a broad range of situations to be dangerous and not only those similar to the context in which the crime occurred. Twenty-three per cent had a 'total fear' reaction. This is characterised by a greatly increased perception that the world is dangerous and that every situation is potentially dangerous. Women here would often say that they were always afraid (Scheppele and Bart, 1983: 69–71). Rape may also lead to a lack of sexual desire, which may cause relationship difficulties (Burgess and Holmstrom, 1974). Women who are assaulted by their partners seek to change their own behaviour so as to try and avoid future beatings, this may involve complying with the man's wishes, or avoiding the man when possible. Some may also either temporarily or permanently leave their partners (Dobash and Dobash, 1979; Norris and Feldman-Summers, 1981). A study of women who have been raped by their husbands reveals that after leaving their husbands, these women may decide never to marry again (Russell, 1990). Stanko and Hobdell's (1993) study of male victims of physical assault illustrates how some men chose a period of isolation, while others armed themselves for future encounters. Indermaur's (1995) study illustrates that violent property crime can also have a major impact upon individuals' behaviour, since in all cases individuals increased their home and personal security. Some of the victims in this study also resigned from their jobs, whilst others moved home. Burglary victims may also move home. A study by Dugan (1999) reveals that being the victim of a property crime increases the likelihood of moving home within the following year by 12 per cent (Mawby, 2001: 47). Mawby (2001) stresses, however, that not everyone will have the resources to move, and so people from socially and economically deprived areas are more likely to be imprisoned in places where they feel unsafe. Raped women may also move home as a result of feeling unsafe where they live, or due to fear of retaliation from the offender (Katz and Mazur, 1979). Individuals who have been sexually harassed at work may leave their jobs, or their work performance may decline (Russell, 1982).

Behavioural responses such as those illustrated above may have a positive impact upon an individual's ability to cope, as they can provide an individual with a sense of control, thereby minimising their perception of vulnerability (Janoff-Bulman and Frieze, 1983). At the same time, however, they may cause unnecessary restrictions to a person's life. Other types of behavioural change in the aftermath of a victimising event can be very harmful for the individual concerned, especially where a victim consumes alcohol or other types of drugs in order to try to minimise the psychological and emotional harm that is experienced. Russell's (1990) study of women raped in marriage reveals how a significant proportion of women used alcohol in order to cope with their situations.

Victimisation: the physical impact

The physical effects of victimisation can range from mild injuries, to severe internal and external injuries (Stanko and Hobdell, 1993). Many victims require medical help, which may be provided by a hospital casualty department, a police doctor, or the victimised individual's general practitioner (Shapland *et al.*, 1985). Women who have been raped may suffer irritation to the throat as a result of forced oral sex, also vaginal injury or rectal pains and bleeding. Headaches, nausea and fatigue are also symptoms which have been documented (Burgess and Holmstrom, 1974). A study of 153 women who attended a sexual assault service in Newcastle Australia between 1997 and 1999 reveals that non-genital injuries were found in 46 per cent of the women examined (although these were mostly minor injuries) and genital injury was found in 22 per cent of women (Palmer *et al.*, 2004: 55). Women who have been raped may become pregnant as a result and this may lead them to undergoing abortions or placing their babies into adoption (Katz and Mazur, 1979; Russell, 1990).

A particularly distressing physical effect of victimisation may be that of self-destructiveness. This is where the victimised individual may try and kill her/him self. In cases of wife battering, for instance, women may blame themselves for the violence committed against them to the extent that they may take, or attempt to take, their own lives (Dobash and Dobash, 1979). Often, women think of committing suicide but do not do so 'for the sake of their children' (Hoff, 1990). Women raped by their husbands may also try and take their own lives. These women often experience physical and sexual violence from their husbands and committing suicide is the option used by these women as a means of ending this (Russell, 1990). Women suffering physical and sexual violence from their partners may also try to kill their partners when there appears to be no other solution to their problem (Dobash and Dobash, 1979). In cases of father–daughter incest, women may also attempt to take their lives. According to Silver *et al*'s (1983: 85) study, 46 per cent of the women interviewed reported attempting suicide.

Victimisation: the financial impact

Victims may incur substantial financial losses as a result of the costs involved in going to the police, the court, seeking legal advice, or lobbying in Parliament (Shapland *et al.*, 1985). Time spent in physical or psychological recovery may lead to a substantial loss in income due to the individual being unable to return to work. Studies about women who have been raped reveal that they can experience significant financial losses due to being unable to return to work. Some women may also become pregnant as a result of the attack on them, and so may then have to bear the cost of bringing up the child (Katz and Mazur, 1979; Russell, 1990). Burglary victims may also take time off work to recover (Mawby, 2001). Victims of domestic violence who leave their homes may be thrust into poverty due to no longer having the partner's wages to rely upon. This is particularly acute when children are involved, since if the woman goes to work she will have to pay for childcare facilities. The families of murder victims often have to cope with significant financial difficulties. The individuals concerned may be unable to return to work for a considerable amount of time due to their grief, and if they are self-employed this means that their income stops altogether. Death certificates are necessary where families want to make withdrawals from the deceased's bank accounts. Death certificates are also necessary for claiming insurance policies, tax rebates and unpaid salaries. However, these may take many months or even years to obtain, depending upon how many post-mortems are carried out and whether or not an offender has been apprehended. Additionally, extra costs have to be met, such as funeral expenses, the expense of going to the mortuary, to court and so forth (Brown *et al.*, 1990).

Victims can also incur significant costs in trying to increase their security. For example, rape victims may buy new doors and locks for their homes (Katz and Mazur, 1979). Burglary victims may also spend large sums of money trying to make their homes more secure (Maguire, 1982). A substantial proportion of burglary victims may also not be insured. According to data from the British Crime Survey 2000, only 48 per cent of victims of burglary with entry were insured. Victims are less likely to be insured than non-victims because they are over-represented among poorer people, and so cannot afford to pay insurance premiums. Indeed, those individuals who do not have household insurance are more likely to be divorced, single, separated, living in rented accommodation, unemployed, Asian, Afro-Caribbean and inner-city dwellers (Mawby, 2001: 42). Insurance payouts may not reflect the real value of the goods stolen, since insurance companies might dispute the value of listed items. At the same time, victims may have to pay out the first £50 or £100 before they receive any type of insurance payment. There is also the additional issue of the sentimental value of stolen goods, since certain items that are taken may be irreplaccable, such as, for example, jewellery or photographs (Mawby, 2001).

Case study

Post-traumatic stress disorder (PTSD) has long been associated with warfare. The syndrome was first identified in the survivors of trenches in the First World War, it was increasingly recognised in bomber crews and infantry during the Second World War and then studied intensively by US researchers during the Vietnam War. This research established that the longer that people are exposed to conflict, the more likely they are to experience psychiatric damage. In May 2003 British army veterans brought a court case claiming for compensation for the after-effects of trauma suffered in active service in the Falklands, Northern Ireland, Bosnia and the 1991 Gulf War. They lost the case, however, as a High Court judge ruled against the accusation that the Ministry of Defence had failed to adequately prepare personnel for the inevitable exposure to the horrors of war. Had the claimants been successful, it could have led to compensation of up to £100 m being paid.

Question

Should a distinction be drawn between someone who suffers PTSD as a result of their job, and a person who suffers from PTSD due to being the victim of a crime?

Summary

As illustrated in the discussions overleaf, the experience of victimisation involves a wide range of psychological, emotional, behavioural, physical and financial impacts. Research further suggests that a variety of factors will influence the severity of these experiences, and so these are now addressed.

Influences upon the severity of the impact of victimisation

Research studies looking at the factors that might influence the severity of a particular victimising event have generally focussed upon three areas: pre-victimisation factors (which consist of the demographic and psychological characteristics of victims, the quality of their relationships and chronic life stressors), factors which relate to the specific characteristics of the victimising event itself, and post-victimisation characteristics (which include factors such as the amount of time following the event, and formal and informal systems of support).

Pre-victimisation factors

Victim characteristics such as age, marital status, employment, education and sexuality have been examined to see whether these have any effect. With respect to burglary, the results show that age, gender and socio-economic status are important variables in terms of how individual victims experience the crime committed against them. According to Maguire (198: 131), 62 per cent of the most severely affected of people victimised by burglary were separated, widowed or divorced. Maguire (1982) concludes that the reason for these findings may be that these individuals were already experiencing a number of stresses in their lives. Using data from the 1988 British Crime Survey on burglary victims, Mawby and Walklate (1994) highlight how women, older people, those living in households with no other adults and divorced victims were most affected. Those on lower-incomes, those living in rented accommodation and individuals belonging to minority ethnic groups were also worst affected. In a cross-national study directed by Mawby (1992 in Mawby, 2001), which compared the experiences of burglary victims in cities in five countries: Plymouth and Salford (England), Munchengladbach (Germany), Warsaw and Lublin (Poland), Miskolc (Hungary) and Prague (Czech Republic), the research here revealed that whilst there was no clear pattern with regard to older victims, those under 30 were significantly less likely to be affected. Women consistently described themselves as being more affected, as did individuals from single-parent households and from socially and economically deprived backgrounds (Mawby, 2001: 48).

In a research review of rape victims, Sales *et al*. (1984) found that marital status did not seem to influence the impact of the crime, and that neither did employment status, education nor religion. Sales *et al*., found that age has an impact, although in quite a complex way. In the immediate post-assault period, younger women demonstrated higher levels of symptoms, however, these were of quite a short duration and six months later younger women were experiencing less difficulty than older women. Age may thus have quite a different impact according to the time period since the act of victimisation. This may also be the case for other demographic variables. Sexuality may influence the severity of an experience of victimisation. Where a lesbian or gay man has 'come out' prior to their victimisation, this may lead to a less severe response in the individual. This is because such a person may already have supportive groups and community resources to help them through their experience (Curry and Stanko, 1997). Such a person may also be able to balance their victimisation experience against many other positive aspects to their sexuality (Herek, 1992). Pre-existing problems of drug-use, alcoholism and learning difficulties may lead to greater impact of victimisation (Burgess and Holmstrom, 1974). Similarly, pre-existing neuroses may increase the severity of the impact of victimisation (Sales *et al*., 1984). Social deprivation in terms of unemployment and low income may also affect the ability of individuals to survive (Burgess and Holmstrom, 1974; Young and Matthews, 1992).

Factors relating to the victimisation event

The context in which the victimising event occurs may also influence the impact of the experience. Researchers examining the impact of sexual violence upon women argue that women's ability to mitigate the harms depends upon the context in which the abuse occurs. Where the violence occurs in a place previously viewed by the woman as safe, then this may have a more severe impact upon a woman than if the violence occurs in a place which was regarded as being unsafe (Janoff-Bulman and Frieze, 1983; Scheppele and Bart, 1983; Kelly, 1988). In cases where the offender is known to the victim, the severity of the impact is more severe. Contact with the offender may not necessarily stop after the victimisation, which may cause great distress since contact will not necessarily end with the offence (Shapland *et al*., 1985). The severity of the event also has an influence on the impact upon the person, and the greater the level of violence involved the greater the impact upon the victim tends to be. For instance, a study of women who had either been raped or who had managed to avoid being raped, found that a higher proportion of raped women exhibited severe fear and distress levels than those who had avoided being raped (Scheppele and Bart,

1983: 75). In a further study by Norris and Feldman-Summers (1981) of 179 female rape victims, it was found that as the severity of the assault increased so did the psychological, emotional and physical impacts.

Post-victimisation factors

The time period following the victimising event has also been found to influence the severity of the psychological, emotional, behavioural, physical and financial effects. At first there is likely to be a crisis period, where the severity of the symptoms is greatest. This may then eventually be followed by a reorganisation phase, whereby the victimisation becomes increasingly assimilated and the survivor tries to continue with his/her life. Studies of rape victims have often tended to document the short-term impact of rape, followed by the woman's attempts to restore 'equilibrium'. It has been argued by some researchers that some women will go back to 'equilibrium' while others will continue to show fear, anxiety and confusion. However, many observers (Lewis and Sarrell, 1969; Peters, 1976) have found that rape often leaves a permanent impact upon the woman, which may lead to marital problems, illness and suicide. Similarly, Sales *et al.* (1984) found that at no time during the three years that they spent documenting rape victims' reactions did their symptoms return to their pre-assault level. This is also likely to be the case with other types of crime. In a study of individuals whose partners or children had died due to a traumatising, sudden event such as a hit-and-run, individuals' lives changed dramatically, and individuals experienced painful upsurges of grief (Wortman, *et al.*, 1997). In Stanko and Hobdell's (1993) study, some of the male victims revealed how they felt that the assault had radically altered their lives and, to some extent, their personalities. A study of women who, as children, had experienced sexual abuse from their fathers, revealed that for 65 per cent of the women, memories, thoughts and pictures regarding the incest continued to invade their minds for years after the abuse had taken place (Silver *et al.*, 1983: 92). Moreover, the images that they recalled were still vivid, as the following words of an older woman illustrate: 'I am 72 years of age and I can still "see" as if it just happened, my mother scolding me that day' (Silver *et al.*, 1983: 87). Terms such as 'recovery' or 'resolution' when documenting victimisation are therefore highly problematic, and indeed, do not reflect many individuals' experiences. Victimisation often involves long-term effects, and individuals may remain changed forever.

Support and coping

A helpful social support network might help individuals to cope with the detrimental impacts of crime (Cobb, 1976; Kutash, 1978; Bard and

Sangrey, 1979; Silver and Wortman, 1980; Sales *et al.*, 1984; Kelly, 1988). A supportive social network may consist of friends and family, as well as agents working for a wide range of criminal justice, victim support, and health and welfare organisations. These can provide emotional support, allowing individuals to discuss their experiences, as well as providing victims with practical, problem-solving advice. For instance, in the case of victims of domestic violence, responses from others may involve providing the woman with temporary accommodation, helping her to take care of her children, accompanying her on a visit to a doctor, lawyer, social worker, police station and so forth (Dobash and Dobash, 1979). Victim Support schemes offer significant help to the victims of crime.

A study examining the impact of a visit from a victim support volunteer found that the main objective had been to encourage the victim to express his or her feelings about the crime. Almost two-thirds of the victims said that the visits had made some difference, and 12 per cent had said that they had made a 'very big difference' to how they had coped with the emotional impact of the crime. The authors of the study conclude that a group of individuals who were visited by Victim Support scheme volunteers, when matched against a group of individuals who weren't visited, tended to 'recover' better. The visits seemed to show people that at least 'somebody cared' (Corbett and Maguire, 1988).

However, it is important to bear in mind that responses from other people and agencies may be negative, and this may increase the severity of the victimisation. For instance, in Hoff's (1990) study of battered women, many reported receiving negative responses from professional agencies, and the counselling which they received was often inadequate. Stanko and Hobdell's (1993) study of men victimised by assault revealed that most of the men injured at work experienced a lack of support from their employers. Dissatisfaction with their treatment in court was also expressed by some (Stanko and Hobdell, 1993). When considering victim support groups, many people may feel uncomfortable discussing their plight with strangers. Furthermore, most groups are made up entirely of women because it seems that men may be more reluctant to express their emotions. This may make it problematic for a man to join a victim support group. Individuals may also find it overwhelming in a support group situation to encounter so many people who have had their lives shattered. This may reinforce an individual's view that the world is an 'evil place' (Wortman *et al.*, 1997). With respect to lesbians and gay men, the police and physicians may assume that the victim is heterosexual and so display insensitivity when interacting with the victim (Herek, 1992). Thus, it seems that some responses to victimisation may be inadequate and may not provide significant help for some individuals.

Summary

The studies presented in this chapter so far, provide a general overview about the experience of victimisation. However, it is important to bear in mind that this framework has largely developed from an examination of the experiences of individuals affected by events that are defined as criminal by the state. Events which may be injurious but which may not be defined as crime by law or wider society have tended to be overlooked. Indeed, Newburn and Stanko (1994: 153) argue that victimology is a 'stagnant' discipline as a result of social scientists treating the label 'victim' unproblematically, often adopting taken-for-granted assumptions about which experiences constitute 'victimisation'. Elias (1994) further maintains that researchers have largely confined themselves to officially sanctioned categories of crime. As a result, less detail is known about the experience of victimisation in relation to harms caused by 'non-traditional' crimes such as white-collar offences or institutional violence. These are focussed upon in greater detail in later chapters of this book.

Another crucial limitation to the work presented in this chapter, is that although some attention has been paid to factors such as gender, age, income and sexuality and how these influence victims' experiences, this only constitutes a small proportion of the total work on victimisation, and there is a lack of in-depth research that focuses on documenting how particular communities, based on ethnicity, gender, class, religion and so forth, experience victimisation. This should be of great concern, since a significant proportion of research on victims has a policy and practice focus, whereby a common, underlying theme in many of the studies highlighted in this chapter is that of acquiring knowledge about the victimising process so as to use this to respond effectively to victims' needs.[2]

Diversity amongst victims

Within the literature there seems to be an assumption that the experience of victimisation is generally the same for all people, regardless of significant differences in individuals' class/gender/ethnicity/religious/sexuality subject positions. This means that for individuals whose self-identities occupy positions that lie outside of the dominant norms around which the general experience of victimisation is understood, there is not much knowledge about, nor awareness of, their particular experiences nor how best to develop policy and practice around their specific needs.

Male victims have generally generated little interest from researchers, policy makers and agents of the criminal justice system. This is partly due to stereotypical imagery associated with victimhood, whereby older people, children and women often receive a more sympathetic response to their victimisation than males, and so men are rarely seen as victims (Elias, 1990). Stanko and Hobdell's (1993) study of male victims of assault highlights how individuals experienced their victimisation primarily as men, and so to understand the impact of the offence on them, it was important to situate this within notions of masculinity. The study found that a loss of self-confidence was particularly acute, because many men grow up with an idealised image of manhood as being strong and 'macho'. This means that the victimising experience questions the man's supposed strength. In Stanko and Hobdell's (1993) study, men often articulated the need to be able to take care of themselves and their families. The victimising experience thus caused them to feel vulnerable, and this might be interpreted as an affront to their masculinity. Similarly, Indermaur (1995) discovered that the men who had been physically overcome during a violent property crime had developed a low self-confidence, since they no longer saw themselves as being able to 'look after themselves'. Studies of male victims have also shown that men generally experience more intense anger and a greater desire for revenge than women (Stanko and Hobdell, 1993; Mawby, 2001). According to Herek (1992), male rape may challenge men's assumptions that this crime does not happen to men, leaving them feeling particularly vulnerable and helpless. For this reason, some men may find it difficult to accept that they have actually been raped.

Men's experiences of victimisation is just one area that research needs to focus more specifically on, if differences between victims are to be acknowledged more fully. Another significant, under-developed area, is that relating to individuals belonging to minority ethnic communities and their experiences of victimisation. Following a number of racist murders in the 1990s, the impact of racially motivated crime upon victims has generated substantial research interest (Clancy *et al.*, 2000). As illustrated in the Chapter 4, this has typically involved quantitative methods via the use of local crime surveys examining the extent and level of racist violence. Thus, according to a study carried out by Bowling (1999: 196) in North Plaistow, in the London borough of Newham, 21 per cent of African and Afro-Caribbean women, 19 per cent of Asian men, 18 per cent of Asian women and 17 per cent of African and Afro-Caribbean men had experienced some form of racial harassment, in comparison to 8 per cent of white men and 7 per cent of white women. Victims' reactions included anger, feeling shocked and being fearful. Bowling (1999) further describes how victims might move house, might avoid certain places (e.g., football matches, the pub), and they might invest in crime prevention techniques such as shatterproof glass and fireproof mailboxes. Collective responses to victimisation from within communities may also occur, such as movements opposing racist organisations such as the National Front or the British National Party. Webster's (1995) study shows that young Asian men defending particular parts of territory in Keighley, West Yorkshire, was their way of responding to racial hostility and violence. Bowling's (1999, Bowling and Phillips, 2003) work has produced many important insights into the experience of racist violence, one being the conceptualisation of this via a 'continuum of violence'. This theme has been taken from feminist work on women's experiences of sexual and physical violence, and involves approaching victimisation as a process, which connects everyday acts of abuse with severe forms of violence (Kelly, 1988). This approach also acknowledges that victims of racist violence are often repeat victims, and so individuals' everyday lives are framed by actual, or the perceived threat of, racist acts of abuse and violence (Bowling and Phillips, 2003). The impact of racist crime is particularly severe. Findings from the British Crime Survey (2000) indicate that a much larger proportion of victims of racial incidents said that they had been very much affected by the incident (42%) than victims of other sorts of incident (19%) (Clancy *et al.*, 2000: 37).

Work examining the process and extent of racist victimisation is extremely important, and indeed, Bowling and Phillips (2003) suggest directions that future investigations should take in this area. Nonetheless, research looking at minority ethnic communities' experiences of victimization should not concentrate solely on racist violence, or the racial component of a crime, as this may serve to marginalise minority voices from mainstream analyses of experiences of victimisation. As a result, services supporting the victims of crime, developed largely from these mainstream analyses, will insufficiently help victims who belong to minority ethnic communities. Whilst a significant proportion of offences against blacks and Asians may contain a racial component,[3] other aspects of the process of victimisation should also be explored for a wide range of crimes, so that appropriate services for minority ethnic victims can be developed. Feminist research looking at sexual and physical violence against minority ethnic women (including domestic violence) suggests that there is a substantial and significant cultural context to the offences that take place, and to victims' experiences, their understandings and their survival strategies, and yet mainstream victim support services often fail to take ethnic and cultural differences into account.

In the first detailed survey of domestic violence as experienced by black women, conducted by Mama between 1987–88, it was found that some men might invoke 'tradition' or 'religion' to justify their violent actions, and that some women were also battered through justifications that they were too western. Women also often referred to 'tradition', in that they had tried to conform to idealised notions of a dutiful wife. Extended families are likely to have a more significant role in minority ethnic women's experiences of victimisation, and these may sometimes intervene positively, although they can also make the situation worse. Choudry's (1996:1) study of Pakistani women's experiences of domestic violence further reveals that the Pakistani women who took part in this project felt they faced dishonour and rejection within their own community if their marriages failed, and that language difficulties and restrictions of their personal freedom outside the family home made it very difficult for women to seek help from external agencies. Mama (2000) argues that evidence from her research challenges western feminist understandings of domestic violence, since many of the minority ethnic women that she has studied have often been assaulted by men who are economically dependent upon them, thereby contradicting feminist arguments that relate domestic violence to economic marginalisation and dependence upon men. This argument is also evident in the work of American black feminists such as Richie (2003) and Stark (2003), with Stark (2003: 176) maintaining that 'color blindness works to conceal the unique constellation of culture and psychology that defines the experiences of black victims'. With respect to the issue of why some women stay with violent partners, research suggests that black women may have pity for their partners due to the specific stressors in black men's lives, some may feel that contacting the police is a betrayal of community values, some may also believe that the family unit should be maintained, and this belief might be reinforced by the church (Stark, 2003).

Researchers exploring the impact of rape upon victims have tended to ignore ethno-cultural variables when documenting victims' experiences and processes of recovery (Neville *et al.*, 2004). An important study by Wyatt (1992 in Neville *et al.*, 2004), compared Black and white women's experiences of sexual assault, and found that Black women were generally less likely to disclose the incident and they were more likely to believe that Black women are generally at higher risk of being sexually assaulted than white women. A study by Neville *et al.* in 2004 revealed that race and cultural factors contribute to post-rape recovery. Cultural attributions about why they were attacked were stronger in Black women than their white counterparts. The Jezebel image, a race-gender stereotype of Black women as sexually loose, which has been identified by Black feminist academics, appeared to be internalised by the Black women taking part in this study and identified as a reason why they were raped. Neville *et al.* argue that the more powerfully this image was internalised, the greater was the victim's self-blame, and the lower the level of their self-esteem.

Belief systems and victimisation

When studying the victimising experiences of minority ethnic women, critical black feminists have introduced the concept of 'spirit injury' or 'spirit murder' in order to explain and to try to understand the full impact of racism and sexism upon women's lives (Davis, 1997; Williams, 1997). The continual, daily harassment on the basis of race and gender that black women experience amounts to harm that goes beyond the psychological, emotional, behavioural and physical impacts of crime as documented by researchers. Embedded within the notion of 'spirit injury' is an assertion of the interconnected nature of the self, so that common and recurrent experiences of racist and sexist abuse amounts to a brutalisation of an individual's self-identity and their dignity. If the self is regarded not in isolation (as westernised understandings of self-hood would perhaps have us believe) but as connected to other people and broader social systems, then where racist or sexist abuse is encountered, it will have a substantial impact upon the victim's sense of who they are. Spirit murder can be considered to be the product of an accumulation of a myriad of micro-processes that constitute aggressive, racist, sexist language and behaviour from the 'uncontrollable, powerful, external observers who constitute society' (Davis, 1997: 199). The concept of 'spirit injury' also allows us to think about the impact of racism and sexism upon the wider audience of people, who may not directly be victimised in this way, but who nonetheless are indirect victims because their subject positions link to aspects of society that denigrate parts of their self-identity.

Concepts like spirit injury or spirit murder need to be further explored, and should not be confined within the boundaries of critical race theory. An acknowledgement of spirit injury with respect to people's experiences of victimisation has some important implications when providing support to the victims of crime, since therapies aimed at a more spiritual level, such as the use of alternative forms of healing for example, might be more appropriate in some cases. This area is discussed in greater detail in Chapter 8 of the book.

Individuals' religious affiliations and beliefs should also be increasingly acknowledged when documenting experiences of victimisation. According to Haug (1998: 181), a 1990 Gallup poll in America found that 94 per cent of Americans believe in God, with 60 per cent considering faith to be the most important influence in their lives. According to a study carried out by the University of Michigan, 44 per cent of Americans attend church once a week (Swanbrow, 1997). In Britain, in 2001 the National Census included, for the first time, a voluntary question on religious affiliation. Just over three-quarters of the UK population reported having a religion, with Christianity being the most common faith cited, Islam being the second most common faith (National Census, 2001). People belonging to minority ethnic groups are significantly more likely to view religion as being an important aspect of their self-identities and their lives. A report based on the findings of a Home Office *Citizenship Survey* (2001), highlights the interconnected nature of religion and ethnicity. In contrast to 17 per cent of white respondents who said that religion was important to their self-identity, 44 per cent of black and 61 per cent of Asian respondents said that religion was important. For Muslims, religion was ranked second only after family in terms of the importance to their self-identity (O'Beirne, 2004: 18). O'Beirne (2004) stresses that religious affiliation and ethnicity should be considered together rather than separately when carrying out research and when making policy decisions. Members of faith communities may be victimised by religious hate crime. Muslim communities, for example, are not only likely to experience racist crime, but also crime that is motivated by religious hatred. But whilst we have some understanding of the impact of racist crime upon victims, we do not know how crime that is motivated by religious hatred is experienced by victims, nor do we know its incidence and prevalence. As a result, it is of vital importance to investigate religious hate crime and its impact upon victims so that adequate services can be developed to cater to victims' needs and also so that victims can be encouraged to report their experiences to the police or to other, more suitable, agencies. Religion can also act as an important support mechanism for victims, and Spalek's (2002) study of the victimisation experiences of Muslim women reveals that prayer and meditation were common responses to crime. For example, one interviewee who had experienced burglary on more than one occasion, said that in addition to buying a burglar alarm, her father had gone to the local Imam to ask for special prayers of protection. Also, for some African American women taking part in a study carried out by Shorter-Gooden (2004: 408), participation in a congregation or spiritual community was part of their coping strategies against the debilitating consequences of racism and sexism.

The discussion above adds further weight to the argument that research into the experience of victimisation needs to consider more carefully the role of religion and belief in people's lives, particularly in relation to diversity, and the documentation of minority ethnic groups' experiences. The better the understanding that we have of how specific groups of individuals react to crime, the better will service delivery be informed. The following section discusses work carried out with minority ethnic groups that challenges dominant victimological knowledge constructions of the process of victimisation.

Challenging dominant knowledge constructions

As highlighted earlier in this chapter, researchers argue that a fundamental part of the experience of victimisation is that of the 'shattering of cognitive assumptions' about the world. Prior to the negative event occurring, social psychologists argue that an individual holds a 'belief in a just world', a world where people generally get what they deserve (Lerner, 1980; Janoff-Bulman, 1985; Furnham, 2003). Therefore, it is argued that following an experience of victimisation, the victim may feel a loss of a sense of control over their lives, as they attempt to confront a world that they thought was stable and orderly but which in fact is chaotic and uncontrollable. It seems that mainstream organisations that offer help and support to the victims of crime follow this model of victimisation, since they value giving control back to the victims of crime, since crime is seen as taking control away from the victim. For example, according to a publication by Victim Support, *Helping People Cope with Crime*, which aims to provide people with information about victimisation and what help is available, 'many victims feel that they have suffered a fundamental loss of control in addition to other losses that may be involved' (2000: 4). However, this work may be underpinned by western values and assumptions. It may be the case, for example, that individuals who follow a faith believe that the world is unpredictable and that they have little control over it since God and other forces are at play (Spalek, 2005a). Furthermore, cross-cultural comparisons of a 'belief in a just world' framework of understanding suggest that this belief system is stronger in individuals who have property, wealth or power (Furnham, 1991).

A study by Calhoun and Cann (1994), which assessed the assumptions that individuals make about their own personal worlds or the world in general and assessed whether these assumptions differ for members of a majority or a minority group, found that individuals from the majority group saw their personal worlds as less random, more just, and more benevolent than they saw the world in general. People belonging to minority ethnic groups, on the other hand, saw their personal worlds, as well as the world in general, as less benevolent and less lucky. Furthermore, according to Calhoun and Cann (1994), in the United States, African Americans perceive that they have less control over outcomes that are linked to social or institutional processes than European Americans. In a study of 2628 Californians, Hunt (2000) revealed that Black minority groups held the lowest scores for the 'belief in a just world' construct, moreover, white males occupying a low socio-economic status showed greater support for the 'belief in a just world'. Researchers suggest that differences between minority and majority groups' perceptions might be linked to minority groups' direct and indirect experiences of injustice and victimisation, both at an individual and group level (Furnham, 2003). This discussion illustrates that the constructs used in academic disciplines may be so general that they have little validity when exploring the experiences of specific groups of individuals. Researchers should therefore be encouraged to critically explore the inherent biases that may be present in the socially constructed worldviews that underpin research. Thus, although we can say that we have a very general overview of the process of victimisation, how victimhood is actually experienced by specific individuals, particularly in relation to their subject positions, is largely unknown.

Conclusion

This chapter has reviewed the research looking at the impacts of crime and the process of victimisation. At a very general level, it seems that a victimising experience often involves significant psychological, emotional, behavioural, physical and financial impacts. Nonetheless, this work is both theoretically and empirically rather limited. Differences between individuals have been insufficiently captured and explored, and the norms and assumptions underpinning the research have rarely been made visible and then deconstructed.

The framework of understanding about the nature of victimisation has been constructed largely through documenting the experiences of people who have been affected by events that are defined as criminal by the state. As such, little is known about the consequences of harms caused by 'non-traditional' crimes such as white-collar offences or institutional violence. Also, within the literature there seems to be an assumption that the experience of victimisation is generally the same for all people, regardless of significant differences in individuals' class/gender/ethnic/religious/sexual orientation and other subject positions. Nonetheless, men's experiences of victimisation may be significantly different, and also there is likely to be a substantial cultural context to victimisation. For instance, critical black feminists have introduced the concept of 'spirit injury' in order to explain and to try to understand the full impact of racism and sexism upon women's lives. Also, individuals' religious affiliations and beliefs should be increasingly acknowledged when documenting experiences of victimisation, as participation in a congregation or spiritual community can be part of how a victim copes in the aftermath of a crime. Social psychologists have argued that following an experience of victimisation, victims may feel a loss of a sense of control over their lives, as they attempt to confront a world that they thought was stable and orderly but which in fact is chaotic and uncontrollable. However, this may not apply to all people, and it may be the case, for example, that individuals who follow a faith believe that the world is unpredictable and that they have little control over it since God and other forces are at play. These kinds of limitations in the research about victimisation have important consequences for policy and practice issues when seeking to help the victims of crime. Chapter 6 will examine developments within the official victims' movement and the victim initiatives that have emerged here.

Questions

1 In what ways can crime impact on victims?
2 Why might the impact of crime on men be particularly traumatic?
3 What issues are raised by the diversity to be found amongst victims?

6

Official Responses to Victimisation

Introduction

Over the last forty years, victim services, aimed at addressing victims' emotional, practical, financial, psychological and social needs, have rapidly expanded. In Britain, these developments include the introduction of the Criminal Injuries Compensation Scheme, the formation of Victim Support, and many initiatives arising from the Victims' Charters of 1990 and 1996, which have placed new obligations upon agencies of the criminal justice system to make their practices more inclusive of victims' concerns. These services form part of a broader official victims' movement, which is the main focus of this chapter.

The official victims' movement is so-called because initiatives tend to be funded largely through government. At the same time, the agencies that put these initiatives into practice tend not to be too critical of government policy, but rather, try to persuade government of the need for change, whilst working within the parameters that have been set by politicians and civil servants. But perhaps the most defining characteristic of the official victims' movement is the construction of victimhood that lies at its core. Essentially, the notion of a 'neutral', 'deserving' victim underpins many initiatives, which means that the wider structural context to victimisation is often ignored and victims are viewed from the perspective of them being individuals rather than belonging to broader group collectivities. Victims are also seen as 'innocent', having played no part in their plight, and as being distinct from offenders, and as having experienced harm from events defined as criminal by the state. This means that individuals who are victimised by events that occupy an ambiguous status in social and political arenas, such as the victims of white-collar crime or institutional violence, are omitted. This framework of understanding regarding the nature of victimhood has important repercussions in terms of the help that is provided to individuals, and this chapter examines some of the initiatives that have developed out of the official victims' movement and highlights the predominant models of victimhood that prevail.

Victim support

In Britain, during 2002–03, 1.75 million people were offered help by Victim Support, which is a network of affiliated charities in England, Wales and Northern Ireland, each of which run court and community based services aimed at helping the victims of crime (Victim Support, 2003a: 2).[1] The roots of Victim Support lie in Bristol, when in 1974, as a result of inter-agency discussions about the impact of crime on individuals (Tudor, 2002), which included the National Association for the Care and Resettlement of Offenders (NACRO) and local probation officers, the first Victim Support Scheme was established. The organisation rapidly expanded, so that by 2003, there were approximately 400 community-based services and 480 court-based services across the country (Victim Support, 2003a: 4). The structure of Victim Support is such that it is a registered charity, under the name of the National Association of Victim Support Schemes (NAVSS), based in London. The NAVSS consists of affiliated members in the form of Victim Support Areas, with coverage of one or more counties, and small local schemes. Membership of the NAVSS is conditional on members meeting the requirements of a nationally agreed Service Level Agreement, incorporating Victim Support's Code of Practice in relation to issues such as training and service provision. Victim Support has two core objectives: to provide support and assistance to victims and witnesses of crime, their relatives and friends, through all appropriate means; and to raise public awareness and recognition of the effects of crime by research into relevant issues and to disseminate the results of such research (Victim Support, 2003a: 4). Local victim schemes differ according to the specialist help that they provide, which will depend upon a number of factors such as the local context to crime that a particular scheme operates within. So, for example, in areas where there is a significant minority ethnic population, then focus may be placed upon supporting the victims of racist crime. The availability of volunteers to carry out work with victims is also likely to a have a significant impact upon the work that a particular scheme carries out, and in socially and economically deprived areas this may be of particular relevance, since researchers have found that high rates of crime and disorder are likely to deter individuals from volunteering their services (McManus, 2001).

The NAVSS receives the majority of its funding directly from government, via the Home Office, and it then re-distributes this to local Victim Support charities to pay for staff, offices and other costs (Victim Support,

2003a: 5). Other money is received via donations and fundraising activities. Thus, for example, for the period 2002/03, the NAVSS received £29 million from the Home Office and £1.09 million in grants and donations from other sources (Victim Support, 2003a: 3). However, later that same year, the Government announced plans to devolve funding to Local Criminal Justice Boards.[2] Little is known yet of the detail or implications involved here (Victim Support, 2003b: 20). Victim Support employs staff to coordinate local schemes and also to work for the National Office, however, by far the majority of people involved with Victim Support are volunteers. In 2002, over 13,500 volunteers supported the victims and witnesses of crime (Victim Support, 2002a: 12).

Whilst remaining true to its original purpose, to help and support the victims of crime, Victim Support has grown significantly not only in terms of its size, but, more importantly, in terms of the services that it provides to people, and also in terms of an increased focus upon influencing the development of victim-focussed policies. Originally, Victim Support concentrated resources upon helping the victims of burglary, who would be referred to local victim support schemes via the police. For example, in 1984–85, around 80 per cent of referrals were of victims of burglary, with only 8 per cent of victims being victims of violent crime (Mawby and Walklate, 1994: 117). In recent times, however, Victim Support services have been targeted at a wider range of victims, so that now male and female victims of sexual assault, rape, the bereaved families of murder victims, and the victims of hate crime including racist crime, homophobic crime and disablist crime, can be supported. At the same time, services to young people have been expanded so that some local Victim Support schemes might be involved in anti-bullying projects. Volunteers are trained to understand victims' reactions, such as their anger and distress, but additional training is also available to experienced volunteers who may be providing more specialised support to distinct categories of victims, such as those listed here. Indeed, volunteers and staff can now work towards achieving nationally recognised qualifications such as the Community Justice National Vocational Qualification (NVQ) in working with victims, survivors and witnesses (Victim Support, 2003b: 13).

Victim Support has also entered into, and developed, working partnerships with other organisations such as Support After Murder and Manslaughter, Womens Aid, RoadPeace, the Campaign Against Drinking and Driving, and Kidscape. This can act as a two-way flow of information and as a mechanism through which organisations can be mutually supported (Victim Support, 1995). However, voluntary sector organisations may be competing over the same pool of clients, and so the development of working relationships between organisations is not always clear-cut and can be rather erratic (Mawby and Walklate, 1994). Most referrals still come via the police, for example, for the period 2002/03 the police supplied nine out of ten referrals to Victim Support, whilst the total number of self-referrals was just under 2 per cent of total referrals (Victim Support, 2003a: 20). Automated referral systems have been introduced in Manchester, Hertfordshire and Surrey, whereby referrals from the local police are transferred directly to Victim Support computers, which can save a significant amount of time (Victim Support, 2003b: 9). The following is a breakdown of referrals that were made to Victim Support in England and Wales for 2002/03 according to offence type: homicide: 1240 referrals; rape 5768 referrals, robbery 73,029 referrals, burglary 397,884 referrals; racially motivated crimes 2180 referrals (Victim Support, 2003a: 18–19). As these figures clearly indicate, helping burglary victims continues to be a major focus for Victim Support.

Contact with victims includes home visits or telephone calls. Whilst most people who are visited will be visited only once, for serious crimes such as homicide, volunteers expect to visit the victim on a number of occasions over a much longer period of time (Victim Support, 2003a). A study examining the impact of a visit from victim support scheme volunteers found that the main objective had been to encourage the victim to express his or her feelings about the crime. Almost two thirds of the victims said that the visits had made some difference, and 12 per cent had said that they had made a 'very big difference' to how they had coped with the emotional impact of the crime. The authors of the study conclude that a group of individuals who were visited by Victim Support scheme volunteers, when matched against a group of individuals who weren't visited, tended to recover better (Corbett and Maguire, 1988: 29).

Victim Support also operates a Witness Service within both Crown and Magistrates courts in England and Wales. This service was first set up as a research project in seven Crown Courts in 1989. In 1999, it was decided that all magistrates courts would also be covered by the scheme by 2002 (Victim Support, 2002a: 11). The Witness Support Service also operates in the Youth Court. People are referred to the Witness Service via agencies such as the police or the Crown Prosecution Service, however, they can also refer themselves for help. The Witness Service aims to provide victims and witnesses with emotional and practical support, and information before, during and after the trial. This may include a pre-trial visit to help people familiarise themselves with the court surroundings. After the trial, individuals may be referred for further help from Victim Support or other agencies to help reduce the stress of giving evidence. Following the implementation of the Youth Justice and Criminal Evidence Act 1999 to criminal courts in the summer of 2002, which extended the range of Special Measures from young witnesses to include all vulnerable and intimidated witnesses, for people regarded as being vulnerable or likely to be intimidated, the Witness Service will, with the consent of the witness, inform the court of the need to implement special measures (Victim Support, 2003a).

The results of the *Witness Satisfaction Survey* 2002 reveal that eight out of ten witnesses are offered help by the Witness Service, with there being many young people using the service – 85 per cent of witnesses under 17 in 2002 received help via the Witness Service, compared to just 46 per cent in 2000 (Victim Support, 2003b: 10). For the period 2002/03, the Crown Court Witness Service supported 151,086 people, three-quarters of whom were witnesses for the prosecution (Victim Support, 2003a: 20–21). For the same period, the Magistrates Courts Witness Service supported 181,103 people. Again, witnesses for the prosecution made up the majority of individuals supported (Victim Support, 2003a: 21). Forty-two per cent of all referrals between 2002–03 were for the crime of violence against the person, 2 per cent were for robbery, 2 per cent were for sexual offences, 2 per cent were for burglary, with the remaining 51 per cent being for 'other' offences, including criminal damage, arson, theft and fraud (Victim Support, 2003a: 21). Ninety-five per cent of individuals using the Witness Service were satisfied or very satisfied with it (Victim Support, 2003a: 2).

Victim Support also operates a Victim Supportline, which is a national telephone line to provide victims with emotional and practical support. The Supportline can pass on to people details of the Victim Support scheme, or the Witness Service, operating in their own local area (Victim Support, 2003a: 22). The Supportline is run from the National Office in London, with there being approximately 7 members of staff and 42 volunteers involved in its operation (Victim Support, 2003a: 42). During 2002/03, the national telephone helpline received just under 19,000 calls. Forty-nine per cent concerned a violent crime, 16 per cent of which were either rape or other sexual crime. 2,014 calls were made in relation to domestic violence, whilst the number of calls about racial harassment was just 99 (Victim Support, 2003a: 22). The latter statistic suggests that minority ethnic groups are not necessarily accessing the services provided by Victim Support. Indeed, as indicated earlier, the majority of victims are referred to Victim Support via the police. This means that the majority of victims of racist crime are unlikely to be referred for help, due to the significant level of under-reporting of this type of crime to the police (Bowling, 1999). This is borne out by the figures provided earlier on in this chapter in relation to referrals to Victim Support by crime type, whereby in comparison to 5768 rape referrals, 73029 robbery referrals, and 397,884 burglary referrals, only 2180 referrals were made for racially motivated crimes (Victim Support, 2003a: 18–19). Nonetheless, statistics suggest that the Witness Service, in both Crown Court and Magistrate Court, is accessed fairly well by minority ethnic communities. 13 per cent of people referred to the Crown Court Witness Service between 2002/03 were from ethnic minorities, whilst 9 per cent of people referred to the Magistrate Court Witness Service belonged to a minority ethnic community (Victim Support, 2003a: 20–21).

Some local Victim Support schemes are attempting to encourage the greater take up of their services by employing racist incidents officers, or hate crime managers, who work in partnership with other agencies such as the police and race equality councils, in order to highlight the work that Victim Support do, and also to increase the level of reporting of racist incidents alongside other types of hate crime. It is argued that whilst victims may not be comfortable in going to the police to report a hate crime, they may nonetheless be more comfortable reporting this to Victim Support, as well as to other agencies. So, for example, Northamptonshire Victim Support has helped to develop and publish a leaflet called Stamp Out Hate Crime. This includes a self-report form that individuals can use to provide details about a racist, homophobic or disablist incident, and they can indicate whether they would like further help from a variety of agencies, including the police, the race equality council and Victim Support. The leaflet has been distributed to housing offices, GP surgeries, schools, libraries, post offices, hospitals and local councils. Northamptonshire Victim Support has also helped to establish a web-based reporting form for the victims of hate crime, so that people can file reports quickly by making statements online (Victim Support, 2003b: 5). In many of the local Victim Support schemes in London, including the boroughs of Hackney, Camden, Croydon, Enfield, Greenwich and Islington, hate crime workers or racial incident officers, can also be found. In Lincolnshire, Victim Support has been a member of the Rainbow Forum, this being a collaboration between local agencies set up to address the issue of homophobic violence. The forum has also encouraged more victims to come forward by leaving self-report forms in public venues such as libraries, hospitals and colleges (Victim Support, 2003b).

The examples provided above illustrate the ways in which Victim Support has developed as an organisation. A greater emphasis is now placed upon developing partnerships with local authorities, health services, fire services, the police, probation boards, and businesses due to the implementation of the Crime and Disorder Act 1998. Under this legislation, Crime and Disorder Reduction Strategies have been drawn up by local authorities and the police who have joint responsibility for the formulation of these. Crime and Disorder Reduction Strategies set out a range of objectives and targets to be met, which may include aims like reducing the number of offending youth, tackling drug-related crime and reducing the fear of crime, and Victim Support is also involved with many of these initiatives. However, partnerships can be problematic, as highlighted by Garland and Chakraborti's (2004) study of rural racism, which included an analysis of the workings of two anti-racist inter-agency forums. The authors argue here that there can be a lack of clear aims and objectives, so that an impression of vagueness is created, and many key organisations may not even be present at meetings as they not may have been invited to attend.

Victim Support has also become increasingly political, attempting to influence policies and practices aimed at the victims of crime. The National Association has a Research and Development Department, which carries out and commissions research into good practice and on how to improve services to victims and witnesses. This department also collects data to monitor the performance of services across the country, and issues guidelines for helping young victims of crime, the victims of domestic violence and hate crime (Victim Support, 2003b). Victim Support also arranges, and takes part in, conferences and independent working parties on a wide range of victim issues such as domestic violence, rape and sexual assault, road deaths, reparation and compensation (Victim Support, 2003b). Victim Support also responds to draft legislation and is often consulted by the Home Office on victim issues. Victim Support has worked to shape the Victim's Charter and the Government's (2003) Victims and Witnesses Strategy. In 1995, Victim Support issued a policy paper on The Rights of Victims of Crime whereby it was argued that victims have the right to receive information and explanation about the progress of their case, the right to receive compensation and the right to receive respect, recognition and support (Victim Support, 1995: 8–10). In 2002, Victim Support published the document Criminal Neglect (2002b), whereby many instances of the insensitive treatment of victims by employers, public officials and administrators were highlighted. This paper raised political awareness of victims' needs in relation to a broader context, so that in the Government strategy document, A New Deal for Victims & Witnesses: national strategy to deliver improved services (Home Office, 2003c), victims' experience of the National Health Service and local authorities is included. Victim Support has also played a significant role in the development of the Victims' Code of Practice (Victim Support, 2003a), legislation that came into effect in 2005, and this is expanded upon later in this chapter.

The Criminal Injuries Compensation Scheme

The financial compensation of victims by the state has a relatively long history, with the world's first compensation scheme being set up in England in 1964, being called the Criminal Injuries Compensation Scheme (Cook *et al.*, 1999: 83). This was established by the Home Office in order to provide discretionary payments to the victims of unlawful violence. In 1996, a second Criminal Injuries Compensation Scheme was introduced, replacing the 1964 Scheme, this being designed to be simpler than the previous scheme. Under the new system, a tariff of injuries was introduced so that the non-financial impacts of crime relating to physical and mental pain and suffering had defined sums of money to be paid as compensation. In 2001, a third Criminal Injuries Compensation Scheme was set up, this replacing the 1996 scheme, but retaining the tariff-based system that was introduced earlier under the 1996 scheme. The 2001 scheme (and previously the 1996 scheme) is administered via the Criminal Injuries Compensation Authority (CICA), which came into force on 1 April 1996. This is a public body that covers compensation claims throughout England, Scotland and Wales – Northern Ireland has its own authority. Approximately 550 staff from both the Home Office and the Scottish Executive are employed by the CICA in offices in Glasgow and London (CICA, 2004: 3).

The Criminal Injuries Compensation Scheme allows financial awards to be made to victims to 'recognise their physical and mental injuries caused by a violent crime; in certain circumstances to compensate for past or future lost earnings or special expenses caused by a violent crime; and for the death of a close relative as a result of violent crime' (CICA, 2004: 3). Whilst there is no legal definition of the term 'crime of violence', this will usually involve a physical attack on a person such as an assault, wounding or sexual attack, and may also include arson. This means that a victim sustaining a mental injury from a crime such as burglary, which did not involve violence, will not be granted compensation (CICA, 2004: 20). A claimant may be paid compensation for an injury sustained in trying to prevent an offence, however, only in exceptional circumstances. For example, a police officer who trips over whilst chasing an offender is not likely to receive compensation (CICA, 2004: 21). The Criminal Injuries Compensation Scheme also will not compensate people for any injuries that they received abroad, which means that in these situations victims have to find out if there is a similar compensation scheme operating within the country in which the injury was sustained and will have to apply directly to that scheme (CICA, 2004: 18).

The tariff award for physical injury already includes an element of compensation for the mental injury that a victim has incurred as a result of their physical suffering, which means that if a separate award is sought for mental injury, the claimant must show that the mental injury that was suffered was clearly greater than would normally be expected (CICA, 2004: 19). To get any compensation, a victim must quality for at least the minimum award that is paid under the scheme, which is £1000. However, this may be reduced by the CICA, so that in practice a victim can receive less than £1000. The maximum award is £500,000. The sums awarded are applied to the injury rather than the person applying. This means that if a number of people apply following the death of a person, then the maximum that they can receive in total is £500,000 (CICA, 2004: 38). The tariff of injuries paid by the Criminal Injuries Compensation Scheme includes the following awards:

> burns (affecting multiple areas of body covering 25% of skin area, with significant
> scarring) standard award is £33,000; infection with HIV/AIDS (may be paid in
> addition to other awards) standard award is £22,000; loss of foetus, standard award
> is £5,500; permanent mental illness, seriously disabling (confirmed by psychiatric
> prognosis), standard award is £27,000; minor injuries: multiple (will qualify only
> where applicant has sustained at least 3 separate physical injuries, at least one of
> which must still have had significant residual effects 6 weeks after the event, injuries
> must also have necessitated at least 2 visits to or by a medical practitioner within that
> 6 week period), includes grazing, cuts, bruising, black eye, bloody nose, standard
> award is £1,000. (Home Office, 2001a: 25–28).

In future, offenders may be forced to pay back to the CICA the money that
it has paid to victims, together with the costs of administering that payment. In 2004, the Government signaled the desire to arm the CICA with
new powers to get money back from offenders, through the civil courts, via
a consultation document Compensation and Support for Victims of Crime.

The philosophy underpinning the Criminal Injuries Compensation
Scheme is that victims have no direct right to compensation. This means
that in practice, only certain types of victimised persons receive compensation, those regarded as 'deserving'. The CICA will scrutinise the victim's
behaviour, before, during and after the criminal event, to help determine
what kind of compensation they should receive, if anything at all. Failing
to cooperate with the authorities, for example, by refusing to make a statement, by refusing to go to an identity parade or by refusing to go to court,
will result in no compensation being paid to the victim (CICA, 2004: 26).
The dynamics of a crime event will also be assessed to scrutinise the
victim's culpability. In a case whereby an injury has been caused during a
fight that the victim had agreed to take part in, or if there has been a history
of assaults involving both sides, or if the victim had drunk too much alcohol or used illegal drugs and this had contributed to the attack which
caused the injury, then compensation will be reduced or refused (CICA,
2004: 27). The victim's character will further be examined to see if they
have any previous criminal convictions. Any convictions that are 'spent'
(i.e., convictions that do not have to be declared) under the Rehabilitation
of Offenders Act 1974, will be ignored. However, 'unspent' convictions
will be taken into account, the rationale here being that a person who has
committed criminal offences has imposed costs upon other victims, as well
as upon wider society, and so should not subsequently receive any compensation (CICA, 2004: 28). The more serious the penalty the offender
received, and the more recently it was given, the longer the conviction

takes to become spent. A conviction leading to a prison sentence of thirty months or more can never become spent. However, the CICA operates a 'penalty points' system whereby the more recent the conviction, and the more serious the penalty, the more penalty points the conviction will attract. The greater the number of penalty points, the larger the percentage of reduction applied to an award. However, under this system, there is some discretion. For example, if the penalty points total indicates a refusal of an award, an award can still be made if the injury resulted from helping the police, or helping someone else who was being attacked. Similarly, a low number of penalty points is no guarantee that an award will be made, especially where an applicant's criminal record includes violent or sexual offences (CICA, 2004: 27).

Originally, compensation for violence within the family was not paid. However, following a Home Office Working Party in 1978, this exclusion was modified so that from 1 October 1979 victims of crimes of domestic violence can make claims for criminal injuries (Mawby and Walklate, 1994). However, compensation is unlikely to be paid if there is a 'continuing link between the victim and the offender which makes it likely that the offender would benefit from the award' (CICA, 2004: 32). This means that in cases of domestic violence, an award will only be made if the offender has been prosecuted or if the offender does not live in the same household as the victim, and the relationship is one of estrangement, before a claim for compensation is made (CICA, 2004: 32).

The Victim's Charter sets the CICA the aim of issuing a decision within 12 months of receiving an application, although this may not always be possible due to delays in awaiting the outcome of a trial or in awaiting a medical prognosis. Nonetheless, a fairly high percentage of claims are processed within 12 months of receipt, the figures for 1998–1999 showing that out of 78,651 new claims received, 90 per cent of applications were processed within that time frame (CICA, 2000: 9–10). All applications are first decided by a claims officer within the CICA. If the applicant disagrees with the first decision, a request for it to be reviewed at a higher level in the Authority may be made within 90 days. If the applicant is dissatisfied with the outcome of the review, an appeal may be made within 30 days to the independent Criminal Injuries Compensation Appeals Panel (CICAP) (CICA, 2000: 13).

A significant number of cases are rejected by the CICA, and interestingly, a good proportion of disallowed claims are a result of a failure to report the incident without delay and/or cooperate with the police (see the case study overleaf). This is likely to have a disproportionate impact on minority ethnic communities, since these communities have lower levels of confidence in the police,[3] which may deter them from reporting an incident or from cooperating with the police in their investigations.

Case study

In 1998/99, awards were made in 53.7 per cent of all claims that were received, and this includes cases that were reviewed and appealed, as well as those cases that were finalised on first decision (CICA, 2000: 14). Out of the disallowed claims, the most common reasons for refusal were that the injury that was sustained was not serious enough for the minimum award (32.3% of cases); there was a failure to report the incident without delay and/or cooperate with the police (23.9% of cases); no crime of violence was established (12.4% of cases); as a result of the applicant's conduct before, during or after the incident (11.2% of cases); and as a result of the applicant's criminal record (7.6% of cases) (CICA, 2000: 16).

Question

Do you think that it is problematic to disallow claims on the basis that victims failed to report the crime without delay to the police, or that victims failed to cooperate with the police?

In November 2003 Victim Support published a policy document about the Criminal Injuries Compensation Scheme, entitled Insult to Injury: how the criminal injuries compensation system is failing victims of crime. Of particular interest here is that implicit within Victim Support's critique of the Criminal Injuries Compensation Scheme is the notion of the deserving victim, as 'innocent' and therefore worthy of compensation. The argument provided in Victim Support's document is essentially that the Criminal Injuries Compensation Scheme discriminates against some victims, resulting in their re-victimisation. For example, it is argued that because there is no definition of a crime of violence, this gives the CICA much discretion over what kinds of victims are compensated. Victim Support argues that all victims of sexual offences should be entitled to compensation, whether or not physical violence is used. The case of Laura is provided, who was sexually abused at school by a teacher 20 years older and who reported the crime 12 years later. At the end of a 3-day trial the perpetrator was found guilty of the indecent assault of a minor. However, the CICA rejected Laura's claim for compensation because it did not accept that she had not consented, despite being under 16 at the time and being incapable of giving consent in law (Victim Support, 2003c: 5). Victim Support also highlights how a child, whose parent is murdered, may be denied compensation if that parent had criminal convictions. Similarly, parents whose murdered children had convictions may also be denied compensation. What is so apparent within this document is that Victim Support are not campaigning to make it easier for all victims to gain compensation, otherwise the fact that the victim's lifestyle, character and their actions before, during and after the criminal event, are scrutinised by the CICA, would be criticised, since this leads to claims being reduced or refused. Rather, Victim Support seems to focus upon those categories of victims who conform to the prevailing model of innocence, and so seems generally supportive of the idea that victims can be judged in terms of how deserving they are of compensation. As highlighted in Chapter 2 the idea that victims are 'completely innocent' is a social construct, and can be a gross over-simplification of the dynamics of crime. It might be argued that to gain a fairer system of compensation for everyone, we need to first deconstruct idealised notions of victimhood, as these serve only to disadvantage real-life victims.

Compensation orders

As well as the state providing financial compensation to the victims of crime, via the Criminal Injuries Compensation Scheme, offenders can also be required to pay under a Court Compensation Order. Significant pieces of legislation here include the 1982 Criminal Justice Act, which required that where courts ordered compensation to be paid by the offender, alongside a fine, then compensation should be given priority (Mawby and Walklate, 1994: 83). More recently, under the powers of the Criminal Courts (Sentencing) Act 2000, a court is under a duty to consider compensation whether or not an application has been made. Where compensation is not ordered, sentencers are required to give reasons why (Home Office, 2004h: 12). However, in practice, most victims do not receive any financial compensation from 'their' offenders, and there are many reasons for this. One reason is that the courts must take into consideration the offender's ability to pay when imposing a Compensation Order. As many offenders do not have the means to pay, perhaps because they are unemployed or sentenced to immediate custody, they are unlikely to be told to compensate the victim. Where an offender is sentenced to custody, compensation may also not be ordered because this is perceived as being disproportionately severe by sentencers. Also, in some cases the calculation of what the offender can afford to pay is so low that this might result in re-victimising the victim, and so again a compensation order is unlikely to be imposed (Home Office, 2004b). Another difficulty with the Compensation Order is that offenders may be given a long time to pay the compensation, and so this can cause considerable distress to victims, who may have to wait before they can replace damaged or stolen items, for example. For these kinds of reasons, the Home Office is seeking to find ways of increasing the extent to which compensation orders are used, through the consultation paper, Compensation and Support for Victims of Crime (Home Office, 2004b).

The Victim's Charter

In 1990, the Conservative government in Britain introduced a Victim's Charter. Although it referred to victims' rights, in reality it articulated standards of services that victims should receive from agencies of the criminal justice system. In 1996, a second Victim's Charter followed, and this refers explicitly to 27 service standards that victims can expect to receive. The Victim's Charter also provides guidance to agencies of the criminal justice system, such as the Police, Probation and Crown Prosecution Services, on how they can improve their treatment of victims, by, for example, setting targets that agencies are expected to meet. A Victim's Steering Group monitors the performance of the overall system, and this is chaired by the Home Office and includes representatives from all agencies whose work includes a focus on victims. In 2001 the Government reviewed the Victim's Charter in relation to issues such as the format of the Charter (e.g., whether it is too long, and whether public awareness of the Charter can be improved as it has been acknowledged that awareness is low), whether service standards should continue to be the focus of attention or whether a rights-based approach should be taken, and whether further measures can be introduced to support the victims of hate crime (Home Office, 2001b: 11). The viewpoints of victim organisations, agencies of the criminal justice system and researchers were sought. Following on from this process of consultation, the *Victims' Code of Practice* was published in December 2003, and this came into effect in late 2004, when the *Domestic Violence, Crime and Victims Act* received Royal Assent in November 2004. The Code of Practice continues to focus upon the service standards that victims can expect to receive from agencies of the criminal justice system working in England and Wales, such as the Criminal Cases Review Commission, the CICA, the Crown Prosecution Service, all police forces, the Parole Board, the Prison Service, Victim Support and Youth Offending Teams. The Code of Practice effectively builds on from the services set out in the Victim's Charter 1996, providing greater details about the exact responses that victims can expect to get. For example, the Code states that in the case of the families of murder victims, the police must assign an appropriate family liaison officer to the relatives and they must make a record of the assignment. The police must also provide close relatives with the Home Office packs 'Advice for bereaved families and friends following murder or manslaughter'. Where victims are not satisfied with the service that they have received, they should first contact the service provider(s) concerned. If they remain dissatisfied, then their complaint can be investigated by the

Parliamentary Commissioner for Administration under the Parliamentary Commissioner Act 1967, as amended by Schedule 1 to the Domestic Violence, Crime and Victims Act 2004 (Criminal Justice System, 2003: 2). However, the Victims' Code of Practice does not include service standards for all types of victim. For example, for work-related incidents, where people may be injured or killed as a result of health and safety law violations, and hence the incident will become subject to a Health and Safety Executive (HSE) investigation and prosecution, then the Victims' Code of Practice does not apply to victims here (Criminal Justice System, 2003: 5).

Victim statements

Since 2001, after the implementation and evaluation of a series of pilot projects by the Home Office, Victim Statements have been introduced across Britain (Edwards, 2001: 40). This reflects similar developments in the United States and Australia. In the United States, victim impact statements can be made to the judge prior to sentencing and also at parole board hearings before the release of the offender (Garland, 2001). In South Australia, the Victim Impact Statement (Amendment) Act 1998 allows victims to read a prepared statement to the sentencing court (Edwards, 2001). Victim statements are regarded as giving victims the opportunity to describe the impact of the crime upon them. In the British scheme, victims can state the physical, financial, psychological, social or emotional effects of the crime on them or on their families, either via a form that is sent out to them, or via a police officer filling in a free-form statement for them. The difficulty with Victim Statements is that there are a number of competing rationales for their implementation into the criminal justice process, yet these rationales are rarely clearly articulated by policy makers, which leads to confusion and this can detrimentally affect victims (Edwards, 2001). So, for example, if victim statements are introduced into a criminal justice system from the viewpoint that they should be used for cathartic value, whereby the expression of a victim's feelings will make that victim feel better, if the actual victim believes that their statement should be used to influence the sentencing outcome, then they are unlikely to be satisfied with the resulting outcome (see Edwards 2001, for a more detailed analysis here). This is clearly illustrated by the results of a Home Office pilot project, in that although 55 per cent of victims opting to give Victim Statements wanted to influence the case outcome, in practice, these had no effect on sentencing decisions (Hoyle, Morgan and Sanders, 1999: 1). At the same time, reflecting the focus of the official victims' movement upon the individuals who have been victimised by events regarded as being criminal by wider social and political arenas, victim statements do not include all types of victim. Crimes such as domestic burglary, robbery, domestic violence and sexual assault are focussed upon, and these initiatives do not include victims of white-collar crime or environmental damage (Edwards, 2001).

'Victim-Centeredness' and the work of agencies of the criminal justice system

Agencies of the criminal justice system have increasingly focussed upon their interaction with the victims of crime, particularly since the publication of the Victim's Charters of 1990 and 1996, and the Victim's Code of Practice. These documents have led to a series of policy developments within the Police, Probation, Crown Prosecution and Prison Services, and the courts, and agencies have increasingly been given procedures that they must follow and targets that they must meet. The policy developments here have been enormous, and it is beyond the remit of this chapter to examine them all. Therefore, only a few examples of the kinds of initiatives that have been implemented are provided, with the intention of illustrating the difficulties involved for agencies when adopting a more victim inclusive approach.

The police service

In 1982 a documentary by Roger Graef was screened on television called Police, which provoked a public outcry over the treatment of rape victims. This documentary showed a woman who had reported a rape being interrogated by police officers, who asked her questions like 'Have you ever been on the game? How many times have you had sex? How many men have you had sex with? Can you count them on the fingers of one hand?'. The public concern that this documentary aroused led to a series of initiatives being implemented into police forces to handle rape victims with greater sensitivity, such as, for example, better police training, the appointment of more female police surgeons and the introduction of rape suites into many areas (Lees, 1999). According to a research study carried out by Gregory and Lees (1998), these changes have improved rape victims' experiences. Nonetheless, sexist attitudes continue to operate within the Police Service, for instance, police officers may wrongly believe that rape victims make false allegations more commonly than other kinds of victim, and so may 'no crime' cases, particularly in situations where the victim knows their attacker (Gregory and Lees, 1998). This example illustrates that new procedures and policies aimed at being more responsive to victims may not be sufficient to address their concerns, but rather, wider changes need to be made to the occupational culture of agencies of the criminal justice system. This point can further be highlighted by the Macpherson Report (1999) in relation to the racist murder of Stephen Lawrence, which accused the Police Service of being institutionally racist. This led to the introduction of new police training procedures and new policies aimed at increasing the representation of minority ethnic communities within police forces (Sharp, 2002).

Case study

In 1999, a domestic violence prevention project was developed in Merseyside, England. Women who were identified as vulnerable by crime prevention officers and domestic violence workers were issued with quick response pendant alarms. Victims of domestic violence were also offered greater support and the project raised awareness of the problem of domestic violence amongst police officers. The project was deemed successful since the pendants were found to increase the physical and psychological safety of women and children, alerting the police to the removal of the offender. The pendants were also found to act as a powerful deterrent, making the perpetrators of domestic violence less likely to carry out acts of violence on their partners and families.

Question

Do you think that issuing women with alarms sufficiently empowers them?

Court initiatives

The treatment of victims/witnesses in court has gained increasing political attention. Researchers have provided graphic evidence of the often harrowing experiences of victims in court, particularly when being cross-examined by defence lawyers, because under an adversarial justice system, the victim is a witness to an alleged crime, a crime that is regarded as having been committed against the state. This work has highlighted how secondary victimisation is a common aspect of the experience of going to court for many victims, dissuading them from proceeding with their allegations, particularly in cases of domestic violence, sexual assault and rape (Ellison, 2002; Lees, 1996). Research also shows how the victims of domestic violence are often frightened of appearing in court and giving evidence against the abuser, especially when the abuser may be intimidating them physically or mentally in order to try and prevent them from pursuing a criminal prosecution (Bennet, Goodman and Dutton, 1999 in: Ellison, 2000: 849).

In June 1998, a report was published by the Government, entitled Speaking Up for Justice. This contained a series of recommendations for the treatment of vulnerable or intimidated witnesses in the criminal justice system. According to the Victims' Code of Practice, vulnerable or intimidated witnesses include persons under the age of 17, individuals suffering from mental disorder, those individuals who have a history of self neglect or self harm, individuals who have experienced domestic violence, those who have made an allegation of criminal conduct that constitutes a sexual offence or which is racially aggravated or aggravated on religious, homophobic or transphobic grounds, or those who are likely to be, or who have been, subjected to intimidation. Under the Youth Justice and Criminal Evidence Act 1999, some of the recommendations in the Speaking Up for Justice report have been implemented. These include a ban on defendants conducting the cross-examination in person in rape and sexual assault trials, the installation of equipment into the courts to enable vulnerable or intimidated witnesses to give evidence via TV links, and the publication of further guidance to agencies of the criminal justice system, such as the police, to help reduce the burden upon witnesses (Home Office, 2001c: 2). Nonetheless, despite these changes, the difficulties that need to be overcome in order to increase victims' cooperation with the prosecution of cases remain immense, especially in crimes that involve a sexual or domestic component. For this reason, authorities have increasingly sought to develop measures whereby prosecutions for domestic violence are less dependent upon victim cooperation. However, this approach is itself controversial, since it may be seen as disempowering victims (see Ellison, 2000 for further discussion of this).

In 2003, the Sexual Offences Act came into force in Britain. This piece of legislation has been drawn up partly in response to an increasing concern about the low rate of convictions in rape cases. Thus, the conviction rate has dramatically dropped from being 24 per cent of crimes of rape recorded by the police in 1980, to only 9 per cent by 1994 (Gregory and Lees, 1998: 91). The Sexual Offences Act 2003 for the first time contains a definition of consent as 'a person consents if he agrees by choice and has the freedom and capacity to make that choice'. Prior to this legislation, where an offender could argue in court that they had an honest belief in the consent of the victim, even if such a belief was unreasonable, then they had to be found not guilty. The Sexual Offences Act sets out the circumstances whereby it is most unlikely that consent was given, for example where the victim was sleeping or was unconscious. However, because the trial itself is such an ordeal for victims, and due to sexist attitudes that continue to prevail in agencies such as the Police and Crown Prosecution Services (see Lees, 1996; Gregory and Lees, 1998), this piece of legislation may do little to encourage victims to come forward and report their experiences to the criminal justice system, despite providing the possibility for increasing the conviction rate.

Probation work with victims

Victim-focussed work is increasingly being applied within the Probation Service. Under the Criminal Justice and Court Services Act 2000, and according to Probation Circular 108/00, the victims of sexual and violent offenders sentenced to more than 12 months must be given information about the offender's term of incarceration and must be given the opportunity to give their views on proposed conditions surrounding the offender's release. There are some difficulties with this initiative, however, particularly in terms of the problem of responding to victims' needs but also having to obligate offenders' rights. Offenders are entitled to know on what grounds their release conditions have been decided, and so where a victim has influenced these, it may lead to an increased hostility from the offender, causing distress to the victim (Spalek, 2003).

At the same time, establishing an identifiable victim may be problematic. For example, in the case of shoplifting, the victim may be a commercial organisation, also crimes such as drug possession for personal use and soliciting may not involve a victim. This illustrates how a probation officer must decide who constitutes the victim, and this is likely to be influenced by the officer's understandings and views of victimhood (Dominey, 2002). Victim work can be time-consuming and the issue of whether enough additional resources have been made available to the Probation Service is highly relevant (Spalek, 2003).

Diversity issues: challenging official constructions of victimhood

So far, this chapter has presented a brief summary of some of the major initiatives developed within the official victims' movement. A recurrent theme within this book, which has so far only briefly been mentioned here, is that of the diversity to be found amongst victims and whether victimological frameworks of understanding are equipped to adequately deal with this. The following section focuses briefly on whether services aimed at the victims of crime can better cater to the needs of minority groups.

Greater engagement with local communities is being pursued by agencies of the criminal justice system. For example, the Victim Liaison Unit within the West Midlands Probation Service has put together an excellent directory of local minority ethnic community groups, which acts as a way of informing victim liaison officers about groups which are willing to work with them. This also acts to enhance the responsiveness of victim liaison units to the needs of minority and ethnic communities, as it is a means of providing victim liaison officers with the necessary information and local contacts that will enable them to give advice about culturally sensitive support services available to victims from minority ethnic backgrounds. This initiative also helps to raise awareness and the accessibility of probation service victim contact work amongst minority ethnic communities. Similarly, the Crown Prosecution Service (CPS) has drawn up a directory of community groups and contacts, which is available on the CPS intranet.

These initiatives have been brought in as a result of the acknowledgement that uptake by minority ethnic communities of certain mainstream victim support services can be low (see Spalek, 2005a). There are many reasons for this. It may be the case that individuals from minority ethnic communities may be deterred from seeking help from mainstream organisations due to perceived and actual direct or indirect discrimination. Another important factor is likely to be the lack of specialist help specifically catered to the needs of specific communities, since mainstream organisations tend to offer fairly general support targeted at a general audience. Another related factor appears to be the under-representation of Black and Asian volunteers and members of staff in many organisations, which is likely to influence service uptake from minority ethnic groups. A study carried out by the Home Office looking at the experiences of young Black men as victims of crime suggests that these young men infrequently have any contact with formal agencies that help the victims of crime, such as Victim Support for example. Awareness of Victim Support was poor, and a minority of the young Black men viewed Victim Support as being for older, more privileged and less street-wise people (Yarrow, 2005).

There may also be significant cultural differences in the ways in which particular communities address experiences of being victims. As highlighted in Chapter 1, many writers suggest that in contemporary western society a 'cult of victimhood' operates, whereby individuals are increasingly identifying themselves with notions of victimhood. However, in contrast to the self-confessional approach increasingly dominant in western society, individuals from 'traditional minority communities' may prefer not to speak, or wish to disclose information, about negative or traumatic events because of the belief that in doing so, this may exacerbate the problem, or at least not benefit the situation (Spalek, 2005a). This more reserved approach to victimisation means that not only will many individuals be unlikely to approach mainstream organisations for help, but they are also likely to seek help from within their own communities, for example, by speaking to religious leaders, or by going to seek advice from healers who may use alternative forms of therapy, which may include a spiritual or religious component. Indeed, it is also pertinent to note that within the general population, increasing numbers of people are seeking help from, and trying out, different forms of spirituality (McManus, 2001: 3).

Mainstream victim services are secular in nature, which means that people's religious and spiritual needs are not addressed. This is likely to have a profound impact upon uptake of service delivery by minority ethnic communities, since research shows that religious affiliation is a much more fundamental aspect of the self-identity of minority ethnic groups when compared to many White Christians (O'Beirne, 2004: 18). Yet religion has rarely featured as an aspect of self-identity within responses to victimisation. For example, within responses to hate crime, there has rarely been a focus upon the hostility, abuse and violence that might be experienced by a person due to the religion that they follow. This can be traced back to the secular nature of the race relations movement, whereby race and ethnicity have predominantly been focussed upon, and not religion, when attempting to find ways of alleviating disadvantage and discrimination. Nonetheless, following the introduction of a religiously aggravated element to crime, under the Anti Terrorism Crime and Security Act 2001, local partnerships between the police and other statutory and voluntary agencies have increasingly focussed upon religiously aggravated offences, so that religious hate crime is increasingly being incorporated into policy developments. Support services for the victims of domestic and sexual violence also generally lack an appreciation of the centrality of faith in some women's lives. This means that for women who have a religious belief, they may choose to stay in their abusive relationships rather than go and seek help from an organisation which, at best, will ignore women's religious requirements, or at worst, will judge them for conforming to what are prejudiced assumptions about the controlling and patriarchal nature of religion (Ahmad and Sheriff, 2003).

The model of the neutral victim, underpinning the official victims' movement, can also indirectly discriminate against victims from minority communities. The model of neutrality separates the victim from the wider socio-structural context to their victimisation. This approach essentially views crime as an incident, rather than as an insidious feature of people's everyday lives, because the wider racist, sexist, homophobic (and other) structures that help to create, sustain and maintain repeat patterns of victimisation, are largely unacknowledged, such that people are seen to lead largely crime-free lives, which nonetheless may, now-and-again, be shattered by violent or non-violent offences. This model can be seen in partnership work that takes place between different organisations aimed at boosting the reporting of hate crime and helping the victims here. Macpherson's definition of a racist crime is used as the template for approaching hate crime, this being, 'any incident which is perceived to be racist by the victim or any other person'. This means that leaflets targeted at the victims of hate crime ask the following types of questions: 'Was the incident homophobic, racist, disablist?' 'When did the incident occur?' 'Where did it occur?' 'What actually happened?' (Stamp Out Hate Crime leaflet, Victim Support).

Within this kind of framework of understanding, is the 'belief in a just world' construct that has been influential in developing knowledge about the consequences of crime upon victims, as highlighted in Chapter 4. However, this model about the process of victimisation may be a construct that has developed from research by, and about, people occupying positions of relative power, and hence may not be particularly relevant to minority groups' experiences. Indeed, researchers have shown that hate crimes against racial and ethnic groups and women and gay communities are rarely one-off events, but rather, are a common feature of the everyday lives of many individuals (Kelly, 1988; Phillips and Bowling, 2003). Therefore, trying to fit people's lived experiences into a generalist model of victimisation that fails to consider specific structural contexts is likely to deter uptake of services, since victims may not see the relevancy of those services to their lives.

Summary

The discussions above have a number of implications for service delivery. Policies that on first appearance seem 'neutral' due to their secular, apolitical nature, are indirectly discriminating against particular communities due to the lack of relevancy to individuals' lives, so that service uptake is poor. This then raises the question of how to make the services that are offered to victims more inclusive of minority communities so that individuals have a greater choice over the types of support that are available to them. But it is also important to bear in mind that increasing the funding given to mainstream victim support services, such that they are able to offer more choice, should not take place without developing services that lie outside of the official victims' movement, since this will further disadvantage those individuals from minority groups who wish to continue using those specialist services.

Mainstream victim support services should consider widening the range of organisations that they suggest people contact, so that spiritual and/or religious guidance and support can be obtained by victims, which may be of significant comfort to them.[4] Homeopathic therapists are increasingly aware that underlying the symptoms that their clients present themselves with, there may be a history of violence and abuse, and so techniques to tackle the impact of sexual and physical violence are also applied. Homeopathy, which can include, for example, the use of reiki techniques or massage, can be used alongside counselling and other forms of support that people receive from organisations like Victim Support (Moss, 2004). Therapists are also increasingly including a spiritual dimension to the techniques that they use. Therapists' 'spiritual literacy' enables them to 'non-judgementally and respectfully open space for the discussion of religious or spiritual content that is important to clients' (Haug, 1998: 185). Mainstream victim support services, and the people working for them, need to be more aware of these kinds of developments and perhaps incorporate these into the work that they do.

Mainstream organisations should also be encouraged to form partnerships with a wider range of organisations, so that the needs of a broader range of victims can be taken into account more effectively. For example, in Britain, some Victim Support schemes have developed good links with locally based Muslim charities so that the volunteers who run these charities have the opportunity to be trained on how to provide support to victims by Victim Support. By training the Muslim charity volunteers, this can empower them to offer practical and emotional support to the victims of crime from within their own communities (Spalek, 2005a). However, before this can realistically be achieved on a larger scale, specialist organisations need to be properly funded. Many of these organisations are charities, and so rely heavily on donations for their activities, and the fund-raising that they need to do can take up a significant amount of their time, time that could more effectively be used on helping people. For example, the Muslim Women's Helpline, which provides support to Muslim women for a wide range of issues including divorce, domestic violence, arranged marriages, sexual abuse and incest, does not receive funding from Government. Muslim welfare organisations have found that the fact that they cater to individuals' religious and spiritual needs means that there is a large demand for their services from, for example, secular women's refuges, mental health services and schools (Ahmad and Sheriff, 2003). However, projects to fund local housing, welfare and crime reduction initiatives are unlikely to subsidise Muslim groups to meet Muslims' needs because they cannot support projects for religious groups due to the focus upon race and ethnicity. This means that the Muslim Women's Helpline; Mushkil Aasaan, which develop religious and cultural primary care packages that service providers can purchase; and the An-Nisa Society, who offer numerous services which include accredited training in Islamic Counselling, all struggle to maintain services with scarce resources and are dependent on voluntary contributions (Spalek, 2005a). Funding is therefore a key issue to address when developing a greater focus upon partnership work.

Conclusion

This chapter has examined some of the core initiatives that have been developed for victims, most of which contain characteristics that define the official victims' movement. Clearly, these initiatives do not cater to all of victims' needs, nor do they cater for all types of victim. The philosophy underpinning the Criminal Injuries Compensation Scheme, for example, is that victims have no direct right to compensation. This means that in practice, only certain types of victimised persons receive compensation, those regarded as 'deserving' because they have no criminal records or have fully supported the police in their investigations. Under the *Victims Code of Practice*, published in 2004, victims of health and safety law violations at work are not included.

Uptake of mainstream victim support services by minority ethnic communities also tends to be low. The model of the neutral victim, underpinning the official victims' movement, can indirectly discriminate against victims from minority communities since this separates the victim from the wider socio-structural context to their victimisation. As such, victimhood is seen as a one-off incident rather than as an insidious feature of people's everyday lives. Mainstream victim services need to be more sensitive to the needs of individuals and the wider communities that they belong to. Victim support services should consider widening the range of organisations that they suggest people contact, so that spiritual and/or religious guidance and support can be more easily obtained by victims. Mainstream organisations should also be encouraged to form partnerships with a wider range of organisations, so that the needs of a broader range of victims can be taken into account more effectively. To summarise, it is crucial that mainstream initiatives look at the models of victimhood that underpin their responses to victimisation, since although these might appear as non-discriminatory, on closer examination they clearly value some categories of victim over others, and lack an in-depth appreciation of the diversity to be found amongst individual victims.

Questions

1 In what ways does the notion of a 'deserving victim' underpin official responses to victimisation?
2 In what ways might victims' expectations of victim initiatives be raised and then remain unfulfilled?
3 What implications do diversity issues have for official responses to victimisation?

7

Victims' Needs and Victims' Rights

Introduction

As illustrated in Chapter 6, the treatment of victims by agencies of the criminal justice system has attracted much political and research attention. This has involved the identification of victims' needs, an examination of how well those needs are met, and has also led to changes in policy and practice within the criminal justice system. A recurring theme running throughout this work is the issue of whether the harms and trauma suffered by victims can be improved via a greater emphasis upon the development of victims' rights, together with the implementation of clear procedures to seek redress if those rights are not met by agencies working with victims. This chapter demonstrates, however, that enhancing victims' rights through existing legislative mechanisms will not necessarily lead to better and more appropriate responses to victims' needs. Some authors argue that human rights legislation is somewhat idealistic, with there being a significant difference between the rights that new legislation is said to protect and the actual protection that it affords (Smiljanic, 2002). Moreover, as clearly demonstrated by the anti-terror legislation implemented in the United Kingdom in 2001, which involved suspending British obligations to the European Convention on Human Rights, human rights can be challenged and removed by political will, thereby illustrating their fragility (Smiljanic, 2002). At the same time, increasing victims' rights can have negative consequences for offenders. In this chapter it is argued that if victims' needs are to be responded to more effectively, then the issue of victims' rights needs to be conceptualised in a wider framework than that currently afforded by victims' rights legislation.

We must also critically address the ways in which victims' needs have been framed and used by government. It can be argued that victims' needs have been co-opted by government, and imposed upon agencies that work with victims and offenders, in order to pursue broader goals linked to the development and operation of more efficient systems of criminal justice, which attempt to gain people's confidence and trust, acting as disciplinary mechanisms on agencies of the criminal justice system, so that the extent to which victims are directly helped is questionable. The political and social support given to this official victims' movement, is part of a wider 'individualisation of emotionality' that can be found in late modern societies (Karstedt, 2002: 304), whereby emotions are constructed as individual reactions, rather than as collective displays of group identity, to social and political events (Karstedt, 2002). Victims' emotional reactions have essentially been translated into individual need using the discourses of consumerism and active citizenship. Within this approach, although victims' needs are acknowledged, they are framed and used according to the bureaucratic and political goals that prevail. As a result, the help that is afforded to victims is limited, and this has important consequences for individual victims, as well as for the wider gender, class, ethnic, religious and other group collectivities that they may belong to.

This chapter looks at the social construction of victim need, and the issue of victims' rights. Part of this analysis will involve taking a close look at developments within the British criminal justice system, as the theme of victim as consumer/active citizen can be most clearly seen here. However, detailed information about specific victim initiatives will not be provided in this chapter, since the concern here is to highlight and address some core debates around the general issue of victims' needs and their rights.

Establishing and responding to victims' 'needs'

Over the last two decades victims' treatment by agencies of the criminal justice system has been a source of concern for governments, and so victim satisfaction with the police, the courts and with victim initiatives such as witness and victim support schemes has been measured via a wide range of surveys, including the use of national crime surveys such as the British Crime Survey (Shapland *et al.*, 1985; Newburn and Merry, 1990; Mayhew *et al.*, 1993; Kelly and Erez, 1997; Mirrlees-Black and Budd, 1997; Mirrlees-Black, *et al.*,1998). Victims' satisfaction with the police response has been a particular focus of concern, since police officers are often the first point of contact that victims have with the criminal justice system, and so a poor experience here is likely to detrimentally impact upon perceptions of the wider system in general. One common finding in relation to policing has been that whilst victims are generally satisfied with the police at their first contact, the level of victim satisfaction decreases as their case progresses through the criminal justice system, largely due to receiving insufficient information regarding their case from the police. Thus, the flow of information between the police and victims can be poor (Shapland *et al.*, 1985; Newburn and Merry, 1995). For example, in a report stemming from the 1996 British Crime Survey, it was found that whilst the majority of victims were satisfied with police response, only 38 per cent of victims considered that they had been kept very or fairly well informed about the progress of investigations (Mirrlees-Black and Budd, 1997: 4). Results from the 2002/03 British Crime Survey further reveal that victims who reported the incident and who wanted information from the police received it in only one-fifth of incidents. In only 59 per cent of cases that the police came to know about, victims were very or fairly satisfied with the way the police dealt with the matter (Ringham and Salisbury, 2004: 4).

Researchers have previously argued that recognition amongst agencies of the criminal justice system that the reporting and prosecution of a wide range of offences often requires the victim (McCabe and Sutcliffe, 1978; Kelly and Erez, 1997) has acted as a 'bargaining tool' (Zedner, 1994: 1230) in gaining recognition of victims' needs and their interests (Zedner, 1994, 2002). Providing for victims has become a central plank of criminal justice policy and so it is argued that 'the victim has moved from being a forgotten actor to become a key player in the criminal justice process' (Zedner, 2002: 419). However, this argument appears to accept, rather than challenge, the way in which victims' needs have been tied predominantly to processes of the criminal justice system. Acknowledging that negative treatment by, and experiences of, the police and courts may adversely affect victims and therefore may constitute their 'secondary victimisation' (Maguire and Pointing, 1988), and putting into place initiatives to reduce this, is not equal to responding to victim need.

In Britain, when looking at the various initiatives that have been developed within the criminal justice system, particularly since the introduction of the Victim's Charter in 1990, and the second Victim's Charter in 1996, on first appearance it would seem that a more 'victim-friendly' justice system has been created. For example, Witness Services have been established to give help and support to witnesses, as well as to victims of crime, who are called to give evidence in court or who might be attending court for other reasons. Witness service staff and volunteers offer a range of services including providing someone to talk to, giving the opportunity to see court beforehand and giving the opportunity to learn about court procedures, and also offering practical help such as filling in expense claim forms. The agency responsible for managing offenders, the Probation Service, has also been encouraged to incorporate a 'victim perspective' into its work, for example, by providing information to victims about the release arrangements of 'their' offenders, and giving them the opportunity to influence these, also by pursuing restorative justice strategies that might (amongst other things) help victims develop an understanding of why the crime was committed against them. On the Home Office website there is also a virtual tour of the criminal justice system, the aims of which are to 'guide any victim of crime through the processes that they will encounter, from the time a crime is reported, through the police investigation, prosecution decision making, court processes, and sentencing'. Information is also provided on the 'personal support that is available at all stages, including, when relevant, after the court case'. However, when critically examining the developments taking place within victim policy, it would appear that any changes being implemented are more to do with the pursuit of broader government-instigated goals rather than with directly helping victims.

A recurring theme in British politics over the last 20 years has been the pursuit of an agenda seeking to increase the efficiency of the public sector (Mawby and Walklate, 1994). The fact that victims are vital to the reporting and investigation of many cases, and are essential as providers of evidence in court (McCabe and Sutcliffe, 1978; Mawby and Colston, 1979),[1] means that victims are crucial to any government attempts in setting targets to boost the efficiency of the criminal justice system. Victims' needs have essentially been subsumed within a discourse of victim satisfaction, and this has allowed policy makers to pursue their own wider agenda in relation to efficiency whilst at the same time claiming that victims are being helped. The British Government has sought to boost the efficiency of the criminal justice system via the introduction of a series of Public Service Agreement targets that criminal justice agencies are expected to meet. One key target that has been set is that in relation to increasing the number of crimes for which an offender is brought to justice, since there is a large gap between the number of offences that are recorded and the number that lead to an offender being brought to justice. Two further, related, targets include the need to raise public confidence in the criminal justice system, and to increase year after year the satisfaction of victims and witnesses, as it is argued that the justice system relies on public cooperation and involvement to function effectively. Thus, whilst victim and witness satisfaction is featured here, the issue of victim need is not. The list of Public Service Agreements, and the concomitant performance indicators and priorities that lead from this, can be seen as a way of controlling and disciplining agencies of the criminal justice system (see Williams, 1999b). A discourse that is able to link victims' needs to various processes of the criminal justice system enables policy makers to pursue their wider goals whilst at the same time maintaining that they are helping victims, and thereby is of high rhetorical value. Nonetheless, if we approach victimisation from a broader perspective than that linked to process, it becomes clear that in many cases victims' needs are not met.

The first point to make is that the changes in policy and practice that have been implemented across agencies of the criminal justice system, under the guise of the development of a 'victim perspective', have not necessarily led to significant improvements for victims. For example, Spalek (2003) has examined the initiatives taking place under the Probation Service, and has argued that the development of a victim perspective has taken place rather quickly, with little consideration of the tensions and problems that can arise from attempting to respond to both victims' and offenders' needs simultaneously. This means that victims' expectations may be raised about the level of influence that they have over an offender's release, expectations which cannot be fulfilled and which may therefore leave the victim feeling disappointed (Crawford and Enterkin, 1999). The extra demands placed upon probation work as a result of the pursuit of a 'victim perspective', also means that resources are likely to be switched from offender-based services to those catering for victim 'need' (Williams, 1999b). However, if we broaden the perspective through which victimisation is viewed, we see that the categories of 'victim' and 'offender' are not as distinct as public policy discourses would suggest. As highlighted in Chapter 3, offenders and victims are disproportionately male, young, single, and urban residents of lower socio-economic status. An offender, therefore, is also likely to have experienced repeated victimisation, which might take many forms such as physical or sexual violence. This means that it is also important to provide adequate resources to offenders. However, according to Tudor (2002), support services for young males are particularly thin, as are initiatives that are aimed at tackling the victimised pasts of many sexual and violent offenders.

The second point to mention is that the majority of victims do not report the crimes that have been committed against them to the police, and thereby have little contact with the criminal justice system. According to figures from the British Crime Survey 2002/03, only 40 per cent of crime picked up by the survey was reported or came to the attention of the police (Ringham and Salisbury, 2004: 5). Nonetheless, victims are likely to have contact with other statutory, welfare and voluntary organisations, such as hospitals, medical practices, housing associations, schools and businesses. However, it appears that there is less awareness of victim issues amongst agencies outside of the criminal justice system than amongst agencies inside, and few adequate facilities in place to train members of staff, and so victims may be treated inappropriately. For example, a document published by Victim Support (2002c), *Criminal Neglect*, highlights many instances of the insensitive treatment of victims by employers, public officials and administrators. One example that is given in this publication is in relation to a victim who was repeatedly stabbed in her apartment by her ex-partner. When she asked her local housing authority for an urgent transfer to alternative accommodation it was rejected as housing officials there did not seem to recognise how difficult it would be for her to continue to live in the location where the attack had taken place. According to Victim Support, there are many cases whereby the victims of crime have found themselves homeless as a result of being unable to continue living in their homes due to the psychological trauma that they experience. There have also been instances where employees have witnessed violent crime in the workplace, yet their employers have required them to continue working, despite any significant psychological and emotional trauma that may have been endured (Victim Support, 2002c). Findings from the 2002/03 British Crime Survey would suggest that violence at work is a significant issue. Approximately 376,000 workers had experienced at least one incident of violence in the workplace during 2002/03, which might involve physical assaults, verbal threats or non-verbal intimidation. Furthermore, 22 per cent of workers who had contact with members of the public thought it very or fairly likely that they would be threatened at work in the next year (Upson, 2004 1–2). Medical practitioners also may not receive thorough training about victimisation and so victims here may not receive the kind of medical and psychological attention that they require (Victim Support, 2002c).

The third point to make is that individuals who are victimised by 'non-traditional' types of crime, such as those experiencing institutional violence, health and safety law violations or financial crime, often receive little, if any help. Research exploring experiences of white-collar victimisation suggests that the impact of such crime is often severe, and victims experience psychological and emotional impacts and significant financial costs (Spalek, 1999, 2001). Nonetheless, when we look at the issue of whether any substantial help is provided to victims here, we see that beyond some form of financial compensation that may or may not be given, and indeed, may take many years to obtain, individuals are often left to cope on their own. Importantly, 'secondary victimisation', whereby individuals are victimised by the subsequent regulatory response, is often significant in cases of white-collar crime. However, in stark contrast to the attention paid by policy makers and agencies of the criminal justice system to the secondary victimisation of victims of street and property crime, under the guise of responding to victims' needs, victims of white-collar offences are often ignored. This point can be illustrated by drawing on a study carried out by Spalek (2001), which examined the impact of the closure of the Bank of Credit and Commerce International (BCCI) in 1991 upon employees of the bank. Spalek's (2001) study shows that former employees felt victimised by the subsequent regulatory response to the crimes that were committed at BCCI, rather than the actual crimes themselves. However, little consideration was paid to the needs of former employees by the regulatory authorities, such as the Bank of England and the liquidator. Spalek (2001) argues that this may partly be explained by the ambiguous nature of 'white-collar crime' when individuals caught up in 'white-collar scandal' may not be viewed as 'victims' by regulatory authorities (Elias, 1990), and so their needs are not considered. In addition to this, because the former employees were largely superfluous to the investigations and prosecutions carried out by the regulatory authorities, the regulators did not have to consider their concerns. Evidence against BCCI was gathered through undercover operations carried out by customs officers, and through intelligence agencies such as the CIA and MI5. Accountants Price Waterhouse were also asked by the Bank of England to gather evidence when auditing BCCI's accounts. When prosecutions were carried out against this bank and some of its former employees, only a very small proportion of employees were required to give evidence. Moreover, these employees occupied high-ranking positions, as more junior employees would not have had any evidence of corruption to present at court (Passas, 1996). This means that most former employees of BCCI, many of whom had not been aware of the illegal operations and surveillance that had been occurring over the years, were unimportant to the prosecutions carried out. As a result, their experiences of secondary victimisation were overlooked and individuals had to find their own support mechanisms in order to fight the damaging repercussions of the closure of BCCI (Spalek, 2001). This case study illustrates that discourses which suggest that victims' needs are increasingly being met refer predominantly to victims of events that traditionally have been viewed as criminal, persons victimised by 'non-traditional' types of crime, on the other hand, such as victims of white-collar offences, remain outside prevailing discussions of victims' requirements.

Summary

Clearly, as indicated in the preceding arguments, there are many instances where victims' needs are not being met with the appropriate responses. Indeed, the analyses above illustrate the very narrow focus of the debate around victims' needs, resulting in little improvement to the experiences of the majority of individuals affected by both traditional and non-traditional types of crime. This leads on to the consideration of whether a greater focus upon victims' rights would ensure that victims' needs are better catered to.

The development of victims' rights

As highlighted in Chapter 2, victims' rights legislation has been drawn up in many different countries. In the United States, for example, in 1997, Congress passed the Victims Rights Clarification Act to clarify existing federal law allowing victims to attend a trial and to appear as 'impact witnesses' during the sentencing phase of both capital and non-capital cases. This allowed victims and survivors of the bombing of the Alred P. Murrah Federal Building in Oklahoma City to observe the trial and also to provide input later at sentencing (US Department of Justice, 2000). In Canada the

Criminal Code sets out victims' rights, which include the rights to safety, security and privacy (Department of Justice Canada, 2003). In Britain, the Government referred to victims' rights when it published the first Victim's Charter in 1990, which was subtitled as 'a statement of the rights of victims of crime' (Williams, 1999b). Victims' rights have also been referred to by intergovernmental organisations such as the United Nations and the Council of Europe. For example, the United Nations document, entitled Declaration of Basic Principles of Justice for Victims of Crime and Abuse of Power, provides guidelines and standards that individual member States should follow, relating to the recognition of, and respect for, the rights of victims of crime and of abuse of power, in terms of access to justice and fair treatment, restitution, compensation and assistance. In 2001, the Council of Ministers of the European Union agreed the Framework Decision on the Standing of Victims in Criminal Proceedings, setting out minimum standards for the treatment of victims of crime that should apply throughout the European Union: victims have the right to access to justice, compensation in criminal proceedings, they have the right to give and receive information, to protection, to understand and be understood (Victim Support, 2001: 4). Also, in terms of the European Convention on Human Rights and Fundamental Freedoms, incorporated into British law by the Human Rights Act 1998, although this does not refer specifically to victims, it nonetheless has been established that articles relating to the protection of life, liberty and security of the person may be used in relation to victims (Zedner, 2002). This kind of legislation is symbolically compelling, since it gives the impression that victims are being empowered in some way. However, upon closer examination of the issues raised by the subject of victims' rights, it becomes clear that there are many significant limitations to the implementation of victims' rights legislation.

First, within the area of human rights in general, there is much discussion and debate, and a general lack of clarity, over how we are to understand, interpret and safeguard individuals' rights. There is no one definition of human rights, and so there are different ways of interpreting these, which might include a legalistic understanding examining what rights are protected by law, or ethical or legal debate around which rights should be afforded protection (Smiljanic, 2002). This lack of clarity can clearly be seen when looking at victim legislation, since policy makers may refer to victims' rights without explaining what they mean by this phrase, nor giving clear procedures for implementing such so-called rights. Indeed, when the phrase 'victims rights' is utilised, it is often in relation to services that victims can expect to receive from the criminal justice system, rather than in relation to any new or existing social, political or economic rights that victims might have. This was clearly the case with the first Victim's Charter in Britain in 1990, in that although it referred to victims' rights, in reality this document articulated service standards. Indeed, when the second Victim's Charter was launched in 1996, the phrase 'the rights of victims of crime' was dropped from the heading, and replaced by the phrase 'service standards for victims of crime' (Williams, 1999b). The provision of services was considered in relation to the following four general areas: the provision of information to victims, taking victims' views into account, treating them with respect and sensitivity at court, and providing them with support. In 2004 the Home Office published the Victims' Code of Practice, which 'represents a minimum level of service in England and Wales' that victims can expect from agencies such as the Crown Prosecution Service, the Courts, the Prison Service and all police forces.

Couching victims' rights in terms of the services that individuals can expect to receive from the criminal justice system has a number of important implications. One area of concern is that victims are encouraged to think of themselves as individual consumers of a criminal justice system, who have certain requirements. If those requirements are not met, individuals are then encouraged to complain via the detailed grievance procedures that are issued by Government. However, grievance procedures are directed towards the specific criminal justice agencies themselves rather than the wider political and social context that agencies operate within. Yet it can be argued that it is often the broader political and social context that impacts upon individuals' experiences as victims, and so victims' rights legislation should be viewed more broadly than the current focus upon core services that victims should expect to receive from the criminal justice system. At the same time, the services that agencies of the criminal justice system provide to victims are themselves heavily constrained by political factors, which influence the level and type of resources allocated to agencies, also impacting upon the particular priorities and targets that agencies are expected to pursue. Victims' dissatisfaction with the treatment that they receive is thereby channelled into making complaints against particular agencies of the criminal justice system, and these can then be used by central government as a reason to reform these particular agencies according to the government's own political agenda, which may have little to do with responding effectively to victims' needs (Williams, 1999b).

Case study

The following is an example of some of the service standards laid out by the Victim's Charter 1996:

You Can Expect a crime you have reported to be investigated and to receive information about what happens.

Case study (cont'd)

The police will respond to your report as quickly as they can.

The police look into all crimes reported to them. If you phone them to tell them about a crime they will send an officer to see you if necessary.

The police will give you the name and phone number of the officer or 'crime desk' responsible for your case.

The police are normally your first point of contact. If you have any questions at any time you can contact this person, who will either answer your question or put you in touch with someone who can.

Question

In what ways, if any, do the service standards laid out by the Victim's Charter empower victims?

Sometimes, the phrase victims' rights might be used in the context of giving victims a more active role in the criminal justice system, for example, by participating in decisions affecting the prosecution and/or sentencing of offenders. Indeed, many countries have now introduced Victim Impact Statements, allowing victims to explain the impact of the crime that has been committed against them. However, whether these kinds of initiatives benefit victims is debatable because some victims may not want the additional burden of getting involved more closely with the criminal justice process. Indeed, it might be argued that victims should have the right to be free of the burden of decisions relating to the offender (see Victim Support: The Rights of Victims of Crime, 1995). Furthering victims' rights may also have the additional negative outcome of curtailing defendants'/offenders' rights, thereby questioning the legitimacy of a criminal justice system that is supposed to be underpinned by notions of 'due process'. Indeed, Zedner (2002) argues that the balancing of victims' rights with those of the rights of the defendant is likely to be a recurring source of academic and legal debate. At the same time, in jurisdictions where Victim Impact Statements are not to be used to directly influence offender management (including punishment) decisions, this may leave victims feeling even worse, since their expectations may have been raised about the extent to which their voices can influence the criminal justice system, when in reality they continue to occupy a marginalised position. For example, in contrast to the United States, where victims have some influence over the sentences that offenders receive, in the UK victims can express how a particular crime has affected them, using Victim Statements (as introduced under the Victim's Charter 1996), although this should not be used to decide the sentence that an offender receives. In a study of a pilot project relating to Victim Statements in Britain, it was found that around 30 per cent of victims invited to state what physical, financial, psychological, social or emotional effects the offence had on them or their family opted to do so. Of this 30 per cent, around one-third felt better. However, a significant minority, 18 per cent, were upset by the process, while the rest were indifferent (Hoyle *et al.*, 1999: 3). 55 per cent of victims opting to give Victim Statements wanted to influence the case outcome, however, in practice these had no effect on bail or prosecution decisions (Hoyle *et al.*, 1999: 1). Another example of where victims' rights legislation may not necessarily lead to improvements for victims is when looking at the area of sexual violence. In recent years, many initiatives have been implemented by police forces in order to lessen the trauma that victims of sexual assault face when having to provide evidence. Special interview suites have been created in police stations and specially trained officers may also be provided to victims. However, Zedner (2002) argues that despite these changes, a general lack of resources and a prevailing police culture means that victims continue to be treated insensitively. An example of where victims' rights legislation can directly impact detrimentally upon victims is in relation to the death penalty in Texas, where the families of murder victims are entitled to view the execution of the murderer. This may have the unintended outcome of traumatising victims even further because the accounts of those who have witnessed executions suggest that victims' reactions include post-traumatic stress (Brewis, 2001). Therefore, victims' rights legislation does not necessarily mean improving victims' experiences of the criminal justice system, nor does it automatically mean that there will be emotional, psychological or financial benefits. This point has been highlighted by Smiljanic (2001), who argues that there is a case to be made that human rights legislation is rather idealistic, with there being a huge gap between the rights that any new piece of legislation claims to safeguard and the actual protection that it actually does provide.

Another obvious limitation to victims' rights legislation is that it does not protect individuals from being victimised in the first place. By virtue of them being victims, individuals' human rights have already been violated, since it can be argued that crime constitutes an infringement of a human right, and the person whose right is impinged constitutes the victim (Schwendinger and Schwendinger, 1975; Elias, 1986). Legislation setting out individuals' rights, such as the Human Rights Act 1998 for example, which sets out precise and legally enforceable human rights (taken from the European Convention on Human Rights), does not prevent those rights from being violated.[2] It has been argued, for example, that human rights law generally is not equipped to handle interpersonal violence, as when one person attacks another (Smiljanic, 2002). Also, states can abuse individuals' human rights, despite the supposed protection afforded by human rights legislation. States can also abrogate, or suspend, individuals' rights. This means that the implementation of victims' rights legislation will not lead to fewer victims, nor will it necessarily mean that people will feel any safer.

Crime-related anxiety is a common feature of contemporary modern society. National and local surveys consistently show that women suffer higher levels of fear of crime than men. For example, according to a Home Office Citizenship Survey that was carried out in 2001, women were five times as likely as men to say that they never went out after dark (15% of women as opposed to 3% of men). Women were also more than three times as likely to say that they felt very unsafe if they did go out after dark (10% of women as opposed to 3% of men) (Prime *et al.*, 2001: 2). If a feminist perspective is taken in relation to women's anxiety around crime, it can be argued that underpinning women's anxiety is the fear of male violence, since women often have to live around daily harassments and threats to personal security from male intimates, acquaintances and strangers. Women routinely engage in avoidance strategies in order to reduce their risk of being victimised (Hanmer and Stanko, 1985). Taking this as an example, victims' rights legislation in relation to issues such as domestic violence and sexual assault is not likely to influence women's management of their personal safety, nor their feelings of insecurity. Rather, broader cultural, social and political changes are needed in order to enable women to feel safer, these relating to issues such as, for example, the construction of masculinity and links here with the male propensity to violence. At the same time, if we take the view that patriarchy underpins the state and legal system, then any responses to women's victimisation, whilst appearing to be helpful to women, may in reality do little to alleviate any power inequalities and injustices stemming from these. As such, a focus upon individual victims' rights may do little to address women's collective rights (Mawby and Walklate, 1994). This discussion therefore highlights that to truly protect people from victimisation, and from high levels of fear of crime, we need to take a broader perspective than purely focussing upon the notion of individuals' rights. Although the phrase 'victims' rights' is potent as it suggests that victims are being empowered in some significant way, racial, sexual and economic (alongside other forms) of equality are dependent upon wider cultural, social, political and economic processes.

Case study

In 1995, following pressure from victims' support groups, the Texas Board of Criminal Justice passed a rule that allows family members of murder victims to be present at the execution of 'their' murderers if they feel that seeing this will help them. The offender is strapped to a bed and lethally injected. One woman, who watched the killer of her two daughters executed, said, 'It was scary because I will see his face forever now. The most difficult bit was he looked so pitiful'.

Source: K. Brewis (2001) 'Witness for the Execution' *The Sunday Times Magazine* 22 April.

Question

To what extent should criminal justice policy makers listen to the voices of victims?

Victims as individual consumers and as active citizens

In Britain, the debate about victims' rights has arisen within a particular political climate seeking to impose a culture of 'customer service' upon the public sector, whilst at the same time re-defining the nature of the relationship between the state and the individual in terms of 'consumerism' and 'active citizenship'. In the early 1990s, under a Conservative Government headed by Prime Minister John Major, Citizen Charters were drawn up for a number of government agencies and public utilities, such as the National Health Service, the rail industry and the criminal justice system (the latter, e.g, included the Victim's Charter 1990 and the Court Users' Charter, 1994). These set out the standards of service that individuals should receive from various agencies, highlighting that individuals have both rights and choices. Importantly, the charters defined service users as individual consumers, who have civil citizenship rights, and not wider political, social or economic rights (Williams, 1999b). Individuals are seen as being equal, as being able to freely choose the type of service that they need, and they should encounter as little state interference as possible. At the same time, individuals are viewed as having certain responsibilities, under the notion of 'active citizenship', whereby people should be encouraged to offer their skills and knowledge to public service (Mawby and Walklate, 1994). This approach is consistent with New Right ideology of pulling back the contours of the State and encouraging individual freedom. Under the subsequent Labour Government, headed by Prime Minister Tony Blair, these themes have continued to be pursued by policy makers. As highlighted earlier, under the Home Office Victims' Code of Practice, which 'represents a minimum level of service in England and Wales' that victims can expect, the 'victim' is understood solely as 'a person entitled to receive services under this code'. Within the Labour Government, a strong emphasis has also been placed upon active citizenship and community involvement in the delivery of community justice, as evidenced by the formation of the Civil Renewal Unit, the Faith Communities Unit and the Active Citizenship Centre, which have been established in order to 'ensure that policies and practices consistently take into account the need to advance citizenship, strengthen communities and deliver in partnership with communities' (Home Office, 2003a). An Active Community Unit has also been set up by Government, to promote the development of the voluntary and community sector and encourage people to become actively involved in their communities, particularly in deprived areas.

The notions of victim as 'consumer' and as 'active citizen' mutually reinforce each other, and are underpinned by similar philosophies. Essentially, they serve to de-politicise victims, to individualise and neutralise their experiences, so that victims are seen as individuals who have certain 'rights', but also who have certain responsibilities towards their communities and the neighbourhoods in which they reside. Taking first the notion of 'victim as consumer', from this perspective, victims are viewed as having individual needs, relating to processes of the criminal justice system, which must be satisfied. Individuals are seen as equals, as having equal choice, despite there being significant differences in terms of their purchase power. The language of consumerism also gives the impression that victims are largely willing consumers of the criminal justice system, even though this, clearly, is not the case (Mawby and Walklate, 1994; Williams, 1999b). The notion of active citizenship ignores wider social and economic inequalities, emphasising the obligations of individual citizens rather than those of state institutions (Mawby and Walklate, 1994). Individuals are encouraged to identify and define the problems that their communities face and to put forward solutions to those problems. All citizens, regardless of the inequalities that they may experience, can get involved in order to build safer, more tolerant communities, as the following quotation from the Home Secretary's Scarman Lecture, delivered at the Citizens' Convention on 11 December 2003, reveals:

> I set out a philosophy of civil renewal. At the heart is a vision of strong, active and empowered communities – increasingly capable of doing things for themselves, defining the problems they face and then tackling them together. People should be encouraged to solve their problems themselves.

And according to the Civil Renewal website in 2004:

> Civil renewal can happen anywhere, from the most deprived communities to the most affluent. It takes place when people become actively engaged in the well-being of their communities and are able to define the problems they face and tackle them together with help from the government and public bodies.

Citizens are thereby viewed as individuals who belong to politically neutral communities, separate from broader structural inequalities relating to class, gender, race and so forth. The Home Secretary wants to encourage people to take part in Neighbourhood Watch Schemes, also he wants more people to get involved in policing, as Special Constables (Home Office, Scarman Lecture, 2003d). This echoes the 'community-based, anti-dependency volunteer philosophy' of the previous Conservative Government, during which Victim Support schemes expanded across the country and were financially and politically supported by government due to the model of the neutral victim that Victim Support adopted (Mawby and Walklate, 1994: 173). The ideal of 'active citizenship' also echoes the rise of the new criminologies (O'Malley, 1992; Garland, 1994: 458), whereby responsibility for crime is placed squarely on to both victims and offenders, as exemplified by the popularity of, for example, situational crime prevention initiatives. Thus, individuals are encouraged to protect themselves from the risks of crime by, for example, investing in security measures. The impression that individuals have some degree of choice and control over the risks that they are exposed to, and that they can act to avoid becoming the victims of crime, is thereby created and perpetuated. Significant differences in the structural positions that individuals occupy are left outside of the prevailing discourse, despite the fact that these structural differences influence people's risks of being victimised, since crime is not equally spread out amongst the general population (Mawby and Walklate, 1994; Williams, 1999b). So there are many constraints upon individual choice. For example, if a person becomes the victim of a burglary, then this may be because they live in a high-crime area and lack the resources to move away, equally they may lack the resources to afford effective security measures. Similarly, in a world that privileges 'whiteness' (Frankenberg, 1993; Lewis and Ramazanoglu, 1999), there is little choice over the risks that a black person is exposed to in relation to race hate crime. These examples highlight the necessity of placing individual experiences of victimisation within a broader social, political and economic context.

Victim identities, emotions and self-governmentality

The notion that victims are consumers of the criminal justice system, whose needs should be met by the provision of certain basic services, lies at the core of a 'civilising process' that serves to depoliticise and individualise victims' emotions, so that the shock, anger, disgust, fear (alongside other emotional reactions documented by researchers) felt by victims are not placed within their broader structural context, but rather, are translated into largely a bureaucratic discourse that is part of a wider governmental machinery measuring, and setting targets for, victim satisfaction. This serves to disempower victims since they are encouraged to think about themselves as individuals with needs that are linked to criminal justice process, which then becomes part of their process of feeling. If we take a Foucauldian perspective that views the exercise of governmental power via the subjectification of individuals, this means that the discourses of consumerism and active citizenship belong to 'technologies of the self', that might be willingly adopted by individual victims, which shape individuals' subjectivities, so that they are aligned to specific governmental aims and objectives (Garland, 1997: 175).[3] Thus, for example, under the prevailing victim discourse found within government, black victims of racist violence might be encouraged to think of themselves as deserving of services such as Victim Support and compensation, and where their needs are not effectively satisfied they might be encouraged to complain to the service provider(s) concerned. The dominance of the consumer discourse might mean that it is less likely that black communities will see their victimisation within a wider context of social and economic deprivation and racist, oppressive structures. Rather, they are encouraged to focus on the services offered by the criminal justice system instead. The government's approach to civil renewal and active citizenship also encourages individuals to view themselves in politically neutral ways, since the prevailing ethos seems to be that people should be encouraged to solve their own problems through the empowerment of local communities via help from government and public bodies. However, in the government's approach to active citizenship there appears to be no critique of socio-structural inequalities, rather, there is an implicit acceptance of these via the belief that individuals, working together, can overcome the problems that they face.

Governmental power shapes active subjects, seeking to 'align their choices with the objectives of governing authorities' (Garland, 1997: 175). Discourses of 'consumerism' and 'active citizenship' can be viewed as governmental technologies, belonging to wider processes that threaten the formation of collective identities and the collective expression of emotion, thereby individualising experiences of victimisation. Technologies that serve to subjectify victims as individual consumers and as active citizens are so pervasive and compelling precisely because the impression that they create is that victims are being helped and that their needs are being catered to under the ethos of 'customer care', also that individual victims can work to reduce their risks from victimisation and to better their lives. Instead, however, they constitute a threat to victims and may serve to disempower them since they may neutralise how individuals see themselves, influencing people's actions so that they behave in politically safe ways, ways that are consistent with government objectives.

Nonetheless, and perhaps encouragingly, findings from the 2002/03 British Crime Survey would suggest that there is some resistance to discourses that view victims as consumers of the criminal justice system. According to the 2002/03 British Crime Survey, the majority of victims (75%) do not want any form of advice or support (Ringham and Salisbury, 2004: 4). In this survey, victim need has been framed by policy makers by asking victims whether they would want the following types of support or advice: information from the police, advice on security, practical help, someone to talk to, help with insurance/compensation, protection from further victimisation, and help in reporting. It might be argued that four out of the seven options given to victims here are process-based, since they can be linked to the wider government goals of increasing efficiency and confidence in the criminal justice system highlighted earlier in this chapter. This means that it should not be assumed that the survey indicates that victims do not want any help per se, rather, it seems that victims are indicating here that they do not require the forms of support identified in the survey, which can be linked to wider government aims.

The marginalisation and lack of financial support provided to victim support groups that belong to the unofficial, or hidden, victims' movement further threatens to erode the emotional space and the formation of collective identities that might be found amongst individual victims of crime. Nonetheless, and despite severe resource shortages and the significant strains encountered by individual volunteers, the unofficial victims' movement continues to thrive, so that there continue to be many cases whereby individuals will group together to form victim support and/or action groups. Examples that can be quoted here include: the Islamic Human Rights Commission, the Muslim Women's Helpline and the United Families and Friends Campaign, but there are many more. It might be argued that individuals' subject positions in terms of their class, gender, race (etc.) play a significant role in group identity, formation and the help and support that is provided in these groups. This theme is pursued further in Chapter 7, when the 'unofficial victims' movement' is examined in closer detail.

Research exploring the volunteer activities of people belonging to minority ethnic groups suggests that people's subject positions appear to be important in the kind of work that they do. A study by Britton (2000: 32), for example, found that in a sample of black volunteers working for a black voluntary organisation, 54 per cent were graduates and undergraduates, whilst 37 per cent of volunteers were employed in managerial or professional positions. Nonetheless, race identity and politics were important motivating factors, with the most significant motivating factor being the project's aims, which included achieving justice for black people and serving the needs and interests of black people. 30 per cent of the sample also considered race to be a motivating factor to volunteering, whilst a quarter of the volunteers insisted that being black was central to their decision to volunteer for the project. Individuals also revealed a commitment to a diverse range of black issues and community initiatives (Britton, 2000: 47). These findings mirror the results of a previous survey on black volunteering, carried out by the Black Perspectives in Volunteering Group, which found that a quarter of the black volunteers surveyed wanted to meet the needs specific to black people and that they had to rely on black organisations for adequate volunteering opportunities. Three-quarters of the volunteers here revealed that being black had some influence on how and why they came to participate in the project (Britton, 2000: 36).

Clearly, individuals' self-identities and subject positions influence the type of community work and political action that they engage in. Victim action and support groups, which constitute the unofficial, or hidden victims' movement, are examples of the formation of collective identities within which victims' reactions, including their emotions, are shared and embedded within groups' responses to their experiences of victimisation. It would appear that the public policy debate around victims' needs has taken place at a rather superficial level, and has failed to grasp the importance of individuals' cultures, identities and sense of marginalisation. Williams (1999) argues that the focus upon service standards by government agencies implicitly infantilises victims and patronises them. As a technology of governance, however, individualising victims' reactions to crime through the discourses of 'consumerism' and 'active citizenship' constitutes a powerful threat to how individual victims may view themselves, and can work through individuals so that they respond to crime in ways that act to sustain government priorities. Nonetheless, the proliferation of victim action and support groups, constituting the unofficial victims' movement, acts as a powerful challenge to governmental technologies and objectives, illustrating that people do not necessarily view themselves as distinct individuals, but rather, see themselves as being connected to others, as well as to broader social systems of inequality.

Conclusion

This chapter has unpicked the notions of victims' needs and victims' rights within contemporary criminal justice and victim policy. It has been argued that victims' needs have been subsumed within a broader political discourse of victim satisfaction, to pursue the government goal of boosting the efficiency of the criminal justice system. However, if the lens through which victims' needs are viewed is broadened, to look at individuals' experiences of agencies that lie outside of the criminal justice system, such as victims' experiences of hospitals, medical practices, housing associations and businesses, then it is clear that individuals' needs are often unmet. At the same time, if the experiences of individuals victimised by non-traditional types of crime, like financial crime or other types of white-collar offences, are taken into account, then again, it is clear that their interests are often ignored. It is therefore important to challenge the ways in which victims' needs have been constructed and tied predominantly to processes of the criminal justice system. As highlighted in this chapter, the acknowledgement that negative treatment by agencies of the criminal justice system constitutes individuals' secondary victimisation, and the development of initiatives to reduce this, is not equal to responding to victim need.

Victims' rights legislation, despite giving the appearance of empowering victims, is often put together in terms of the services that victims can expect to receive from agencies of the criminal justice system. This means that individuals' political, economic and social rights are not enhanced, and so inequalities in relation to race, class and gender (alongside other inequalities) remain. In Britain, the debate around victims' rights has been underpinned by the notions of 'victims as consumers' and 'victims as active citizens'. Both of these act to depoliticise victims, civilising their reactions, serving to threaten the formation of collective group identities which may develop out of shared experiences of victimisation that can be linked to wider social inequalities. Nonetheless, the strong presence of the unofficial victims' movement, as exemplified by a wide range of victim action and support groups that can be linked to race, gender, class (and so forth) inequalities, illustrates how victims do not necessarily view themselves only as individuals who have certain expectations of the services provided by the criminal justice system. Rather, similar histories and experiences of victimisation that can be linked to shared aspects of identity positions continue to galvanise human action. Chapter 8 focusses upon the unofficial victims' movement, in order to highlight how experiences of victimisation are closely linked to, and part of, wider structures of inequality based on race, class, gender, ethnicity and so forth. As a result, these responses to victimisation constitute a powerful challenge to the model of the neutral, deserving victim that tends to be perpetuated by official responses to victimisation.

Questions

1 In what ways is the debate around victims' needs narrowly focussed?
2 What is meant by the phrase 'victims' rights'?
3 In what ways are victims consumers of a criminal justice system?

8

Unofficial Victims' Movements: Re-defining Victimhood

Introduction

Outside of the developments and initiatives that can be conceptualised as belonging to an official victims' movement, whereby reactions to crime are firmly located within individuals, collective responses to victimisation can be found, which can be classified as being part of an unofficial victims' movement. This bears witness to injustices arising from wider social structures of oppression, and so constitutes a powerful form of resistance against the ever-present movement towards the individualisation of victims' pain as evident within late modern society, and highlighted in Chapters 1, 2, 6 and 7 of this book.

A wide range of organisations and groups make up the unofficial victims' movement, and these can consist of single-issue victim action and support groups, which are likely to be transient in nature, existing only for a specific period of time, dissolving once the specific injustices that played a large role in the groups' formation have been resolved. At the same time, however, some of the groups to be found here may be engaged in activities that go beyond the remit of a particular issue, and so their claims-making activities will be less transient and more broad-reaching in scope. These latter types of initiatives may also belong to a wider coalition of interests based on shared group collectivities that make up a 'social movement', within which particular views of the nature of victimhood may be located, and the activities undertaken by the separate groups here may be directed at achieving common political and social goals.

The following chapter will look at examples of victim action groups belonging to the unofficial victims' movement in order to highlight how victims' reactions to crime are not solely confined to, or solely expressed within, individuals. Rather, commonalities of experience between individual victims' reactions can be found, and these may relate to aspects of individuals' subjectivities that they have in common with other victims. These shared aspects of identity can lead to the formation of action and support groups, and can inform and underpin the work carried out by group members. At the same time, where victim identities extend beyond the confines of individual groups, then these may be part of a wider 'collective consciousness' based on race, class, gender, ethnicity, religion, disability and so on which informs and underpins a broader 'social movement'.

This chapter focusses on victimisation arising from white-collar deviance, hate crime and institutional violence. These three areas are explored in some detail because they comprise instances of victimisation that have traditionally been excluded from social and political debates about the 'crime problem', because they clearly show how wider social structures can create, and/or impact upon, experiences of victimisation, and the cases used in this chapter also highlight the centrality of identity issues when conceptualising the developments within the unofficial victims' movement.

Victim subjectivities and white-collar victimisation

Compared to the extensive amount of work that has been carried out examining the impact of 'street crime', a category that includes crimes like physical and sexual assault, robbery and homicide, white-collar victimisation is an under-researched phenomenon. This can partly be attributed to the hidden nature of white-collar deviance, whereby, for instance, official crime statistics tend to focus on street crime and burglary, and government departments tend to offer only vague information. For example, Tombs (2000) argues that the police and the Home Office do not hold information on safety crimes and so other sources of information must be found to try to assess how many people are killed or injured at work as a result of health and safety law violations. However, reliance upon the enforcement or prosecution data produced by regulatory authorities, such as the Health and Safety Executive for example, is highly problematic because this data is generally unreliable and open to a number of biases (Tombs, 2000). Also, as highlighted in Chapter 4, victim surveys have rarely included, or focussed upon, white-collar deviance, and so whilst a large amount of data is available regarding the risks that 'street crimes' pose and the human costs of these, little similar information is available about white-collar victimisation.

Nevertheless, some attempts have been made to examine the physical, psychological, financial and emotional costs of white-collar deviance. For example, criminologists have estimated the cost to human lives as a result of health and safety law violations (Box, 1983; Pearce and Tombs, 1992) and case studies of incidents such as Agent Orange, the Bhopal Disaster and the Dalkon Shield (Mokhiber, 1988; Grabosky and Sutton, 1993) highlight the physical violence that white-collar crime wreaks, illustrating that this damage is as harmful as, if not more harmful than, the damage caused by street crime and burglary. The financial cost of white-collar crime is also considered to dwarf the costs of the latter types of crime (Box, 1983; Levi, 1987; Snider, 1991; Coleman, 1994). Some studies have focussed upon documenting the psychological and emotional suffering encountered by victims of white-collar deviance. The general finding in these studies is that the psychological and emotional consequences of white-collar crime are similar to those of street and property crime, and include confusion, shock, helplessness and anxiety (Moore and Mills, 1990; Shover *et al.*, 1994; Spalek, 1999, 2001).

Directly accessing victims to speak about their experiences of white-collar crime can be problematic. In cases of white-collar deviance, individuals may not necessarily be aware that they have been victimised, since the offender may be in a separate location, far-removed from the victim. In cases involving environmental pollution or industrial disease, it is often difficult to establish a clear connection between the white-collar crimes that may have been committed and the actual human impact, since victims' illnesses may take many years to develop and companies will hide and obstruct sensitive material linking their practices to any harmful effects. Victims may therefore not necessarily connect their experiences with the notion of corporate deviance.

Action and support groups offer the researcher the potential to gain access to victims so as to document, and develop a rich and valuable insight into, the process of white-collar victimisation. Action and support groups also enable the researcher to explore the ways in which groups of individuals come together to claim victim status, and to study what aspects of individuals' self-identities are shared by other group members and how these influence experiences of, and responses to, victimisation. Spalek (1999, 2001), for instance, has carried out in-depth interviews with members of two victim action groups in relation to white-collar deviance: the Maxwell Pensioners' Action Group and the Bank of Credit and Commerce International (BCCI) Employees Action Group. Her work reveals some interesting aspects of white-collar victimisation, and these will now be addressed in more detail below.

The Maxwell Scandal

Over the last two decades, a series of high-profile financial scandals have arisen, including the cases of Lloyd's, Barings, Maxwell, BCCI, Morgan

Grenfell and Daiwa Bank. More recently, in the United States, energy firm, Enron, was declared bankrupt in December 2001, whilst in June 2002 WorldCom, the second biggest long-distance telephone company in the US, admitted a $4 billion hole in its accounts. These scandals have created large-scale victimisation, affecting a wide range of victims, including thousands of investors and employees, and so it is both timely and appropriate to consider some of the responses of some of these victims to their plight.

Robert Maxwell, a multi-millionaire and head of a global business empire, disappeared from his yacht on 5 November 1991, amid rumours that he had perhaps committed suicide, or had perhaps been assassinated. Following his death, in Britain the lives of 30,000 pensioners were affected by the discovery that Robert Maxwell had used the pension fund assets of the companies belonging to his business empire as collateral for bank loans, and so hundreds of millions of pounds had disappeared from the company pension schemes, leaving the Maxwell pensioners with an uncertain future (Bower, 1994). Indeed, the uncertainty surrounding individuals' pensions lasted almost four years, since it wasn't until 1995 when pensioners were guaranteed the full payment of their pension entitlements (Spalek, 1999: 217).

In the aftermath of the scandal, Maxwell Pensioner Action Groups were formed, consisting of people who had formerly worked for Robert Maxwell, in a wide range of locations, including Dunstable, Watford, Leeds and Manchester. Action groups performed a number of roles, including offering emotional support to victims and campaigning for their pension money to be secured, as well as for changes to be made to pensions legislation. Importantly, interviews with members of the Dunstable Action Group reveal that underpinning victims' responses to the scandal, and embedded within the work that group members carried out, were their shared identities relating to individuals' subject positions as older people, as working-class, former Maxwell, printing employees, and as members of a partial 'welfare state' that individuals assumed would look after them in their old age.

Within action group members' accounts of their victimisation was a sense of them belonging to a community of print workers fragmented by relatively recent social and economic changes that can be linked to late modernity, which had impacted upon members' sense of well-being, with Robert Maxwell being symbolic of these changes. Individuals contrasted the previous stability and prosperity that they and earlier generations of their families had gained from their employment within print with their present insecurity brought on by the decline in print. Taking a brief look at the history of print, since the introduction of the first printing press in 1450 (Steinberg, 1996) print has been a craft, requiring skilled craftsmen to operate the machinery (Cockburn, 1983). Moreover, although technological advances have been made throughout the centuries, it wasn't until the

1970s that the industry experienced change and decline on an unprece-
dented level, in line with many other British industries. Intensified
competition from foreign imports, together with the rise of in-plant
reprographic departments meant that much work was taken away from
British printers, and so throughout the 1970s and 1980s thousands of jobs
were lost in general print (Marshall, 1983) and so the Maxwell pensioners,
who were working throughout this period, had directly experienced these
changes.

Action group members related the changes taking place in print to the
wider social context, whereby they would talk about the factories that have
been closed down in their local areas. For instance, a common theme that
featured in the interviews was that of how the local landscape has changed,
due to large manufacturing firms being shut down and supermarkets being
built in their place. They therefore seemed to be grieving the sense of
community associated with having worked for a major industry.

For many of the pensioners, Robert Maxwell was an integral element to
the changes taking place in print, since many of them accused him of
'asset-stripping' their companies and 'not caring' about the future of their
industry. Indeed, Robert Maxwell bought up the British Printing and
Communications Corporation, one of Europe's largest printing groups, and
then reduced the workforce by half in a process of rationalisation (Bower,
1994). Individuals' accounts of their experiences of victimisation at the
hands of Robert Maxwell were therefore littered with accounts of their
working lives and their experiences of working for a fraudulent employer.
For example, one pensioner said:

> Maxwell was only there to take money, he wasn't there to make it for the industry. I
> mean, he's let it go to pieces really.

Members of the action group appeared to demonise Robert Maxwell,
thereby drawing a clear distinction between themselves, the 'innocent' victims, and Robert Maxwell, the 'evil offender'. This distinction between
'good' and 'bad' has been found to occur in other support groups (Rock,
1998), and it has been argued that this does not convey the 'reality' of
crime, where the contours between offender and victim are often blurred.
However, in the case of white-collar deviance, where much ambiguity
surrounds white-collar crime, whereby the criminal status of offences and
offenders are open to question, then perhaps demonising offenders serves
to empower victims, and serves to stress the criminal nature, and the
devastating consequences, of the acts that have been committed.

Maxwell pensioners' accounts illustrate that it is not possible to separate
out their experience of being victimised by Robert Maxwell from the
broader socio-structural context. Pensioners' accounts reveal a sense of
community around the notion of being 'working-class' and belonging to a

printing union, the decline of which was linked to the pensions scandal that had hit them. For example, one pensioner argued:

I said to our MP, 'It's the Conservatives' fault all-round'. He said, 'Oh you can't blame the Conservatives for what one man does'. I said,' Well I can and I do'. I said, 'In the first place they put in all these new laws about the trade unions. If that had not happened the unions would have been fighting Robert Maxwell and it wouldn't have happened'.

The local organisation of a printing union was called the 'chapel', and the shop steward of that was known as the Father of the Chapel. One action group member felt that as the shop steward, he should have shielded the workers from the impact of the loss of the pension scheme:

I should have done more. But the terrible part of it was that I was the Father of the Chapel, I was the Father that the boys looked upon for some sort of guidance. And they have never accused me of this but I should have, I had means of getting in touch with people but you wasn't to know.

The support of trade unionism by former Maxwell employees clearly reflects their working-class origins and the solidarity that they felt as workers. Their reflections about union power echoes the real reduction in union power which has occurred over the last 30 years. In the past, printers had considerable influence over matters such as wages, the numbers of hours worked, the number of apprenticeships on offer and so forth. However, the number of print unions, and subsequently union member-ship, has been decreasing, allowing managers to assert control over the work process more readily (Cockburn, 1983).

Interviews with members of the Dunstable Action Group also reveal that a significant number of these individuals felt that they belonged to a political system where people's social and economic needs in retirement are taken care of by government. As such, prior to the scandal, they thought that their pensions were safe, secured by legislation. The pensions scandal, therefore, also caused pensioners to re-evaluate their relationships with, and views of, government, so that they increasingly saw themselves as individuals who must manage the risks that they are exposed to under an 'actuarial regime' in late modernity. In an actuarial regime, individuals must themselves increasingly manage the risks posed by things like sick-ness and unemployment, through investing in private insurance schemes, pension schemes and other financial products. The notion of individual responsibility has firmly been in place within the financial regulatory framework of the 1980s and 1990s and so white-collar deviance is viewed as a risk that individual investors must manage (Spalek, 2004). The Maxwell scandal, therefore, illustrated to the Maxwell pensioners that their pensions are also at risk from fraudulent activity. Part of the campaigning that action group members therefore engaged in was to bring about changes to pension legislation, so that company pension schemes would, in future, be afforded greater protection. The Pensions Act 1995 came into force on 6 April 1997, which put a number of mechanisms into place to try and reduce the likelihood of another Maxwell scandal occurring.

The Bank of Credit and Commerce International

The Bank of Credit and Commerce International (BCCI) was a global bank that was first established in 1972. It quickly expanded into an organisation that contained over four hundred branches in seventy-three different countries, employing approximately eleven thousand people (Gauhar, 1993). However, on 5 July 1991 BCCI was closed down by the Bank of England, as a result of large-scale fraud and corruption that had occurred at the bank – the founder of BCCI and some high-ranking employees of the bank were accused of engaging in false accounting, drugs money laundering, fraud and conspiracy (Kochan and Whittington, 1991). Branches were closed, deposits were frozen and staff members were made redundant.

Upon the closure of BCCI, former deposit holders and employees of the bank formed action groups. The effects of the closure upon victims were severe and multi-faceted, including psychological, emotional, physical and financial costs. When BCCI was closed down, employees were made redundant. Although they received redundancy payments, these were considered to be too low by former employees. At the same time, many of the employees held mortgage accounts with BCCI, which means that when the bank was closed down they effectively owed this money to the liquidator. The liquidator in turn charged a high rate of interest on mortgages, and in many cases former employees were unable to pay since they no longer had any income (Spalek, 2001). Interviews suggest that the liquidator was unsympathetic to the plight of former employees, charging a high rate of interest on their mortgage accounts and threatening many with repossession. By October 1997 there were approximately two hundred former employees in Britain who owed around £40 million to the liquidator as a result of outstanding mortgages and loans. Keith Vaz, MP condemned the response of the liquidator as being aggressive. Victims' emotional reactions to the closure of BCCI included depression, anxiety and anger and these were directed more towards the regulatory response than at any actual crimes that had been committed (Spalek, 2001):

> In case of frauds, only the individuals involved or responsible for frauds should be punished. BCCI should never have been closed in order to save other innocent members of staff and customers from any losses, for no fault of their own.

Of significance to the discussions presented earlier in this chapter, is how action group members' identities can be linked to the process of victimisation. Interview data with members of the BCCI Employees Action Group reveals that underpinning individuals' accounts of their experiences were their subject positions as employees of the bank. In the aftermath of the scandal, the liquidator spoke of the bank as being rotten to the core, and the Governor of the Bank of England pronounced that 'the culture of the bank was criminal' (Kochan and Whittington, 1991: 168). Employee action group members therefore argued that these comments demonised the entire bank and so stigmatised all employees formerly associated with this financial institution. As a result, their activities included the pursuit of compensation for loss in earnings due to having stigma attached to them, which they argued prevented them from gaining new employment. However, the Court of Appeal eventually rejected this claim (Spalek, 2001).

Another dimension to the BCCI case was in relation to the ethnicity of employees and their perceptions of the scandal. Some of the Pakistani and Iranian members of the Employees Action Group taking part in Spalek's (2001) study argued that BCCI was a non-Western financial institution that helped business in the developing world:

> BCCI provided the resources for honest hard-working people. Not one, there were quite a few people which I met and said the same thing ... Western banks did not lend to blacks or Asian communities in those countries, they took deposits from them, they were not as liberal as BCCI, BCCI could take risks.

These action members' accounts included the notion that BCCI threatened the West's dominance over the financial sector, and the power held by western institutions such as the International Monetary Fund, and so because of this, BCCI was closed down. Effectively, these action group members argued that BCCI was an important alternative source of funding for the developing world, which understood non-Western ways of doing business, and so was shut down by the West so as to maintain its hegemony over developing countries. Former employees claimed that the corruption at BCCI provided the Bank of England with an ideal reason for shutting down an expanding Asian bank (see Spalek, 2001 for further details).

Summary

The two case studies examined above clearly illustrate the centrality of individuals' subject positions to their experiences of victimisation, their claims-making and campaigning activities. How individuals felt about, and responded to, their victimisation can be linked to broader social and economic structures relating to individuals' class, race and age positions.

These case studies highlight the complexity of subject positions that victims may occupy, since victims will have multiple identities and so drawing out and unpicking these is likely to be challenging for researchers when studying victimisation. These case studies also illustrate that the individual victims did not respond to their experiences in individualistic ways, but rather, gained comfort from a sense of belongingness provided by the action groups, since the groups' activities were grounded in shared aspects of identity, shared histories and shared understandings of individuals' plight.

Of course, the notion of 'belongingness' is problematic, since group identities are formed and re-invigorated through the 'threat and practice of exclusion' (Bauman, 2004: 21). This raises a number of issues. One relates to the question of the extent to which action group members' reactions and responses are representative of a wider population of victims. There is a danger in assuming that the thoughts and experiences of action group members are somehow shared by the other victims that are involved in a particular case of harm. Since the two action groups described here were formed by employees in response to the fraudulent activities of their employers (as well as the subsequent regulatory response), then perhaps it can be argued that it is likely that the individuals here will have commonalities of experience relating to their work environments shared by the wider population of employee victims involved in these particular case studies. At the same time, the members of these action groups shared similar class, age and race positions, and so perhaps these positions might also be shared by other individuals from the wider population of Maxwell and BCCI victims, thereby suggesting that action group members' reactions are not atypical. However, this may not necessarily, or always, be the case. Certainly, more research is needed to explore what aspects of self-identity link different action group members together, how individuals' subject positions relate to the work carried out by victim action and support groups, and whether these subject positions extend out to a broader community of victims as well as to a broader collectivity based on race, gender, class, religion and so forth, which may be part of a wider social movement.

The emergence of action groups that are underpinned by, or based around, a sense of belongingness to a wider collectivity that may be based on race, gender, class and so on identities has drawn some criticism, with writers viewing this as being socially divisive with the potential to create intergroup conflict (Jacobs and Potter, 1998). Laws that are instigated that benefit some groups of people over others may indeed cause social disharmony and resentment. The following section explores the area of 'hate crime', where identity politics has played a key role in the ways in which legislation has been put together, and it is shown that certain identities of victim have clearly been excluded from the laws that have been implemented.

Hate crime, identity politics and victimisation

Since the 1980s, particularly in the US, the idea of 'hate crime' has gained increasing ground. Within this approach to crime, agencies of the criminal justice are required to take into consideration victims' identities and their perceptions when considering the motivation of an offender, so that crimes motivated by racial, religious, as well as other forms of, hatred are dealt with more severely. In the United States, for example, Congress passed the Hate Crime Statistics Act (HCSA) of 1990, so that the Federal Bureau of Investigation (FBI) collects data, taken from local law enforcement agencies, on the numbers of hate crimes that are committed, and this includes information about victims' identities in terms of, for example, their religion or sexual orientation. The HCSA of 1990 defines hate crime as 'manifest evidence of prejudice based on race, religion, sexual orienta-tion, or ethnicity, including where appropriate the crimes of murder, non-negligent manslaughter, forcible rape, aggravated assault, simple assault, intimidation, arson, and destruction, damage, or vandalism of property' (US Department of Justice, 2001: 2). The HCSA was later amended in 1994 to include crimes motivated by bias against individuals with physical or mental disabilities (McVeigh *et al.*, 2003: 844). However, across differ-ent states in the United States, different definitions of hate crime are in fact used (US Department of Justice, 2001), and the available figures indicate that 46 states have hate crime laws, 29 of which have provision for hate crimes related to sexual orientation or disability (McVeigh *et al.*, 2003: 855). According to FBI reports, in 1998, 7755 hate crime incidents were reported to law enforcement agencies nationwide, with the largest percent-age of bias-motivated offences being motivated by racial hatred (US Department of Justice, 2001: 1). However, statistics collected by agencies of the criminal justice system do not represent an accurate reflection of the true extent of hate crime, since the level of under-reporting is severe, and there may be procedural and administrative differences between the approaches to data collection taken by different law enforcement agencies based in different geographical locations (Iganski, 2002). Surveys carried out by action groups and by social scientists tend to show a higher prevalence of crimes motivated by prejudice (Iganski, 2002).

In Britain, the Crime and Disorder Act 1998, and provisions made under the Anti Terrorism Crime and Security Act 2001, can be considered to be 'hate crime' legislation. The Crime and Disorder Act 1998 introduced higher penalties for offences that are racially aggravated. Whilst the maximum sentence for common assault is six months and/or a £5000 fine, the maximum for racially aggravated common assault is two years and/or an unlimited fine. Under the Anti Terrorism Crime and Security Act 2001, a religiously aggravated element to crime was introduced, which again involved imposing higher penalties upon offenders who are motivated by religious hatred. In 2003, reflecting the incorporation of a more diverse range of peoples within hate crime legislation in Britain, the Criminal Justice Act 2003 was implemented. This provides an increased sentence for offences involving or motivated by hostility based on disability or sexual orientation. However, although a judge is required to state in court any extra elements of a sentence that they are giving for an offence aggravated by hostility in relation to sexual orientation and disability, this may not automatically lead to an increased punitiveness towards offenders, and the Crime and Disorder Act 1998 and the Anti Terrorism Crime and Security Act 2001 afford victims of racial or religious hate crime more protection.

The developments highlighted above have been linked to the activities carried out by victims' movements that have been formed around identities in relation to race, gender, sexuality, disability and so forth. Jacobs and Potter (1998) argue that in the United States, federal hate crime legislation has been significantly influenced by groups whose individual members shared a wider 'group consciousness' based on their identity politics, groups like the Anti-Defamation League, the Anti-Klan Network, the Institute for the Prevention and Control of Violence and Extremism, the International Network for Jewish Holocaust Survivors, the National Gay and Lesbian Task Force, the Organisation of Chinese Americans and the Japanese American Citizens League. Similarly, Jenness (2002) claims that the black civil rights, women's rights, gay and lesbian rights and disabilities rights movements have played a key role in the emergence of the concept of hate crime.

Punishing offenders more severely on the basis of their motivations rather than the actual crimes that have been committed has generated considerable debate, particularly in the United States. Some writers have questioned whether it is fair for crimes to be treated differently on the basis of offenders' motivations (Jacobs and Potter, 1998). Advocates of hate crime legislation argue, however, that this can be justified on the basis that hate crimes impact upon the wider communities that individual victims belong to, since an attack based on the identity of a victim has a significant impact on others who share a similar identity. Also, hate crime legislation is justified as being symbolically important, since this sends out a clear message that society does not tolerate violence based on a hatred of particular races, ethnicities, religions and so forth (Lawrence, 2002; Tatchell, 2002).

Hate crime legislation, however, is not aimed at all communities, and those groups that are included by the legislation appear to be those that have been able to mobilise social and political support more effectively. Morgan (2002, 25) argues that the groups that lack 'political clout, have insufficient moral status, or who see hate crimes legislation as an ineffective way of dealing with their particular concerns' are those that are not recognised as being hate crime victims. Indeed, it has been argued that if all crime victims were to be hate crime victims, then hate crime would lose its 'special symbolic power' (Jacobs and Potter, 1998: 78). Hence different groups may be in competition with each other to feature in laws passed in relation to crimes motivated by prejudice, and some writers view this as being socially harmful (Morgan, 2002). Also, at different periods of time, different identities will become politicised and may impact upon policy-making processes. For example, it has been argued that over the last two decades, Muslim identities within the United Kingdom have emerged, alongside Muslim political activism (Gardner and Shuker, 1994; Modood, 2003). Tatchell (2002) argues that in Britain, a wide range of communities have been targeted by violence that is motivated by hatred, yet these communities have been, or continue to be, excluded from hate crime legislation. These communities include Travellers, transsexuals, refugees and gay and lesbian communities.

Violence against gay and lesbian communities is significant. A series of surveys have been carried out looking at the extent and severity of homophobic hate crime, and the findings here are alarming. For example, according to Stonewall's 1995 study of violence against lesbians and gay men in Britain, entitled Queer Bashing, one in three gay men and one in four lesbians had experienced at least one violent attack during 1990–95. Because of the fear of becoming the victim of homophobic violence, 65 per cent of respondents always or sometimes avoided telling people they were gay, and 59 per cent of respondents always or sometimes tried to avoid looking obviously gay. According to a report published by the National Advisory Group on Policing the Lesbian and Gay Communities, entitled Breaking the Chain of Hate, 65.9 per cent of lesbian, gay and bisexual people taking part in the study had been the victim of at least one homophobic hate crime. 29.4 per cent were verbal abuse, 13.2 per cent threats and intimidation and 22.7 per cent were violent assaults (in Tatchell, 2002: 59). In 2001, a survey of 10,000 lesbians, gays and bisexuals in all parts of the United Kingdom was carried out, and this found that in the previous five years, 25 per cent had been victims of serious homophobic crime, including physical assault, hate mail, rape or sexual assault, blackmail and arson. Moreover, 65 per cent of victims did not report the crime to the police, due to their fear of police harassment, or their belief that the police would be unsympathetic (in Tatchell, 2002: 60).

Interestingly, when human and gay rights activist Peter Tatchell attempted to work with the British government as it was drawing up the Crime and Disorder Act 1998, in order to try to put together hate crime legislation that would be more inclusive of other communities, the Home Office rejected his attempts, claiming that this Act was being designed in order to send out a clear message that racial violence and prejudice is not tolerated, and including other communities would serve to weaken this message (Tatchell, 2002).

Not surprisingly, therefore, the Crime and Disorder Act 1998 has drawn criticism from those communities excluded by this piece of legislation. Muslim groups in particular attacked the Act as it excluded them, since a 'racial group' is, for the purposes of the Act, 'a group of persons defined by reference to race, colour, nationality or ethnic or national origins' (The Crime and Disorder Act, 1998 section 28: 4). This is the same definition as used in the Race Relations Act 1976 and so does not include religious groups, although Jews and Sikhs are covered as a result of case law.

In Britain, religious identity has traditionally been omitted from criminal justice responses to victimisation, and so whilst policies have been implemented to help tackle direct and institutional racism, discrimination and forms of victimisation based on religious affiliation have not attracted as much political or social scientific debate. Nonetheless, a Home Office report published in 2001, entitled 'Religious Discrimination in England and Wales', found that whilst in theory it is difficult to disentangle discrimination based on religious grounds from discrimination based on ethnicity, in practice some of the persons who were questioned in this study did appear to be the targets of discrimination and violence as a result of their religious beliefs and practises (Weller *et al.*, 2001). Also, according to the results of a survey looking at the effects of the events of 11 September 2001 on discrimination and implicit racism in five religious and seven ethnic groups, religion was found to be more important than ethnicity in indicating which groups were most likely to experience racism and discrimination post 11 September. Moreover, this research indicates the existence of modern and implicit religious discrimination. The phrase 'modern religious discrimination' indicates that prejudice against religious communities continues to exist, in a 'post-civil rights politically correct era'. Implicit religious discrimination refers to daily life situations in which covert religious prejudice, such as being treated rudely or not being taken seriously, can be experienced. Of the white people taking part in this study who said that they faced religious discrimination, almost half were Muslim (Sheridan *et al.*, 2003: 19–20).

Following the introduction of a religious element to crime, under the Anti Terrorism Crime and Security Act 2001, in April 2002, the Crown Prosecution Service (CPS) has been collecting information on the number of religiously aggravated prosecutions carried out in Britain. According to the CPS, for offences to be charged as specific religiously aggravated offences, prosecutors have to prove first that the offender committed one of the basic offences (including offences of assault, wounding, harassment, damage and public order offences such as causing people to fear violence or harassment) and then prosecutors have to prove that the offence was religiously aggravated in one of two ways: either that the accused person demonstrated hostility to the victim because the victim was thought to belong to a particular religious group; or the accused person was motivated by hostility towards the victim for the same reasons (Crown Prosecution Service, 2003: 5). There have been relatively few religiously aggravated prosecutions; nonetheless, the majority of victims involved here are Muslim. Thus, between 14 December 2001 and 31 March 2003, out of a total of 18 cases, 10 involved Muslim victims, 2 Sikh victims, 2 Hindu victims, 1 Jewish, 1 Jehovah's Witness, 1 Christian victim and 1 victim whose religion was not stated (Crown Prosecution Service, 2003: 36).

In Scotland, a Hate Crime Working Group was established by the Scottish Executive in 2003, following a proposed amendment to the Criminal Justice (Scotland) Bill 2003. This amendment looked to create an offence in which crimes aggravated by prejudice against social groups because of their age, disability, gender or sexual orientation received a higher sentence. This was not, however, subsequently adopted. Nonetheless, the issue of disability crime has generated increased attention, and the Disability Rights Commission (2005) recently carried out a survey in Scotland asking disabled people, and their carers, a series of questions about their experiences of crime. Out of the 158 completed questionnaires, it was found that approximately half the disabled people who responded experienced hate crime because of their disability. It was also found that 31 per cent of disabled people surveyed who are the victims of hate crime, experienced the attacks at least once a month. Respondents described feeling scared, embarrassed, humiliated and stressed by the attacks. The report stemming from this piece of research, *Hate Crime Against Disabled People in Scotland: a survey report*, recommends that a new law be created which helps to protect disabled people by defining disability crime as a hate crime.

Summary

The discussions above clearly show that for crimes motivated by prejudice, the subject positions occupied by victims will influence the severity of punishment meted out to the offender. Clearly, not all groups of victim are included in hate crime legislation, and especially in Britain, there appears to be a hierarchy of identities in terms of the level of protection afforded to people. In particular, offenders motivated by a hatred of gay, lesbian, transgender and bisexual individuals, or a hatred of people with disabilities, will not necessarily be punished as severely as those offenders motivated by a hatred of race or religion. This means that although initiatives have been developed to try to encourage gay, lesbian, transgender and bisexual communities, and people with disabilities, to report incidents of hate crime to a wide range of agencies, including the police and Victim Support, in the same way that minority ethnic communities are being encouraged to report incidents of race crime, as far as the legislation goes, there are no mechanisms in place to punish offenders as severely as racist offenders. As a result, although the initiatives aimed at encouraging people to come forward to relate their experiences of hate crime give the appearance that all types of victim are equal, in reality there is a large disparity between the legal and criminal justice processes set up to deal with race hate crime and other types of hate crime. In the United States there is also a wide range of people that are excluded from hate crime legislation, and these include the elderly, children and police officers (Jenness, 2002).

But even if more types of prejudice are included in hate crime legislation, the legislation itself does not take into consideration the different structural locations that different communities occupy. This means that, for example, under religious hate crime laws, violence carried out against Muslim communities is treated in the same way as violence committed against Christians. Similarly, attacks motivated by racial hatred on White people are treated in the same way that attacks on Black people are treated (Jenness, 2002). So whilst the campaigns carried out by groups based on identities around race, religion etc. are focussed upon, and concerned with, tackling violence that is carried out against the people that they represent and identify with specifically, and seen as a way of empowering marginalised communities, in reality hate crime legislation operates according to a norm of 'sameness' and so people whose identities are linked to dominant norms, processes and structures receive equal protection as those people whose identities can be linked to subordinate positions. This itself is a contentious issue. At the same time, and related to the point already made here, in hate crime legislation, specific communities, with their own particular histories, are merged within broader, all-encompassing classifications in relation to race, religion, sexual orientation and so on (Jenness, 2002). This means that specificities of experience are overlooked, and yet it might be argued that understanding and acknowledging these specificities is crucial to developing informed approaches to tackling any crimes that are committed on the basis of, or which include an element of, prejudice.

Case study

Billy Jack Gaither, 39, of Sylacauga Alabama was bludgeoned to death by two men on 19 February 1999, then set on fire with automobile tyres because he was gay. On 22 September 2000, a man looking to 'waste some faggots' entered a gay bar in Roanoke, Virginia and opened fire, killing one person and injuring six others. On 4 July 2000, J.R. Warren, 20, who was black and gay, was beaten to death by three men in West Virginia. He was then run over by a car to make it look like a hit and run.

Question

In your opinion, to what extent are the crimes that were mentioned above the product of deviant, violent individuals or the product of homophobia in society?

Institutional violence

Institutional violence is broad-reaching and can take many different forms. Commonly, it is understood as physical violence encountered by individuals at the hands of agents of the state, for example, in terms of police brutality when arresting a suspect, or any physical violence experienced by an individual when in custody, whether that person is being detained in a police cell, or whether they are incarcerated in prison or in any other institution. An action group in Britain, the United Families and Friends Campaign (UFFC), campaigns for justice to the 'forgotten scandal' of deaths in custody. Cases have arisen whereby men arrested by police have died in suspicious circumstances, and some of the inquests into the deaths of these men have concluded that they were 'unlawfully killed'. Nonetheless, in most cases, police officers are not charged or convicted of any crimes. For instance, an inquest verdict of 'unlawful killing' was reached in relation to the case of Roger Sylvester, a 30 year old man from Tottenham in North London, who died after being arrested and restrained by up to eight police officers. Similarly, an inquest ruled that Christopher Alder, a 37 year old man had been 'unlawfully killed'. Alder died in a police cell after being dragged unconscious from a police van in April 1998. As he choked on his vomit, officers stood chatting amongst themselves (1990 Trust Human Rights for Race Equality, 2004). In many cases, the men killed have been Black, and, in the context of institutional racism within the Police Service, this suggests a racist component to the police violence that has taken place.

Violence within prisons is also a significant issue, and perhaps one way of approaching this form of institutional violence is through the lens of identity, because when looking at the harms encountered by prisoners, it seems that individuals' identities are often an important aspect to understanding their experiences. Within prison, a 'hierarchy of identities' can operate, one aspect of which includes the crimes that prisoners have committed and their reputations as 'hard men'. Prisoner autobiographies directly refer to this hierarchy, for example, John McVicar (1982) writes that a prisoner who informs on his attacker to the authorities is condemned as a 'grass', and that this label will place him lower down in the hierarchy than convicted sex offenders. Frank Cook (1998: 41), who has spent many years in many different jails, writes about how, when he first arrived late at night at Manchester Prison, he heard the other inmates calling out 'Who's that?' 'Who's coming?', but that this did not worry him as, being a convicted armed robber, he knew that he would be at the top of the prison hierarchy. A prisoner's status is an important factor since this will influence perceptions of his vulnerability, and again, prisoner biographies reveal that inmates who are thought by other inmates to be 'weak' or 'vulnerable' will be targeted for physical and sexual violence (for example, see Rubin 'Hurricane' Carter, 1974).

Sexual coercion in prison is a significant issue. Researchers estimate that across different penal institutions, the rate of sexual coercion can vary from between 0.3 per cent to 29 per cent (Banbury, 2004: 113). Compared to non-victims, those prisoners who are sexually assaulted or raped report more psychological problems, including depression, shame and anxiety, also they report increased drugs use, self-harm and suicide attempts, and they also run the risk of being infected with sexually transmitted diseases (Banbury, 2004: 128). Other kinds of violence to be found in prison include assault, robbery, threat and cell theft. A survey carried out by Edgar and O'Donnell (1998: 636) revealed a high level of assault in both young offender institutions and adult penitentiaries. Of the young offenders taking part in the study 30 per cent indicated that they had been assaulted at least once in the previous month, whereas 19 per cent of the adult offenders taking part in this study indicated that they had experienced assault in the previous month, leading Edgar and O'Donnell (1998) to conclude that prisons are high risk settings.

Prisons today are also incarcerating an increasingly diverse ethnic, cultural and religious population. In Britain, for example, according to statistics issued by the Home Office, on 30 June 2000, members of minority ethnic communities made up 19 per cent of the male prison population and 25 per cent of female prisoners (Elkins and Olagundoye, 2001: 3). Prisoners are also now following a wide range of religious beliefs, including Hinduism, Buddhism, Jewish, Muslim and Sikh faiths. According to Beckford and Gilliat (1998: 52), since 1975 prisoners registering as belonging to these religions have increased by just under 10 per cent, whilst those registering as Christian have decreased by 31 per cent, with Islam being one of the fastest growing religions in prison. So, for example, on 30 June 2002 there were 5379 male Muslim prisoners, compared to 430 Sikh and 256 Hindu male prisoners in Britain (Home Office, 2003b: 133).

The issue of racism in prisons has long been a feature of academic literature (Genders and Player, 1989; Penal Affairs Consortium, 1996; Bryans and Wilson, 1998). Racism in prison includes racial harassment, abusive language and assault, and involves members of staff as well as inmates. A study by Burnett and Farrell (1994: 9) found that significantly more ethnic minority prisoners complained of racial incidents than white inmates. A third of Asians and nearly half of Blacks said they had been racially victimised by staff. These incidents included assault, bullying, theft, verbal abuse and harassment. In March 2000, Zahid Mubarek, a 19 year-old young offender serving a three month sentence at Feltham Young Offenders Institution, was attacked and murdered by his racist cellmate, Robert Stewart. Robert Stewart was obsessed with symbols of fascism and had a deep-seated hatred of black and Asian people (Bright, 2004). Following Mubarek's murder, alongside other highly publicised incidents at other institutions, the Commission for Racial Equality (CRE) conducted a formal investigation into the HM Prison Service and the Director General announced that the Service is institutionally racist. Mubarek's family also campaigned for a public inquiry to be conducted into his death, to ask questions about why it was that he should be sharing a cell with a racist inmate who had a history of violence. In 2004, this request was granted by the authorities. Mubarek's family hoped that this inquiry would lead to an overhaul of the youth justice system, and that a series of recommendations would be made aimed at tackling racism in British prisons (Bright, 2004).

Religious discrimination is also an issue that has arisen in relation to prison life. Ignorance over the spiritual and practical aspects of certain religions by prison staff may lead to staff feeling that religious requests are a privilege rather than a necessity and may lead to the inappropriate treatment of prisoners who identify themselves with a certain faith. The results of a study carried out by Beckford (2003: 21) show that whilst prison officers were aware of the identity of Muslims and that Muslim prisoners had particular requirements, nevertheless, some officers appeared to be judgemental of Muslim prisoners who broke Ramadan rules or who chatted to friends during prayers.

Institutional violence in relation to imprisonment extends beyond physical and sexual assault, verbal abuse, racism and religious discrimination. Prisoner autobiographies reveal the brutalising aspects of everyday life in prison, and suggest that the concept of a 'continuum of violence', as mentioned in Chapter 4, is applicable here. Bland food, the lack of control over one's daily routine, the regular exposure to verbal, or physical, or sexual, abuse, directly and/or indirectly, or indeed, the constant stress of the potential of being victimised, forms the backdrop to prison life. This dehumanises inmates, so that when released from prison, former prisoners will find it very difficult to settle back into ordinary life. Frank Cook (1998) writes about how inmates become desensitised to the violence in prison so as to be able to cope whilst inside, however, this has the effect of destroying their humanity. Rubin Carter (1974: 141), a professional boxer who was wrongly imprisoned by a racist criminal justice system, writes that Annandale penitentiary in north-western New Jersey in the United States 'didn't waste any time dehumanising its population'. He also suggests that prisons take away human dignity, and kill human spirit, and links the death of an old inmate, and a friend of his, to an incident in prison which 'had driven the spirit right out of his soul, bowing his proud shoulders with a weight that he could no longer bear' (Carter, 1974: 178).

In Rubin Carter's testimony on prison life, on a number of occasions he refers to the 'human spirit' and the detrimental impact of imprisonment on this. Clearly, his upbringing in a devout Christian family, with his father being a senior deacon in a Baptist church, is reflected in the ways in which he experiences his incarceration, and from a research point of view it would be interesting to explore Carter's sense and understanding of 'spirit' in order to expand our knowledge of the detrimental impact of penitentiaries upon prisoners; and Rubin Carter is not the only inmate to have referred to the 'human spirit' or to spirituality more generally. In a book examining the reasons why ex-offenders desist from crime, some individuals here articulate a religious or spiritual base to account for the change in their lives. In the case of Cameron Mackenzie, a former gang member, and now a minister of the Church of Scotland, he describes a particular incident that seems to have had a spiritual component, which led to him re-evaluating his wayward life. He refers to a woman who got into his taxi, whose conversation with him included the words, 'I see a great darkness over you, and the only person that can take that away is God. You must see God' (Devlin and Turney, 1999: 27). In other cases, religion, or support groups that contain a spiritual dimension to their work like Alcoholics Anonymous, for example, can replace crime or other addictive habits that offenders engage in and thereby help to create positive change within offenders. For instance, one ex-offender speaks about trying to practise spiritual principles in his life in order to help him stop drinking, the inspiration for this coming from the self-help group that he joined (see Devlin and Turney, 1999 for more details).

Case study

In December 1994 Shiji Lapite, a Nigerian asylum-seeker and father of two, was stopped by police in Hackney, London for 'acting suspiciously'. Police officers said that they found crack cocaine at the scene. In a struggle one officer held Lapite in a headlock while another kicked him in the head. The coroner found more than forty areas of injury on Lapite's body, including crushed bones at the front of his neck and severe bruising across his back. The jury at the inquest into his death took just 20 minutes to return a unanimous verdict of unlawful killing. However, the Crown Prosecution Service decided not to proceed against the two officers that were involved.

Question

To what extent is police brutality the result of the actions of individual officers or the result of institutional police racism?

Conclusion

The state, through the use of agencies of control like the police and prison services, can victimise individuals. Clearly, this illustrates how the distinction between offender and victim is often blurred, since institutional violence can involve the victimisation of offenders and suspects, who may suffer a wide range of harms. Victimisation here can be linked to abuses of power by the state, thereby broadening the notion of victimhood to include forms of abuse that may not feature in officially sanctioned categories of crime (Elias, 1994).

Identity issues constitute an important element to understanding institutional violence. In prison, for instance, there seems to be a 'hierarchy of identities' that influences individuals' vulnerability and their risk of victimisation. At the same time, an offender's race, ethnicity, religion and so forth can influence the kinds of violence that they experience, and may also influence the ways in which they experience that violence. Sometimes this may include a spiritual component to their suffering and/or the survival strategies that they engage in. Certainly, more work is now needed that includes a greater focus upon individuals' identities and how these relate to the process of victimisation.

Victim action groups that can be found within the unofficial victims movement illustrate that people do not necessarily respond to their experiences in individualistic ways, but rather, may gain comfort from a sense of belongingness provided by such groups. The Maxwell financial scandal, as documented in this chapter, illustrates how individuals came together, and how underpinning their responses to the scandal were their shared identities as older people, as working-class, former Maxwell, printing employees, and as members of a partial 'welfare state' that individuals assumed would look after them in their old age. This case study further illustrates the importance of victim identities to the process of victimisation, and also highlights the complexity of subject positions that victims may occupy, since victims will have multiple identities and so drawing out and unpicking these is likely to be a significant challenge for researchers.

Finally, the discussion of hate crimes featured in this chapter illustrates how the subject positions occupied by victims can influence the severity of punishment that is meted out to offenders. Not all groups of victim are included in hate crime legislation, and especially in Britain, there appears to be a hierarchy of identities in terms of the level of protection afforded to different people.

The issues raised in this chapter have some important implications for future research and work on victimisation, and these will be discussed in the next chapter, which articulates some important themes that need to be increasingly focussed upon if victimology is to develop further as an academic 'sub-discipline'.

Questions

1 What characteristics best describe the unofficial victims' movement?
2 In what ways has hate crime legislation been influenced by the formation of politicised identities?
3 In what ways can the state victimise its citizens?

9

New Perspectives within Victimology

Introduction

The chapters presented in this book so far, provide a general overview of the issues and theories emerging from within the victimological field. Areas that merit further research and exploration have also been briefly suggested, and these will form the basis for the following discussion, which aims to outline new avenues of research for victimology.

The foci of enquiry within victimology are somewhat limited, due in part to the predominance of mainstream understandings of crime as the lens through which to view victimisation, also due to an insufficient consideration of the diversity and differences to be found between individual victims. This narrow focus has important implications, not only in terms of the development of the sub-discipline of victimology itself, but also in terms of policy developments and practice issues for individuals harmed by both criminal and non-criminal events. The following chapter, therefore, sets out some of the main considerations to be addressed, and their methodological implications, if the foci of enquiry are to be broadened so that the victimological field embraces the experiences of a broader range of people.

Areas that will be discussed include victim identities, subjectivities and the wider group collectivities that individuals may belong to, notions of religiosity and spirituality, and emotionality in victimological research. First, however, it is necessary to turn attention to explaining the ways in which victimological work can be viewed as being restrictive, as this will provide the background context to the themes emerging in this chapter.

Victimology: restricted enquiries into, and notions of, victimhood

In what ways, then, is the research that can be classified as belonging within the confines of victimology, restricted? One recurrent theme, which can be linked to the broader debates that have taken place at the International Symposia on Victimology, is in relation to the scope of the subject matter that researchers should concern themselves with. Traditionally, individuals harmed by events considered to be criminal by the state have been focussed upon, so that the direct and indirect victims of crimes like burglary, assault and murder have attracted much research attention, and individuals' psychological, emotional, practical, financial and physical hardships have been stressed with a view to developing mechanisms aimed at reducing the harms experienced by these categories of victim (see Maguire, 1982; Brown *et al.*, 1990; Indermaur, 1995; Dugan, 1999; Mawby, 2001). This work has directly, and indirectly, fed into an official victims' movement so that the categories of victim most easily afforded victim status have been the focus of help. A significant proportion of victimological work has also concentrated upon victim issues that arise within, and emerge from, criminal justice processes and systems (see Shapland, Willmore and Duff, 1985; Newburn and Merry, 1990; Mayhew *et al.*, 1993; Kelly and Erez, 1997; Mirrlees-Black and Budd, 1997; Mirrlees-Black *et al.*, 1998). This work has contributed to enhancing our understanding of 'secondary victimisation', and has played a role in evaluating initiatives aimed at reducing the harms encountered by victims in their interaction with agencies of the criminal justice system. This research has also turned a critical (although somewhat limited) gaze towards the development of policies aimed at enhancing victims' rights, showing that there can be a significant difference between victims' perceptions of a particular piece of legislation and the actual outcomes for them when the policies are implemented (see, e.g., Hoyle *et al.*, 1999 and Edwards, 2001 for a discussion of victim impact statements).

Whilst it is debatable whether the results of research studies are ever used by politicians and civil servants when designing new strategies and approaches to victimisation (Sebba, 2001), what is of concern is how the proliferation of studies focussing upon victim issues with respect to criminal justice, which are also often funded by the state, has profoundly limited the victimological gaze. It can be argued that these developments belong to a positivist victimology, whereby state definitions of crime are taken-for-granted and left unquestioned, and the research here belongs to an 'administrative' tradition, whereby a significant number of the studies are a constituent part of the bureaucratic machinery of government, researching issues that are closely linked to political agendas. This means that researchers are not encouraged to look beyond the confines of positivist victimological frameworks of understanding, and so their work is conceptually, methodologically and theoretically rather limited.

Elias (1994) argues that researchers need to increasingly turn their attention to individuals harmed by events not normally recognised as being criminal, and this might include areas like white-collar, or corporate, crime, state violence and heinous acts against humanity. Importantly, in focussing upon non-traditional forms of victimisation, this may not only lead to the formation of wide-ranging initiatives aimed at helping a broader range of victims, but also, this may lead to many important theoretical and methodological developments, developments that are directly relevant for victimology. This is clearly illustrated in the work carried out by feminists against violence on women and children.

Originally, the victimisation of women and children was not part of state discourses around the 'crime problem', this being viewed largely as something that happens between strangers in the public, as opposed to the private, arena. Feminist work has helped to re-define violence as something that can happen in private spaces, between persons who know each other. The notion of a 'continuum of violence' has also been introduced, whereby it is argued that victimisation is not to be viewed as a one-off event, but rather as a process, so that there is an acknowledgement that women are often repeat victims, and so their lives are framed by actual, or perceived, acts of abuse and violence (Kelly, 1988). Furthermore, feminists include an analysis of patriarchy in their work as the broader social context to victims' experiences. In terms of research strategies, feminist work often involves research participants in the design and analysis of a study, and a non-hierarchical relationship between the researcher and the researched is pursued through an openness when interviewing. Also, feminist research principles call for reflexivity over the research process, this being seen as a key way of ensuring rigorousness and reliability when carrying out research (Harding, 1987; Edwards and Ribbens, 1998). This discussion demonstrates that feminist work has developed novel ways of conceptualising victimisation and has provided much-needed new avenues for research. Feminism has also injected innovative methodological strategies to approaching the study of victimisation.

Within approaches that can be linked to the dominant positivist victimological paradigm, it seems that differences between victims have rarely been acknowledged or fed into research plans, so that generalised accounts of victimisation have resulted. A large volume of work exists that focusses upon documenting the process of victimisation, so that we have a substantial amount of knowledge about the impacts of a wide variety of crime on victims, and this knowledge can be, and has been, used to provide victims with psychological, emotional, practical and financial support (Maguire, 1982; Brown *et al.*, 1990; Indermaur, 1995; Dugan, 1999; Mawby, 2001). However, social scientists here have rarely reflected upon the research strategies that they have used, and have rarely questioned the applicability of generalist frameworks of understanding to individual victims, who may differ according to their class, race, religious, gender (etc.) subject positions. As a result, diversity issues have been somewhat neglected, amidst the use of rather essentialist categories that overlook significant differences between individual victims. It is also important to note here that despite the important methodological and theoretical developments to be found within feminism, black feminists have criticised western feminism for essentialising women's experiences so that white women's lives constitute the norms around which black women's lives are compared and judged (Amos and Parmar, 1997; Harris, 1997; Collins, 2000).

Following on from the issues highlighted in the discussions above, it seems that victimological work must become both broader in its scope and also more specific in documenting individuals' experiences. In this way, a wider range of victims will be captured and a more nuanced approach to the study of victimisation can be pursued, one that includes specificities of experience. However, when opening up the foci of enquiry to include a wider and more diverse range of victims, this raises many critical issues and many potential areas of investigation, some of which will be outlined below.

Victim identities, subjectivities and group collectivities

Social movements and victim research

The subject of identities is relevant to victimology for a number of reasons. Writers exploring identity issues argue that in late modern society identities are not necessarily tied to class affiliations, as a Marxist perspective would previously have maintained, rather, identities can emerge from many different places and new subjects can be constituted on the basis of race, gender, ethnicity, sexuality, as well as many other identity formations. The phrase 'new social movements' has been given to articulate the emergence of these new collectivities of individuals that cut across traditional class and political affiliations, with two commonly quoted examples here being the civil rights movement and the feminist movement, which arose in western society in the 1960s (Woodward, 1997).

These developments are relevant to the area of victimology because within the social movements that emerge there are likely to be demands for a recognition, or greater recognition, of victim status. Alongside these demands, there are likely to be calls for adequate responses to group members' plight, which may involve the development and implementation of wide-ranging victim policies and initiatives. This can clearly be seen in relation to hate crime laws, which emerged as a result of the activities of group collectivities making up a broader social movement. As highlighted in Chapter 7, in the United States, federal hate crime legislation has been significantly influenced by the black civil rights, women's rights, gay and lesbian rights and disabilities rights movements (Jenness, 2002). In Britain, in 2001, hate crime legislation was expanded to include crimes motivated by religious hatred, and this was significantly influenced by the emergence of Muslim identities in the United Kingdom. The secular nature of the race relations movement means that for a long time, Muslims' concerns have been overlooked, and their experiences have been rendered invisible. However, over the last two decades or so, researchers have documented the increasing emergence of Muslim identities and the development of Muslim political activism (Gardner and Shuker, 1994; Modood, 2003). In Britain, this has included demands for religious hatred to be included in hate crime legislation, and so under the Anti Terrorism Crime and Security Act 2001, a religiously aggravated element to crime has been introduced, which involves imposing higher penalties upon offenders who are motivated by religious hatred. Of course, in the context of the 11 September attacks, the Anti Terrorism Crime and Security Act 2001 is likely to be used disproportionately against Muslims, and so this has acted as a bargaining tool for Muslim communities to lobby government so that the issue of religious hate crime has been included in the new legislation. The introduction of religious hate crime legislation has led to the development of new procedures within police forces and the Crown Prosecution Service. Increasingly, police officers have monitored the religious identity of victims (previously, racial, and not religious, identity was often recorded), especially where local partnerships between the police and other statutory and voluntary agencies have focussed upon religiously aggravated offences. In November 2004, for example, a crime reporting scheme, Islamophobia – Don't Suffer in Silence, was set up in the Tower Hamlets area of London. This initiative aimed to encourage Muslims to report any incident that they believe has been motivated by faith, and has been seen as a way of encouraging further links between the police and local Muslim communities. This case clearly illustrates how the mobilisation of identity can underpin victim claims-making activities and can lead to the implementation of new victim initiatives. This means that as researchers, we need to be sensitive to the development and emergence of new identities, especially when those identities belong to broader, politicised, group collectivities. We need to investigate the claims-making activities of these collectivities and, where these activities lead to the development of new legislation and victim initiatives, we need to critically explore these. So, for example, we need to look at the social context to the emergence of a politicised identity at a particular point in time and to examine the likely consequences of this for victim-focussed work and policies.

At the same time, in the same way that the feminist movement led to the incorporation of new research methodologies in order to explore women's lives, the rise of new politicised identities has implications for the development of methodological approaches within victimology and other social science disciplines. In light of the issue of the emergence of Muslim identities, for instance, how can research strategies become more inclusive of these, so that Muslims' experiences and perspectives are adequately researched and understood? For example, both national and local crime surveys have traditionally used the variables of gender, ethnicity and age to inform the sampling process (Walklate, 2001), which means that faith identities have been omitted. As a result, the experiences of crime that religious communities have has been not been sufficiently explored, and so the incidence and experience of the process of victimisation from religious hate crime, as well as other types of crime, has been omitted. McManus (2002) argues that faith communities can experience significant victimisation: arson attempts or acts of vandalism may be carried out against religious buildings, and people in ministry roles have also been the victims of crime. Local crime surveys might be able to capture Muslims' experiences of victimisation through the inclusion of faith identities in sampling, data collection and analysis procedures. Muslim organisations and community representatives might also be included in the design and evaluation of such surveys so that Muslim perspectives are increasingly taken into account. This argument may also be applicable to other faith communities, whose perspectives and experiences have also tended to be overlooked.

Action groups and victim research

Within contemporary western society, a myriad of victim action and support groups can be found. In Britain, for example, the following victim action/support groups have been formed, some of which still operate today: the West Midlands Workers Relatives' Support Group, the Organophosphate Victim Support, the Asbestos Victims Support Group, the Maxwell Pensioners' Action Group, the BCCI Employees' Action Group, Aftermath, and the United Families and Friends Campaign. Research should increasingly focus on documenting the activities of these kinds of groups as they perhaps reflect the establishment of new, victim, identities, which can, at least for a short period of time, provide individuals with a sense of belongingness, this being increasingly difficult to achieve in the fragmented nature of the lives that people lead today (Bauman, 2004). Social scientists need to explore more fully the sense of 'belongingness' that individuals gain from their identification with a particular victim action group, which may be a part of a broader group collectivity. So, for example, how do actors come to think of themselves as being part of a particular group and/or a broader movement? Also, embedded within the responses to victimisation that can be found within victim action and support groups, there may be shared histories relating to individual group members' subject positions. It is therefore important to explore more fully aspects of individuals' identities that link different victim action and/or support group members together, and how these influence individuals' claims-making activities.

Diversity and victim research

A focus upon identity within victimological work is also important in terms of this being a way of enhancing our understanding of the process and experience of victimisation. Elias (1994) has argued that research needs to be more qualitative and context-specific so that the 'human meaning' to experiences of harm is documented. This applies particularly to issues relating to diversity. Although some research has explored the culture-specific aspects to victimisation (see, e.g., Choudry, 1996; Bowling, 1999; Mama, 2000; Shorter-Gooden, 2004), this work appears to predominantly focus upon domestic violence and race hate crime and so the impact of a wider range of crimes upon particular communities is largely unknown and should therefore be increasingly examined. By giving victims' identities a central position within work examining victimisation, this may be a good way of introducing greater diversity and specificity of experience within analyses of the process of victimisation for a broad range of crimes. And, since a good proportion of work examining victimisation is carried out with a view to developing policy initiatives aimed at helping victims, then this may lead to the introduction of more nuanced responses to individuals' needs, responses that acknowledge the diverse range of victim identities.

The greater inclusion of victim identities in research can also lead to work that provides a 'human face' to harms that traditionally have not constituted the 'crime problem' and so can be used to convey the impact of these events more powerfully and so perhaps raise public concern over these issues. For example, white-collar deviance occupies an ambiguous status within social and political arenas (Nelken, 1994). Research here has traditionally focussed upon documenting the social, psychological and financial costs of white-collar violations (Sutherland, 1949; Box, 1983; Levi, 1987; Mokhiber, 1988; Moore and Mills, 1990; Snider, 1991; Grabosky and Sutton, 1993; Coleman, 1994; Shover, Fox and Mills, 1994). However, the human impact of white-collar violations is often lost, and this may partly be attributed to a lack of inclusion, and focus upon, victims' identities. This can be clearly seen in the ways in which victim typologies have been constructed when attempting to highlight the types of victim that can be affected by white-collar deviance. The typologies are rather abstract and do not convey the complexity of victims' subjectivities, or the multiple subject positions that victims can occupy. For example, according to Box (1983), victims can include competitors, the state, employees, consumers and the public, whilst Shichor (1989) suggests that white-collar victims may be the government, the public-at-large, consumers, shareholders, employees, competitors, and business partners; and Croall (1992, 2001) identifies victims as consumers, who might, for example, be overcharged for particular goods, or who might buy faulty goods and services; investors, who may be duped into investing their money into scams; employees, who might be injured or killed as a result of inattention of health and safety regulations; companies, whose workers might steal their assets; and the public in general, who are exposed to an unhealthy diet of toxic fumes and pollution. These rigid and very general categories do not capture the many dimensions to victims' experiences since victims have multiple identities, as Spalek's (1999, 2001) work on white-collar victimisation makes clear.

Research must be open to the many subjectivities that victims may occupy. This position is, however, not unproblematic, because a victim may occupy many different identities and so deciding upon which identities are most relevant to the process of victimisation may, in practice, be difficult to do. For instance, as discussed in some detail in Chapter 7, victims of the Maxwell financial scandal were pensioners; however, they were also working-class, former print employees, and all of these subject positions underpinned their reactions to the crimes that had been committed against them. Also, the researcher may inevitably have to make connections to the broader group collectivities that individual victims belong to, so that an articulation of specific experiences does not lead to the adoption of a wholly relativistic position that loses the political power that might be gained from a focus upon unities based on race, gender, class and so forth (Chakraborti *et al.*, 2004). This means that, as researchers, we need to try and achieve the appropriate balance between documenting specificities of experience and linking these in with the wider group collectivities that individual victims may belong to, as well as acknowledging the wider social processes that frame victims' lives. At the same time, researchers should be encouraged to reflect upon their own multiple subject positions during a piece of work, since different aspects of the researcher's self will come into play at different moments during a study, and whilst some aspects of a researcher's subjectivity can be linked to marginalised, outsider positions, which can help to produce oppositional knowledge, other aspects of self-identity may maintain and re-produce dominant racial, cultural (and so forth) discourses (see Spalek, 2005b).

A focus upon victims' identities suggests that more open-ended forms of data gathering are needed. Identity is a continuing process, identities undergo continual transformations, but they have histories and are dependent upon past and current social positions (Wetherall, 1996). Identities are formed through the ways in which people position themselves, and are positioned by, narratives of the past (Hall, 1990). When examining victims' reactions and experiences, therefore, techniques that elicit their biographies or life histories should be more actively pursued, and these can include the use of oral history, personal narrative or biography (Roberts, 2002). A narrative approach, for example, is different from traditional social scientific interview methods, since the agenda is open to development depending upon the narrator's experiences. Traditional question-and-answer approaches can be accused of suppressing individual participants' stories, since in trying to comply with an interviewer's agenda, the research subject may not communicate what they think is significant. Also, researchers using qualitative research methods have tended to assume that research participants understand themselves, know what they want to say and are willing to tell this to the interviewer. Hollway and Jefferson (2000) question these assumptions, convincingly arguing that subtlety and complexity underpin human communication and that researchers have tended to ignore this. Researchers who have adopted a narrative approach argue that narrative is the primary form by which human experience is made meaningful, since the stories that people tell stay closer to actual life-events than methods that elicit explanations. In telling a story, the narrator explains its significance to the researcher (Hollway and Jefferson, 2000). In adopting a narrative approach, open-ended questions can be used, framed around the theoretical concerns of a study, and when following up on things that the participants say, the participants' own language can be used (Hollway and Jefferson, 2000). Narrative research techniques, therefore, have much to offer victimological work and so can be used to help convey the human meaning to harmful events.

By incorporating more diverse voices and experiences into discourses on victimisation, this necessarily involves widening our frameworks of understanding. For instance, if researching people for whom a belief in God is a fundamental aspect of their lives, who may prefer to seek advice from religious leaders in the aftermath of a crime, or if researching individuals who have a strong sense of their spirituality, who may prefer to seek help for their experience of victimisation from alternative healers, then researchers inevitably have to engage with notions of religiosity and spirituality, as the following section will elucidate further.

Victimhood, religiosity and spirituality

Writers like Cressey (1986) and Fattah (1992) have argued that victimology should be based on objective scientific research and not be ideological or activist-based. Of course, what is taken to be objective and scientific is itself value-laden, and feminist work in particular has questioned the many taken-for-granted assumptions underpinning so-called scientific, objective work, whereby the hidden values and characteristics of the researcher can impact significantly upon the research process (Harding, 1987). The main issue, however, in the context of this discussion is whether social scientific tools of analysis can be used to document the religious and spiritual dimensions to victims' lives. At first glance, it would appear that social science disciplines are ill-equipped to study the notions of religiosity and spirituality, since these subject disciplines are closely linked to the emergence of modernity, whereby scientific rationale (secular rationalism) increasingly came to replace doctrinal outlooks and perceptions. Morrison (1995: 5), for instance, when writing about the social science Criminology, argues that this subject was 'born with the death of God', suggesting that religious and spiritual beliefs and experiences are not open, or indeed relevant, to social scientific investigation.

Nevertheless, religion as an aspect of victims' identities, and therefore part of victims' survival strategies, has attracted some research attention, particularly in relation to the experiences of minority ethnic women. The critique of western feminism, arising from black feminists' work, for its unwillingness to acknowledge differences between women, has included an acknowledgement of the role of religion in some women's lives. For example, Afshar and Maynard (2000) argue that some Muslim women have rejected aspects of mainstream western feminism and used the theological basis of Islam to carve out their own lives. There are also a few research studies that look at the role that religion plays in women's survival strategies following racist, sexist and/or Islamophobic violence and abuse (Kennedy *et al.*, 1998; Spalek, 2002; Shorter-Gooden, 2004). This work clearly illustrates that social scientific research strategies may be used to document and further understand religiosity and its relevance to the process of victimisation. Religiosity has been approached both quantitatively and qualitatively. Quantitative approaches include the use of a questionnaire, whereby respondents are asked to indicate the level of their intrinsic religiosity by responding to questions like 'I read literature on my faith' or 'I try hard to carry my religion over into all other dealings in life' (Kennedy *et al.*, 1998: 327). Within qualitative approaches, researchers give the research participants the opportunity to articulate their experiences in their own voices by using unstructured, or semi-structured, interview techniques that allow research participants to speak about their lives (Spalek, 2002).

However, it must be stressed that this type of work is not unproblematic, since the frameworks of understanding that have developed from within social science disciplines, and which are used to analyse data, are secular in nature, and so may be inappropriate for analysing some aspects of individuals' lives. For example, western feminist explanations of how women negotiate their everyday lives around violence, or the potential for violence, may not be applicable to understanding all women's negotiation of their personal safety. If religious identity is an important aspect of research participants' self-identity, as it is for some Muslim women for example, then feminist frameworks of understanding that focus solely upon the role of societal and cultural traditions in religion may be inappropriate, since it might be argued that these ignore the centrality of faith (Spalek, 2005b). Thus, for many followers of Islam, the Qur'an is the actual word of God that was recorded by Muhammad during the early part of the seventh century (Watson, 1994). This means that explaining Muslim women's behaviour in terms of the transmission of cultural norms is reductionistic and does not give sufficient consideration of women's beliefs or values. Further to this, a researcher who holds little theological knowledge of a particular religion will encounter significant difficulties when trying to understand individuals' interpretations of their religion and their belief systems. In this scenario, the researcher will have to consult the research participants, as well as texts that help to convey the message that a particular faith holds, in order to better understand participants' lives (Spalek, 2002).

The complexity and fluidity of a term such as 'spiritual', and the difficulty of applying scientific techniques to its measurement and exploration, means that researchers have rarely studied spirituality and any connections here with experiences of victimisation. Nonetheless, a number of writers argue that the notion of spirituality as being located within the individual is itself a constituent part of modernity, since the modern era signalled a movement away from pre-modern notions of a divinely structured world located outside persons, that cannot be changed (Gauchet, 1999; Scharff Smith, 2004). According to Haug (1998), spirituality consists of a personal, internalised set of beliefs and experiences that impact upon a person at a cognitive, affective, behavioural and developmental level. According to Morell (1996: 306), 'at the centre of most spiritual traditions (not specific religious ideologies) is a belief that human beings are united as expressions or emanations of a central energy or principle' and there is a recognition of the fundamental relatedness of humanity. Indeed, the many different uses of the word 'spirit' in the English language suggests that there is a cultural and social acknowledgement of an embedded, non-physical essence within humans, which extends beyond individuals, connecting them to each other as well as to wider social systems, as the following Oxford Dictionary definitions would suggest:

The vital animating essence of a person or animal (was sadly broken in spirit).
The intelligent non-physical part of a person; the soul.
A prevailing mental or moral condition or attitude; a mood; a tendency (public spirit, took it in the wrong spirit).
A person's mental or moral nature or qualities (has an unbending spirit).
A person viewed as possessing these: courage, energy, vivacity.
The real meaning as opposed to lip service or verbal expression (the spirit of the law).

According to Kennedy, Davis and Taylor (1998), whilst some research has focussed upon documenting the role that spirituality plays in individuals' reactions to stressful, non-criminal events, such as bereavement for example, virtually no studies have been carried out examining spirituality in relation to individuals' responses to crime. In answer to this, Kennedy *et al.* (1998: 322) looked at changes in spirituality for the female victims of sexual assault. They found that the majority of the female victims (60 per cent) revealed an increased sense of the spiritual in the aftermath of the crimes that had been committed against them. Furthermore, those victims with increased spirituality appeared to cope better than those victims without increased spirituality. Here, spirituality was measured by asking participants to indicate, using a scale ranging from 'strongly increased' to 'strongly decreased', how much a range of statements described their experiences since the crime. Statements like 'My belief that there is a divine plan for the world has' 'My search for spiritual meaning has' and 'My desire to understand events in spiritual terms has' were used (Kennedy *et al.*, 1998: 324–327).

Spirituality is relevant to victimological work because as Kennedy *et al.*'s (1998) work suggests, this may enhance a person's ability to cope with crime. Also, if individuals who have experienced crime, or harms from other events, are seeking therapeutic help from alternative forms of healing that may include a spiritual component, then these must be increasingly examined to see what benefits they bring about for victims. Added, to this, a limited amount of evidence seems to suggest that minority ethnic communities are not necessarily accessing mainstream victim support services, but rather value, and seek out, alternative forms of help that may include a focus upon spirituality (Spalek, 2005a). This means that research needs to examine why minority ethnic communities are seeking alternative forms of help, what benefits they gain from this, and we need to explore ways of funding these alternatives adequately, and perhaps suggest ways in which mainstream victim organisations might incorporate a spiritual component to the work that they carry out. Also, if 'spirit injury' constitutes one important aspect of the process of victimisation, as the work of critical black feminists would suggest (Davis, 1997; Williams, 1997), then researchers need to find ways of exploring this so as to develop a greater understanding of the full impact of criminal and non-criminal events on people's lives. Often, the impacts of crime on victims are written about in terms of the psychological, emotional, physical, financial and behavioural costs, but this still leaves the question of the 'spiritual' impact unexamined, and yet this may be just as important, if not more important than, the other kinds of impacts that victims experience.

Victim research and emotionality

Another area that deserves a greater focus in victimological work is that of emotionality. Work with victims involves asking people to talk about their experiences of suffering, so that emotions are very much a part of any study, and yet researchers have often insufficiently addressed this issue when writing up accounts of their work. Traditionally, a view of the researcher as being 'objective' and 'rational' has been taken within social science (Williams and Bendelow, 1998). However, this position has been increasingly questioned, and, in the context of work with victims, it is difficult to see how this position can be maintained, since when individuals articulate their experiences these are likely to be particularly traumatic, and so it is difficult to see how the researcher can adopt a detached manner and not be emotionally affected by participants' stories. Indeed, in feminist work on domestic violence, researchers' concerns for the safety of victims who participate in their studies can clearly be seen (which are also likely to contain an emotional component), and this has led to work that includes a focus on women's protection (Hoyle, 1998).

A focus upon emotionality can lead to work that is more reflective and more open to the human meaning of victimisation, so that research participants are not objectified, but rather, their humanity comes through the work more powerfully. This may be particularly important when carrying out work on forms of victimisation that have long histories, such as racism or sexism. For instance, in a study carried out by Spalek (2005a), part of which included an examination of the victimising experiences of Muslim British Asians, some of the research participants here spoke angrily about being called a 'Paki'. The use of this particular word by the participants caused the white researcher to feel extremely upset, to the extent to which she reflected upon why this had affected her so much, which led her to reading Ahmed's (2004) account of 'sticky words'. According to Ahmed (2004), stickiness occurs where a word is repeated and accumulates affective value. She argues that the word 'Paki' is a sticky sign that has become an insult through its association with other words that are derisory, which are intrinsic to this sign as a result of past association. As a result, 'the resistance to the word acquiring new meaning is not about the referent; rather the resistance is an effect of these histories of repetition of the word "Paki" ' (Ahmed, 2004: 92). It might be argued that in being white, the researcher here is linked to the history of this racist, sticky, sign, since although the researcher has never used this word herself, the racial structuring of her environment, whereby being white means being located in a privileged position (Lewis and Ramazanoglu, 1999), means that her subject position can be located on a 'continuum of responsibility' in relation to racism, and this is perhaps why she felt so emotionally affected when the research participants used this word, and indeed, this is perhaps why some of the participants verbally articulated the word 'Paki', as a way of holding the white researcher to account.

It appears that social scientists who argue that victimology should be based on scientific principles of study approach emotionality as undermining the study of victimisation, and perhaps equate emotional work with political activism, and this is seen as something that should be avoided. However, this is rather a restricted view of the role of emotion in research. Being emotionally affected by research participants does not necessarily mean the work becomes 'biased'.[1] The emotions that a researcher experiences whilst carrying out a piece of work can be used to reveal hidden decision-making processes which can be linked to power hierarchies inherent in research (Pickering, 2001). An emerging body of feminist work considers emotionality to be a central part of documenting and examining the nature of the researcher's subjectivity. Traditionally, this form of introspection has not been pursued, amid concerns that researchers who explore their feelings might attract accusations of 'unhealthy absorption' or 'emotional exhibitionism' (Pickering, 2001: 486). Nonetheless, increasingly, researchers are examining emotions that they experience as they carry out their work. The emotions that are identified are then used as markers that can help reveal aspects of both the researcher's and participants' biographies that have a significant, if hidden, effect upon the research process. Spalek's (2005b) work with Muslim women reveals that reflecting upon the emotions that she experienced during the research study enabled her to examine the multiplicity of her subject positions and how these influenced the sampling, data gathering and data analysis phases of the investigation. This work shows that a focus upon emotions can help to explore the micro-processes involved in perpetuating dominant knowledge constructions and power relations. As such, within the victimological arena, increased attention to emotions, in relation to both researcher and researched, should be embraced.

Conclusion

This chapter suggests some areas that require greater attention and further development within the victimological field. Within victimology, largely a positivist research agenda has been pursued, whereby state definitions of crime are taken for granted and left unquestioned, and a significant number of studies belong to a broader bureaucratic machinery of government. Moreover, differences between victims are rarely acknowledged or fed into research plans, so that generalised accounts of victimisation have resulted.

Within victimology, new theoretical concepts and innovative research techniques are required. A greater focus upon the emergence of new politicised identities is needed because within these social movements there are demands for a recognition, or greater recognition, of victim status. Alongside these demands, calls are also made for new victim policies and initiatives to be put into place. At the same time, in the same way that the feminist movement led to the incorporation of new research methodologies in order to explore women's lives, the rise of new politicised identities has implications for the development of methodological approaches within victimology and other social science disciplines. In light of the emergence of Muslim identities, for instance, research strategies need to become more inclusive of these.

Researchers also need to explore more fully the sense of 'belongingness' that individuals gain from their identification with a particular victim action group, which may be a part of a broader group collectivity. Embedded within the responses to victimisation that can be found within victim action and support groups, there may be shared histories relating to individual group members' subject positions.

Although some research has explored the culture-specific aspects to victimisation, this work appears to predominantly focus upon domestic violence and race hate crime and so the impact of a wider range of crimes upon particular communities is largely unknown and should therefore be increasingly examined. By giving victims' identities a central position within work examining victimisation, this may be a good way of introducing greater diversity and specificity of experience within analyses. A focus upon victims' identities suggests that more open-ended forms of data gathering are needed, for example, greater use of narrative methods should perhaps be made. Further engagement with the notions of spirituality and religiosity is also needed for a fuller understanding of victims' coping strategies. Finally, victimological work should feature a greater focus upon emotionality, as this can lead to work that is more reflective, and can make visible those hidden decision-making processes within a research study that serve to reproduce dominant knowledge constructions.

Questions

1 In what ways is traditional victimological work restricted?
2 Why are victim identities important to the study of victimisation?
3 What issues does diversity amongst victims raise for victimological research?

10

Conclusion: Future Developments and Implications

Introduction

It is important here to take stock, and reflect upon, the themes raised in the preceding chapters, in order to highlight the core issues that are of central importance to the (sub)discipline of victimology.

Victim issues in contemporary western society

First of all, it is important to emphasise that victim issues will continue to draw media, political and public attention for the foreseeable future. In late modernity, with the increasingly fragmented lives that people lead and the concomitant loss of a sense of 'belongingness', individuals will continue to draw upon victimhood as a way of claiming new identities for themselves. However, rather than viewing this in an entirely negative way, as writers such as Furedi (1997, 1998) have done, it is important to differentiate between victim identities that are 'free floating' and 'ungrounded', which constitute a movement towards the individualisation of pain, and victim identities that belong to, and are expressed within, broader group collectivities, which may be part of a wider social movement seeking to change oppressive social conditions.

An official victims' movement

Individualised responses to harm can be seen in the ways in which victims' experiences have been mass marketed, making up a 'victim industry' which seems to fetishise and therefore objectify human suffering without offering any meaningful solutions to the terrible events that can engulf people's lives. 'Ideal type' victims are constructed within media and political arenas and used to push forward a 'law and order' agenda. This leads to the social control and incarceration of increasing numbers of people, and if we consider institutional violence to be a form of victimisation, oppressing individuals physically, psychologically and spiritually, then state punitiveness leads to ever-greater numbers of victims.

Within the official victims' movement, victims are viewed as being consumers of a criminal justice system, who have certain basic requirements such as the need for financial compensation or for information about the progress of their cases. Whilst providing victims with monetary compensation and with more information may help to alleviate some concerns that they have, there is a danger here that in focussing upon individual need this may serve to civilise and depoliticise victims' reactions. The shock, anger and anxiety felt by victims can be translated into a bureaucratic discourse that is part of a broader governmental project measuring, and setting targets for, victim satisfaction. This serves to disempower victims since they are encouraged to think about themselves as individuals with needs that are linked to the criminal justice process, which then becomes part of their process of feeling, and so may shape individuals' subjectivities so that they are aligned to specific governmental aims and objectives.

Whilst victims' rights legislation gives the impression that victims are being empowered in some way, in reality the policies that have been implemented under the rubric of 'victims' rights' have focussed upon providing victims with certain basic services from agencies of the criminal justice system, and so reflect the governmental understanding of the victim as being an individual consumer rather than a person with wider political, social or economic rights. Furthermore, if the lens through which victims' needs are viewed is broadened, to look at individuals' experiences of agencies that lie outside of the criminal justice system, such as victims' experiences of hospitals, medical practices, housing associations and businesses, then it is clear that individuals' needs here are often unmet. Also, if the experiences of individuals victimised by non-traditional types of crime, like financial crime or other types of white-collar deviance, are taken into account, then again, it is clear that their interests are often ignored. It is therefore important to challenge the ways in which victims' needs have been constructed and tied predominantly to processes of the criminal justice system. The acknowledgement that negative treatment by agencies of the criminal justice system constitutes individuals' secondary victimisation, and the development of initiatives to reduce this, are not equal to responding to victim need.

The victim as individual consumer can be linked to the notion of a 'neutral', 'deserving' victim that underpins many mainstream victim initiatives.

For example, in Britain the philosophy underpinning the Criminal Injuries Compensation Scheme is that victims have no direct right to compensation and so individuals' behaviour before, during and after their victimisation is scrutinised in order to make decisions about the amount of compensation that they receive. A substantial number of claimants do not receive any compensation, either because there was a failure to report the incident without delay and/or cooperate with the police, or as a result of their conduct before, during or after the incident. The former factor is likely to have a disproportionate impact upon minority ethnic communities because research studies show that these communities have lower levels of confidence in the police. As a result, the Criminal Injuries Compensation Authority should monitor its procedures to examine any disproportionate effect upon particular groups of people. For example, young black men may be disproportionately affected because they have a lack of confidence in the police, and so their not reporting crime to the police can serve to severely disadvantage them from receiving state compensation.

According to Yarrow (2005), young black men infrequently have any contact with formal agencies that help the victims of crime. Yarrow's (2005) work reveals that out of 41 men interviewed, none had received help from Victim Support and awareness of Victim Support was very low. This illustrates that although Victim Support has, in recent years, targeted its services at a wider range of victims, certain groups of victims continue to be bypassed. This then elicits the question of whether take-up of Victim Support services by minority ethnic communities should be more vigorously pursued, or whether other, more specialist services targeted at, and arising from within, particular communities, should be developed. Greater emphasis must be placed on partnership work between Victim Support and specialist service providers, but also, government funding must resource specialist services much more adequately.

An unofficial victims' movement

Countering the ever-present movement towards the individualisation of pain, an unofficial victims' movement can be identified, consisting of a mixture of action and support groups which may belong to broader social movements, whose campaigning activities may involve demands for a recognition, or greater recognition, of victim status. But victim status is not necessarily individualistic here, since the different action groups making up each wider social movement may work towards changing wider societal injustices, and these are perhaps more informed, although much longer-term, approaches to reducing, and mitigating the harms caused by, victimisation. It is also important to point out, however, that some of the activities that these social movements engage in can, directly or indirectly, lead to an increased punitiveness towards offenders. For example, hate crime legislation has led to the harsher punishment of offenders motivated by racial or religious prejudice, alongside other forms of hatred. Nevertheless, it might also be argued that campaigns for hate crime legislation have not necessarily been motivated by a 'law and order' agenda, but rather, by the desire to show the importance, symbolically, of group members' identities within criminal justice policy arenas. The limited research examining victim action groups suggests that victim identities, which are likely to be multiple and complex, are central to developing a fuller understanding of individuals' experiences. For example, in the aftermath of the Robert Maxwell financial scandal in Britain in 1991, pensioners came together, and underpinning their responses to the scandal were their shared identities as older people, as working-class, former Maxwell, printing employees, and as members of a partial 'welfare state' that individuals assumed would look after them in their old age (Spalek, 1999).

Social movements, identities and victim research

Social scientists need to be sensitive to the emergence of new group collectivities and identities, since these will have important implications for victim policy and practice, particularly when demands are made for the implementation of new victim legislation. At different periods of time, different identities will become politicised and this will impact upon policy-making processes. For example, over the last two decades, Muslim identities within the United Kingdom have emerged, alongside Muslim political activism (Modood, 2003), and this has led to the introduction of hate crime legislation in relation to faith identities and has led to the development of new victim initiatives.

The emergence of new identities raises important epistemological and methodological issues for victimology. Essentially, victimological work needs to show a greater recognition of, and focus upon, diversity issues. However, national crime surveys, which are a commonplace feature of modern life and play an important role in gathering information about victimisation, tend to group individuals, from a diverse range of different communities, together. The classifications that are used to identify victims, and then the ways in which data is analysed and presented, means that significant differences between different communities are overlooked. For example, in research reports produced from the British Crime Survey, Pakistanis and Bangladeshis may be grouped together with Indians within a broader Asian or South Asian category. This can serve to obscure the particular difficulties faced by Pakistani and Bangladeshi communities, because these groups experience more socio-economic deprivation, and higher offending and incarceration rates, than Indian groups. Moreover, individuals' faith identities are not recorded, so that knowledge about the victimisation of Muslim or Jewish communities, for example, must be found from other sources.

Within academic-based research on the process of victimisation, differences between victims have been insufficiently explored or addressed because of a lack of focus upon victim identities and the multiple subject positions that victims can occupy. This means that within the literature there seems to be an assumption that the experience of victimisation is generally the same for all people, regardless of significant differences in individuals' subject positions. For example, researchers have argued that a fundamental part of the experience of victimisation is that of the 'shattering of cognitive assumptions' about the world because it is maintained that prior to a traumatic incident occurring, individuals hold a 'belief in a just world', a world where people generally get what they deserve. As a result, it is argued that victimisation leads to a loss of a sense of control. This model of victimisation seems to have influenced the practices of mainstream victim organisations, which value giving control back to the victims of crime, since crime is seen as having taken control away from them. At the same time, within this approach crime is viewed as an incident, rather than as an insidious feature of people's everyday lives, because the wider racist, sexist, homophobic (and other) structures, that help to create, sustain and maintain repeat patterns of victimisation, are largely unacknowledged, so that people are seen to lead largely crime-free lives, which nonetheless may, now-and-again, be shattered by violent or non-violent offences. This model of the neutral victim can indirectly discriminate against victims from minority communities, whose lives may be constantly blighted by experiences of harm.

The 'belief in a just world' construct is, however, increasingly being questioned, and it appears that this belief system is stronger in individuals who have property, wealth or power, so that not all groups of individuals will share this cognitive assumption about the world (Furnham, 2003). Also, individuals who follow a faith may believe that the world is unpredictable and that they have little control over it since God and other forces are at play. This suggests that different people can experience the process of victimisation in fundamentally different ways.

Critical black feminists, for example, have introduced the concept of 'spirit injury' to try and capture a rarely acknowledged dimension to black women's experiences of victimhood. The continual, daily harassment on the basis of race and gender that black women experience amounts to harm that goes beyond the psychological, emotional, behavioural and physical impacts of crime as documented by researchers (Davis, 1997; Williams, 1997). The concept of 'spirit injury' also allows us to think about the impact of racism and sexism upon indirect victims, who may not directly be the objects of harm but who nonetheless experience victimisation 'at a distance', as a result of recurrent racist and sexist practices and values that operate in wider society. An acknowledgement of spirit injury with respect to people's experiences of victimisation has some important implications when providing support to the victims of crime, since therapies aimed at a 'spiritual level', such as the use of alternative forms of healing for example, might be more helpful in some cases.

Mainstream victim services are secular in nature, which means that people's religious and spiritual needs are not addressed. This is likely to have a profound impact upon uptake of service delivery by minority ethnic communities, since research shows that religious affiliation is a much more fundamental aspect of the self-identity of minority ethnic groups when compared to many White Christians (O'Beirne, 2004: 18). Some members of minority ethnic groups therefore may prefer to seek help from spiritual or religious leaders/representatives. As a result, researchers need to increasingly examine how and why members of minority ethnic communities might seek alternative forms of help and what benefits they gain from this. Perhaps mainstream victim organisations can also look into incorporating a spiritual component to the work that they carry out by, for example, widening the range of organisations that they suggest people contact, so that spiritual and/or religious guidance and support can be more easily obtained by victims. Therapists are also increasingly including a spiritual dimension to the techniques that they use when working with clients. Mainstream victim support services, and the people working for them, could perhaps be more aware of these kinds of developments. Essentially, much more work needs to be carried out looking at the notions of 'spirituality' and 'religiosity' and their connections with victimisation. In relation to religious hate crime, work needs to increasingly look at the impacts and process of this, as researchers have traditionally looked at the impacts of race hate crimes on minority ethnic communities, thereby omitting individuals' faith identities. When documenting women's experiences of physical and sexual violence and intimidation, mainstream feminist analyses must engage much more fundamentally with the diversity to be found amongst women.

The framework of understanding about the nature of victimisation has been constructed largely through documenting the experiences of people who have been affected by events that are defined as criminal by the state. As such, little is known about the consequences of harms caused by 'non-traditional' crimes such as white-collar offences or institutional violence. Identity issues constitute an important element to understanding institutional violence, in terms of hierarchies of identities that influence vulnerability and therefore risk of victimisation. At the same time, identities linked to race, ethnicity, religion and so forth will influence the kinds of violence experienced by individuals, and also will influence how individuals experience their victimisation, which may include a spiritual component.

Institutional violence clearly illustrates how the distinction between offender and victim is often blurred. Victimisation here can be linked to abuses of power by the state, thereby broadening the notion of victimhood to include forms of abuse that may not feature in officially sanctioned categories of crime (Elias, 1994).

Conclusion

Ultimately, social scientists exploring victimisation must embrace a broader range of experiences, adopting wider definitions of 'crime' and 'harm', and they must also introduce greater specificity into the work that they carry out. A more substantial focus upon victims' identities is needed, and this suggests that more open-ended forms of data gathering should be encouraged, for example, by the use of narrative techniques. Victimological work should also feature a greater focus upon emotionality, as this can lead to work that is more reflective, making visible those hidden decision-making processes within a research study that serve to reproduce dominant knowledge constructions. In this way, the (sub)discipline of victimology will more accurately reflect the diverse range of experiences that can be found within the multi-cultural, diverse societies of late modernity.

Notes

1 Introducing Victimology

1 The term 'Black' used here takes Mirza's (1997: 3) approach as consisting of the shared space of postcolonial migrants of different languages, religions, cultures and classes through the shared experience of racialisation and its consequences.

2 Victimhood, Late Modernity and Criminal Justice

1 These quotations come from the following books: G. Jurgensen (1999) *The Disappearance* London: Flamingo, which tells the story of two young girls who were killed in a car accident; M. Nuttall (1997) *It Could Have Been You* London: Virago, which tells the story of Merlyn Nuttall who survived a rape and attempted murder; and S.Slater (1995) *Beyond Fear* London: Fourth Estate, which tells the story of 25 year-old estate agent Stephanie Slater, who was kidnapped while showing a prospective client around a house and held blindfold for eight days.

2 The families of people murdered by the September 11th attacks in the US were able to claim financial compensation from the September 11th Victim Compensation Fund of 2001, administered by the US Department of Justice. Within twenty-four hours of the attack Congress passed legislation for compensation, in large part due to the potential of victims bankrupting the airline industry if they were to file lawsuits against airlines (Cullen, 2002). Compensation has been determined according to the pain and suffering occurred by direct victims, also in terms of income provisions. This means that there has been a large discrepancy in payouts between the families of low and high income earners, generating some controversy.

3 As an example of the 'ripple effect' of crime, following the bombing of the Alfred P. Murrah Federal Building in Oklahoma City on 19th April 1995, killing 168 people, in a report entitled 'Responding to Terrorism Victims: Oklahoma City and beyond', the US Department of Justice Office for Victims of Crime claims that in the three years after the bombing, 8,869 people received counselling or support group or crisis intervention work.

4 In 1995 the Texas Board of Criminal Justice passed legislation to enable the family members of murder victims to watch the execution of the murderer. K. Brewis 'Witness for the Execution' *The Sunday Times Magazine* 22 April 2001.

5 The patients that Harold Shipman killed were mainly elderly women who were living alone, and who trusted their family doctor.

6 On 12 October 2002 two bombs exploded at a tourist location on the Indonesian Island of Bali, killing at least 183 people. During the trial of the bombers, Imam Samudra (who was found guilty of organising the attacks) said that the bombing was 'justifiable' under Islamic teachings and its purpose was to avenge the killings of Muslims by the United States and its allies. BBC News Timeline: Bali Bomb Trials http://news.bbc.co.uk/1/hi/world/asia-pacific/3126241.stm accessed: 04/01/05.

4 Researching Victimisation: Contesting Victimhood

1 For example, in a report stemming from the British Crime Survey 2001/2002, *Ethnicity and Drug Use,* findings are presented according to the categories Asian, Mixed Background, Chinese/Other, Black and White, and the authors argue that because of the small numbers of people engaged in drug use across the different ethnic groups it is not possible to explore links between drug use, ethnicity, social disadvantage and exclusion. However, they argue that once two or more similar survey years are available, data might be combined to allow further investigation (Aust and Smith, 2003).

5 Understanding Victimisation: Exploring Harms

1 For example, see Gittleson, Eacott and Mehta, 1978; Dobash and Dobash, 1979; Norris and Feldman-Summers, 1981; Maguire, 1982; Baum, Fleming and Singer, 1983; Janoff-Bulman and Frieze, 1983; Miller and Porter, 1983; Perloff, 1983; Silver, Boon and Stones, 1983; Taylor, Wood and Lichtman, 1983; Wortman, 1983; Sales, Baum and Shore, 1984; Janoff-Bulman, 1985; Shapland, Willmore and Duff, 1985; Kelly, 1988; Mezey, 1988; Brown, Christie and Morris, 1990; Hoff, 1990; Lurigio and Resick, 1990; Resick, 1990; Russell 1990; Stanko and Hobdell, 1993; Indermaur, 1995; Dugan, 1999.

2 For example, Resick (1990) reviews the literature that documents the impact of sexual assault upon victims. The author states that a main aim of this chapter is to discuss the implications that victimisation studies have for intervention with adult victims of sexual assault. Similarly, Riggs and Kilpatrick (1990) write about the impact of crime on indirect victims such as the families and friends of murder victims, with a view to helping them through implementing effective victim initiatives. At the end of their analysis, there appears a section entitled 'practical considerations regarding the indirect victims of crime' which discusses the unique problems faced by these individuals and how practitioners should take this into account (Riggs and Kilpatrick, 1990: 132).

3 Indeed, according to Bowling and Phillips (2003), successive sweeps of the British Crime Survey have shown that more than one third of assaults directed against Asians and blacks were considered by respondents to be racially motivated.

6   Official Responses to Victimisation

1   Scotland and the Republic of Ireland are covered by separate organisations (Victim Support 2003: 4).

2   In 2003, the National Criminal Justice Board was created. This is responsible for supporting 42 local criminal justice boards to deliver the Criminal Justice System Public Service Agreements, which are seen to be ways in boosting the efficiency of the criminal justice system.

3   For example, a study by Docking (2003) reveals that minority ethnic groups share a perception that police discriminate against or stereotype them, with young people believing that they are more likely to be stopped and searched than white people. In this study, the older people from minority ethnic groups felt that the police didn't take them seriously when they reported crimes, and they felt that the police did not trust them. Pakistanis and Bangladeshis also indicate the lowest satisfaction with public-initiated police contact and the lowest levels of confidence in the police (Clancy *et al.*, 2003).

4   Choice is a key issue here, since some individuals may specifically want a counsellor/therapist/refuge that understands their specific religious and spiritual needs, whereas others might prefer to seek help from people outside their own communities.

7   Victims' Needs and Victims' Rights

1   For example, in Shapland et al's study (1985) of the experience of victims of violent crime, between 35 per cent and 41 per cent of cases were reported by the victim him/her self. Another fifty per cent were reported by other civilians, such as passers-by, neighbours, friends of those in charge of the places where the offences occurred (Shapland, 1985: 211). While in Newburn and Merry's (1990: 5) study of one hundred victims, sixty-four had contacted the police themselves, and in a further nine cases a member of the victim's household had reported the crime to the police.

2   As an example of this, see Smiljanic (2001) for a discussion of the human rights violations of Muslims despite the implementation of the Human Rights Act 1998.

3   Michel Foucault was a French philosopher during the 1960s to 1980s. Foucault wrote extensively about power and about how governments exercise this. According to Foucault (1978), the art of government in contemporary western society is to shape and normalise individuals' behaviours through their own self-regulation. Language plays a key part in providing individuals with 'shared vocabularies, theories and explanations' (Miller and Rose, 1993: 84), and information created by governmental institutions, practices and agents can work through and upon individuals, shaping, affecting or guiding their conduct (Gordon, 1991).

9   New Perspectives within Victimology

1   A greater interrogation of the term 'bias' is needed, as this is open to interpretation and so raises the question of biased against whom or what?

References

Afshar, H. and Maynard, M. (2000) 'Gender and Ethnicity of the Millennium: From Margin to Centre' *Ethnic and Racial Studies*, Vol. 23 (5), pp. 805–819.

Ahmad, F. and Sheriff, S. (2003) 'Muslim Women of Europe: Welfare Needs and Responses', *Social Work in Europe*, Vol. 8 (1), pp. 2–10.

Ahmed, S. (2004) *The Cultural Politics of Emotion* (Edinburgh: Edinburgh University Press).

Amir, M. (1971) *Patterns in Forcible Rape* (Chicago: University of Chicago Press).

Amos, V. and Parmar, P. (1997) 'Challenging Imperial Feminism', in H. Safia Mirza (ed.) *Black British Feminism: A reader* (London: Routledge), pp. 54–62.

Anderson, S., Kinsey, R., Loader, I. and Smith, C.G. (1994) *Cautionary Tales* (Aldershot: Avebury).

Andrews, M. (2002) 'Feminist Research with Non-feminist and Anti-feminist Women: Meeting the Challenge' *Feminism and Psychology,* Vol. 12 (1), pp. 55–77.

Aust, R. and Simmons, J. (2002) 'Rural Crime: England & Wales', *Home Office Statistical Bulletin*, 1/02 (London: HMSO).

Australian Criminology Institute. (2003) *Rural Crime Surveys* http://www.aic.gov.au/research/projects/0023.html (2003).

Australian Institute of Criminology (2005) *Australian Crime: Facts and Figures 2004* (Canberra: AIC).

Bamfield, J. (2003) 'Stealing from Shops: A Survey of the European Dimension', in M. Gill (ed.) *Managing Security* (Leicester: Perpetuity Press), pp. 125–140.

Banbury, S. (2004) 'Coercive Sexual Behaviour in British prisons as reported by adult Ex-prisoners', *The Howard Journal of Criminal Justice*, Vol. 43 (2), pp. 113–130.

Bard, M. and Sangrey, D. (1979) *The Crime Victim's Book* (New York: Basic Books).

Baum, A., Fleming, R. and Singer, J. (1983) 'Coping with victimisation by Technological Disaster', *Journal of Social Issues*, Vol. 39 (2), pp. 117–138.

Bauman, Z. (2004) *Identity: Conversations with Benedetto Vecchi* (Cambridge: Polity Press).

Beck, U. (1992) *Risk Society: Towards a New Modernity* (London: Sage).

Beckford, J. (2003) *Preliminary Results on Provisions for Muslims in French and British Prisons*, paper presented at the Centre for Ethnic Relations University of Warwick, 12 December.

Beckford, J. and Gilliat, S. (1998) *Religion in Prison: Equal Rites in a Multifaith Society* (Cambridge University Press).

Bendelow G. and Williams, S. (1998) *Emotions in Social Life: Critical and Contemporary Issues* (London: Routledge).

Bennet, L., Goodman, L. and Dutton, M. (1999) 'Systematic Obstacles to the Criminal Prosecution of a Battering Partner', *Journal of Interpersonal Violence*, Vol. 761, pp. 10–36.

Benyon, J. and Solomos, J. (1987) 'British Urban Unrest in the 1980s', in J. Benyon and J. Solomos (eds) *The Roots of Urban Unrest* (Oxford: Pergamon Press), pp. 3–22.

Bergman, D. (1994) *The Perfect Crime? How Companies Escape Manslaughter Prosecutions* (Birmingham: West Midlands Health and Safety Advice Centre).

Boe, R., Motiuk, L. and Muirhead, M. (1998) *Recent Trends and Patterns Shaping the Corrections Population in Canada:1983/84 to 1996/97* (Research Branch Correctional Service of Canada May).

Bolles, A. (2001) 'Seeking the Ancestors: Forging a Black Feminist Tradition in Anthropology', in I. McClaurin (ed.) *Black Feminist Anthropology* (London: Rutgers University Press), pp. 24–48.

Bonczar, T. (2003) *Prevalence of Imprisonment in the U.S. Population, 1974–2001* (Washington: US Department of Justice).

Bottoms, A. (2000) 'The Relationship between Theory and Research in Criminology', in R. King and E. Wincup (eds) *Doing Research on Crime and Justice* (Oxford: Oxford University Press), pp. 15–60.

Bower, T. (1994) *Maxwell the Outsider* (London: Mandarin Paperbacks).

Bowling, B. (1999) *Violent Racism: Victimisation, Policing and Social Context*, revised edition (Oxford: Oxford University Press).

Bowling, B. and Phillips, C. (2003) 'Racist Victimisation in England and Wales', in D.Hawkins (ed.) *Violent Crime: Assessing Race and Ethnic Differences* (Cambridge: Cambridge University Press), pp. 154–170.

Box, S. (1983) *Power, Crime and Mystification* (London: Routledge).

Brewis, K. (2001) 'Witness for the execution', *The Sunday Times Magazine*, 22 April

Bright, M. (2004) 'Revealed: Truth about Victim of a Prison's Race Tragedy', *The Observer* 14 November.

Britton, N. (2000) *Black Justice? Race, Criminal Justice and Identity* (Stoke on Trent: Trentham Books Limited).

Brown, L., Christie, R. and Morris, D. (1990) *Victim Support Families of Murder Victims Project* (London: HMSO).

Brown, D. and Hogg, R. (1992) 'Law and Order Politics – Left Realism and Radical Criminology: A View from Down Under', in R. Matthews and J. Young (eds) *Issues in Realist Criminology* (London: Sage) pp. 136–176.

Bryans, S. and Wilson, D. (1998) *The Prison Governor: Theory and Practice* (Leyhill: Prison Service Journal).

Burgess, A. and Holmstrom, L. (1974) *Rape: Victims of Crisis* (Bowie MD: Brady).

Burnett, R. and Farrell, G. (1994) *Reported and Unreported Racial Incidents in Prisons*, Centre for Criminological Research University of Oxford Occasional Paper 14.

Burnley, J., Edmunds, C., Gaboury, M. and Seymour, A. (1998) 'Theoretical Perspectives of Victimology and Critical Research', in J. Burnley, C. Edmunds, M. Gaboury and A. Seymour (eds) *1998 National Victim Assistance Academy Textbook* (Washington, Department for Justice: Office for Victims of Crime), pp. 1–10.

Burrows, J., Anderson, S., Bamfield, J., Hopkins, M. and Ingram, D. (1999) 'Counting the Cost: Crime against Businesses in Scotland', *Crime and Criminal Justice Findings*, No. 35 (Edinburgh: Scottish Executive Central Research Unit).

Burt, G., Wong, S., Vander Veen S., and Gu, D. (2000) 'Three Strikes and You're Out: An Investigation of False Positive Rates Using a Canadian Sample', *Federal Probation*, Vol. 64 (1), pp. 3–6.

Cain, M. (1986) 'Realism, Feminism, Methodology and Law', *International Journal of the Sociology of Law*, Vol. 14 (1), pp. 255–267.

Cain, M. (1990) 'Realist Philosophy and Standpoint Epistemologies or Feminist Criminology as a Successor Science', in L. Gelsthorpe and A. Morris (eds) *Feminist Perspectives in Criminology* (Buckingham: Open University Press).

Calhoun, L. and Cann, A. (1994) 'Differences in Assumptions about a Just World: Ethnicity and Point of View', *Journal of Social Psychology*, Vol. 134 (6), pp. 765–780.

Carby, H. (1997) 'White Women Listen!', in H. Safia Mirza (ed.) *Black British Feminism: A Reader* (London: Routledge), pp. 45–53.

Carter, H. (2002) 'Armed Police Patrol City in Fear of Guns', *The Guardian*, 30 April 2002.

Carter, Rubin 'Hurricane' (1974) *The 16th Round* (Ontario: Penguin).

Chakraborti, N., Garland, J. and Spalek, B. (2004) 'Out of Sight, Out of Mind? Towards Developing an Understanding of the Needs of Hidden Minority Ethnic Communities', *Criminal Justice Matters*, No. 57, pp. 34–35.

Chambers, G., Curran, J., Millar, A., Moody, S., Tombs, J. and Wozniak, E. (1984) *The British Crime Survey, Scotland* (Scottish Office Research Study Edinburgh Her Majesty's Stationery Office).

Choudry, S. (1996) 'Pakistani Women's Experience of Domestic Violence in Great Britain', Home Office Research Findings No. 43 (London: HMSO) pp. 1–4.

Clancy, A., Hough, M., Aust, R. and Kershaw, C. (2001) 'Crime, Policing and Justice: The Experiences of Ethnic Minorities Findings from the 2000 British Crime Survey', *Home Office Research and Statistics* 223 (London: Home Office).

Clarke, R. (1992) *Situational Crime Prevention, Successful Case Studies* (New York: Harrow & Heston).

Cobb, S. (1976) 'Social Support as a Moderator of Life Stress', *Psychosomatic Medicine*, Vol. 38, pp. 300–314.

Cockburn, C. (1983) *Brothers. Male Dominance and Technological Change* (London: Pluto Press).

Cohen, L. and Felson, M. (1979) 'Social Change and Crime Rate Trends: A Routine Activity Approach', *American Sociological Review*, Vol. 44 (1), pp. 588–608.

Coleman, J. (1994) *The Criminal Elite: The Sociology of White-Collar Crime* (New York: St Martin's Press).

Collins, P. (1998) *Fighting Words* (Minneapolis: University of Minnesota Press).

Collins, P. (2000) *Black Feminist Thought: Knowledge, Consciousness, and the Politics of Empowerment*, second edition (London: Routledge).

Conway Commission on British Muslims and Islamophobia. (1997) *Islamophobia, a Challenge for Us All* (London: The Runnymede Trust).

Cook B., David, F. and Grant, A. (1999) *Victims' Needs, Victims' Rights: Policies and Programs for Victims of Crime in Australia* (Australian Institute of Criminology: Canberra).

Cook, F. and Wilkinson, M. (1998) *Hard Cell* (Liverpool: the Bluecoat Press).

Corbett, C. and Maguire, M. (1988) 'The Value & Limitations of Victim Support Schemes', in M. Maguire and J. Pointing (eds) *Victims of Crime: A New Deal?* (Milton Keynes: Open University Press), pp. 47–59.

Crawford, A., Jones, T., Woodhouse, T. and Young, J. (1990) *The Second Islington Crime Survey* (London: Middlesex Polytechnic).

Crawford, A. and Enterkin, J. (1999) *Victim Contact Work and the Probation Service: A Study of Service Delivery and Impact* (Leeds: Centre for Criminal Justice Studies).

Cressey, D. (1986) 'Research Implications of Conflicting Conceptions of Victimology', in E. Fattah (ed.) *From Crime Policy to Victim Policy* (Basingstoke: Macmillan), pp. 57–73.

Crime and Disorder Act (1998) http://www.hmso.gov.uk/acts/acts1998/19980037.htm

Criminal Justice System (2005) Victims' Code of Practice Consultation (London: Home Office).

Criminal Injuries Compensation Authority. (2000) *Annual Report 1998/99 Third Report Accounts for the Year Ended 31st March 1999* (Edinburgh: the Stationery Office).

Criminal Injuries Compensation Authority. (2004) *Guide to the Criminal Injuries Compensation Scheme 2001* (London: CICA).

Croall, H. (1992) *White Collar Crime* (Buckingham: Open University Press).

Croall, H. (2001) *Understanding White Collar Crime* (Buckingham: Open University Press).

Crown Prosecution Service. (2003) *Racist and Religious Crime – CPS Prosecution Policy* (London: Equality & Diversity Unit and the Policy Directorate, CPS).

Cullen, C. (2002) 'The Victims' Compensation Fund', *The William Joiner Center for the Study of War and Social Consequences*, Vol. V, (1) (Boston: University of Massachusetts).

Curry, P. and Stanko, E. (1997) 'Homophobic Violence and the Self "at risk": Dilemmas of the Public/Private' *Social and Legal Studies*, Vol. 6 (4), pp. 513–532.

Dalbert, C. (1998) 'Belief in a Just World, Well-being and Coping in an Unjust World', in L. Montada and M. Lerner (eds) *Responses to Victimisations and Belief in the Just World* (New York: Plenum) pp. 87–105.

Davis, D. (1997) 'The Harm that Has No Name: Street Harassment, Embodiment and African American Women', in A. Wing (ed.) *Critical Race Feminism: A Reader* (New York: New York University Press), pp. 192–202.

Department of Justice. (2003) *The Nation's Two Crime Measures* (Washington DC: Department of Justice, May).

Department of Justice Canada (2003) *Victims of Crime* http://canada.justice.gc.ca 2003

Devlin, A. and Turney, B. (1999) *Going Straight: After Crime and Punishment* (Winchester: Waterside Press).

Diani, M. (1992 'The Concept of a Social Movement', *The Sociological Review,* Vol. 40 (1) pp. 1–25.

Dijk, J. Van. (1997) 'Introducing Victimology'. 9th symposium of the World Society of Victimology (Amsterdam).

Disability Rights Commission (2005) *Latest News* http://www.drc.org.uk/newsroom/newsdetails.asp?id=598&section=1 accessed January 2005.

Dobash, R. and Dobash, R. (1979) *Violence Against Wives: The Case against Patriarchy* (New York: Free Press).

Docking, M. (2003) 'Public Perceptions of Police Accountability and Decision-Making', *Home Office Online Report* 38/03.

Doerner, W. and Lab, S. (1995) *Victimology* (Ohio: Anderson Publishing).

Dominey, J. (2002) 'Addressing Victim Issues in Pre-Sentence Reports', in B. Williams (ed.) *Reparation and Victim-Focused Social Work* (London: Jessica Kingsley), pp. 160–176.

Douglas, M. (1994) *Purity and Danger: An Analysis of the Concepts of Pollution and Taboo* (London: Routledge & Kegan Paul).

Douglass, J., Bowers, K., Young, C. and Clare, L. (2003) 'If You Don't Call Us, We'll Call You: the Experiences of Business Crime Direct', in M. Gill (ed.) *Managing Security* (Leicester: Perpetuity Press), pp. 21–38.

Dugan, L. (1999) 'The Effect of Criminal Victimisation on a Household's Moving Decision', *Criminology,* Vol. 37 (4), pp. 903–928.

Edgar, K. and O'Donnell, I. 'Assault in prison', *British Journal of Criminology* Vol. 38 No.(4), pp. 635–650.

Edwards, I. (2001) 'Victim Participation in Sentencing: The Problems of Incoherence', *The Howard Journal of Criminal Justice,* Vol. 40 (1), pp. 39–54.

Edwards, R. and Ribbens, J. (1998) 'Living on the Edges: Public Knowledge, Private Lives, Personal Experience', in J. Ribbens and R. Edwards (eds) *Feminist Dilemmas in Qualitative Research* (London: Sage), pp. 1–24.

Ehrlich, H. (1992) 'The Ecology of Anti-Gay Violence', in G. Herek and K. Berrill (eds) *Hate Crimes: Confronting Violence against Lesbians and Gay Men* (London: Sage), pp. 105–111.

Elias, R. (1986) *The Politics of Victimisation* (Oxford: Oxford University Press).

Elias, R. (1993) *Victims Still* (London: Sage Publications).

Elias, R. (1990) 'Which Victim Movement? The Politics of Victim Policy', in A. Lurigio, W. Skogan and R. Davis (eds) *Victims of Crime: Problems, Policies and Programs* (London: Sage), pp. 226–250.

Elias, R. (1994) 'Paradigms and Paradoxes of Victimology', in: C. Sumner, M. Israel, M. O'Donnell and R. Sarre (eds) No. 27 International Victimology, Selected Papers for the 8th International Symposium: proceedings of a symposium held 21–26 August 1994 Canberra: Australian Institute of Criminology), pp. 9–34.

Elkins, M. and Olagundoye, J. (2001) 'The Prison Population in 2000: A Statistical Review', *Home Office Findings*, 154 (London: HMSO).

Ellison, L. (2002) 'Prosecuting Domestic Violence without Victim Participation', *The Modern Law Review,* Vol. 65 (6), pp. 834–858.

Ewald, F. (1991) "Insurance and Risk", in: G. Burchell, C. Gordon and P. Miller (eds) *The Foucault Effect: Studies in Governmentality* (London: Harvester Wheatsheaf), pp. 197–210.

Fagan, J., Piper, E. and Cheng, Y. (1987) 'Contribution of Victimisation to Delinquency in Inner Cities', *Journal of Criminal Law and Criminology*, Vol. 78 (1), pp. 586–609.

Farrall, S. and Maltby, S. (2003) 'The Victimisation of Probationers', *The Howard Journal of Criminal Justice*, Vol. 42 (1), pp. 32–54.

Farrell, G. and Pease, K. (1993) 'Once Bitten, Twice Bitten: Repeat Victimisation and its Implications for Crime Prevention', *Crime Prevention Unit Paper*, No. 46 (London: HMSO).

Farrington, D. and Dowds, E. (1985) 'Disentangling Criminal Behaviour and Police Reaction', in D. Farrington and J. Gunn (eds) *Reaction to Crime* (Chichester: Wiley).

Fattah, E. (1989) 'Victims and Victimology: The f acts and the Rhetoric', *International Review of Victimology*, Vol. 1 (1), pp. 43–66.

Fattah, E. (1992) 'Victims and Victimology: the Facts and the Rhetoric', in E. Fattah (ed.) *Towards a Critical Victimology* (New York: Macmillan), pp. 29–56.

Fattah, E. (1993) 'The Rational Choice/Opportunity Perspectives as a Vehicle for Integrating Criminological and Victimological Theories', in R. Clarke and M. Felson (eds) *Routine Activity and Rational Choice Advances in Criminological Theory* Volume 5 (New Jersey: Transaction Publishers).

Fattah, E. (ed.) (1986) *From Crime Policy to Victim Policy* (Basingstoke: Macmillan).

Fitzgerald, M. and Hale, C. (1996) '*Ethnic Minorities: Victimisation and Racial Harassment: Findings from the 1988 and 1992 British Crime Surveys*', Home Office Research Study No. 154 (London: HMSO).

Forrester, D., Chatterton, M. and Pease, K. (1998) *The Kirkholt Burglary Prevention Project* Rochdale Crime Prevention Unit Paper 13 (London: HMSO).

Foucault, M. (1978) 'Governmentality', in G. Burchell, C. Gordon and P. Miller (eds) *The Foucault Effect: Studies in Governmentality* (London: Harvester Wheatsheaf, 1991), pp. 87–114.

Frankenberg, R. (1993) *The Social Construction of White Women, Whiteness Race Matters* (London: Routledge).

Friedrichs, D. (1983) 'Victimology: A Consideration of the Radical Critique', *Crime & Delinquency*, Vol. 29 (1), pp. 283–293.

Furedi, F. (1997) *Culture of Fear: Risk-Taking and the Morality of Low Expectation* (London: Cassell).

Furedi, F. (1998) 'New Britain – A Nation of Victims', *Society*, Vol. 35 (3), pp. 80–84.

Furedi, F. (2004) *Therapy Culture* (London: Routledge).

Furnham, A. (1991) 'Just World Beliefs in Twelve Societies', *Journal of Social Psychology* 133, pp. 317–329.

Furnham, A. (2003) 'Belief in a Just World: Research Progress Over the Past Decade', *Personality and Individual Differences*, Vol. 34 (1), pp. 795–817.

Gardner, K. and Shuker, A. (1994) 'I'm Bengali, I'm Asian and I'm Living Here, the Changing Identity of British Bengalis', in R. Ballard (ed.) *Desh Pardesh: The South Asian Presence in Britain* (London: Hurst and Company).

Garland, D. (1994) 'Of Crimes and Criminals: the Development of Criminology in Britain', in M. Maguire, R. Morgan and R. Reiner (eds) *The Oxford Handbook of Criminology* (Oxford: Oxford University Press), pp. 17–68.

Garland, D. (1997) 'Governmentality and the Problem of Crime: Foucault, Criminology, Sociology', *Theoretical Criminology*, Vol. 1 (2), pp. 173–214.

Garland, D. (2001) *The Culture of Control* (Oxford: Oxford University Press).

Garland, J. and Chakraborti, N. (2004) 'Racist Victimisation, Community Safety and the Rural: Issues and Challenges', *British Journal of Community Justice*, Vol. 3 (2), pp. 21–32.

Garofalo, J. (1986) 'Lifestyles and Victimisation: An Update', in: E. Fattah (ed.) *From Crime Policy to Victim Policy* (London: Macmillan), pp. 135–155.

Garwood, J., Rogerson, M. and Pease, K. (2000) 'Sneaky Measurement of Crime and Disorder', in V. Jupp, P. Davies and P. Francis (eds) *Doing Criminological Research* (London: Sage), pp. 157–168.

Gauchet, M. (1999) *The Disenchantment of the World: A political History of Religion* (Princeton, NJ: Princeton University Press).

Gauhar, H. 'The Fall Guy Agha Hasan Abedi – September 25, 1922 – August 5, 1995' *Politics & Business*, 22 August 1993.

Genders, E. and Player, E. (1989) *Race Relations in Prisons* (Oxford: Clarendon Press).

Genn, H. (1988) 'Multiple Victimisation', in M. Maguire and J. Pointing (eds) *Victims of Crime: A New Deal?* (Milton Keynes: Open University Press), pp. 90–100.

Gibson, M. (1998) *Order from Chaos: Responding to Traumatic Events* (London: Venture Press).

Giddens, A. (1990) *The Consequences of Modernity* (Cambridge: Polity Press).

Gittleson, N., Eacott, S. and Mehta, B. (1978) 'Victims of indecent exposure', *British Journal of Psychiatry*, Vol. 132, pp. 61–66.

Gordon, C. (1991) 'Governmental Rationality: An Introduction', in G. Burchell, C. Gordon and P. Miller (eds) *The Foucault Effect: Studies in Governmentality* (London: Harvester Wheatsheaf (1973)), pp. 1–52.

Gordon, D. (1973) 'Capitalism, Class and Crime in America', *Crime & Delinquency*, pp. 163–187.

Gottfredson, M. (1981) 'On the Etiology of Criminal Victimisation', *The Journal of Criminal Law & Criminology*, Vol. 72 (2), pp. 714–726.

Grabosky, P. and Sutton, A. (eds) (1993) *Stains on a White Collar: 14 Studies in Corporate Crime or Corporate Harm* (Sydney: The Federation Press).

Greenberg, D. (1981) *Crime and Capitalism* (California: Mayfield).

Gregory, J. and Lees, S. (1998) *Policing Sexual Assault* (London: Routledge).

Hale, C. (1992) *Fear of Crime: A review of the Literature* (Canterbury: Canterbury Business School).

Hall, R. (1985) *Ask Any Woman* (London: Falling Wall Press).

Hall, S. (1990) 'Cultural Identity and Diaspora' in J. Rutherford (ed.) *Identity: Community, Culture, Difference* (London: Lawrence and Wishart), pp. 4–14.

Hanmer, J. and Saunders, S. (1984) *Well-Founded Fear* (London: Hutchinson & Co).

Hanmer, J. and Stanko, E. (1985) 'Stripping away the rhetoric of protection: violence to women, law and the state in Britain and the USA', *International Journal of the Sociology of Law*, Vol. 13, pp. 357–374.

Harding, S. (1987) *Feminism and Methodology* (Milton Keynes: Open University Press).

Harris, A. (1997) 'Race and Essentialism in Feminist Legal Theory', in A. Wing (ed.) *Critical Race Feminism* (New York: New York University Press), pp. 11–18.

Haug, I. (1998) 'Including a Spiritual Dimension in Family Therapy: Ethical Considerations', *Contemporary Family Therapy*, Vol. 20 (2), pp. 181–194.

Hayes, M. (1994) *The New Right in Britain: An Introduction to Theory and Practice* (London: Pluto Press).

Hentig, H. von. (1948) *The Criminal and His Victim* (New Haven: Yale University Press).

Henderson, L. (1992) 'The Wrongs of Victims' Rights', in E. Fattah (ed.) *Towards a Critical Victimology* (New York: Macmillan), pp. 100–194.

Herek, G. (1992) *Hate Crimes: Confronting Violence against Lesbians and Gay Men* (London: Sage).

Hindelang, M., Gottfredson, M. and Garofalo, J. (1978) *Victims of Personal Crime: An Empirical Foundation for a Theory of Personal Victimisation* (Cambridge MA.: Ballinger).

Hochschild, A. (1998) 'The Sociology of Emotion as a Way of Seeing', in S. Williams and G. Bendelow (eds) *Emotions in Social Life* (London: Routledge), pp. 3–15.

Hoff, A. (1990) *Battered Women as Survivors* (London: Routledge).

Hollway, W. and Jefferson, T. (2000) *Doing Qualitative Research Differently* (London: Sage).

Home Office. (2001a) *Criminal Injuries Compensation Scheme 2001*, Issue Number One 4/01 (London: HMSO)

Home Office. (2001b) *A Review of the Victim's Charter* (London: HMSO).

Home Office. (2001c) *Measures to Assist Vulnerable or Intimidated Witnesses in the Criminal Justice System* (London: HMSO).

Home Office. (2003a) *Improving Public Satisfaction and Confidence in the Criminal Justice System Framework Document* (London: Home Office, July).

Home Office. (2003b) *Prison Statistics England & Wales – 2002*. Command Paper M5996 (London: HMSO).

Home Office. (2003c) *A New Deal for Victims & Witnesses: National Strategy to Deliver* (London: Home Office).

Home Office. (2003d) Civil Renewal: A New Agenda (Based on the Home Secretary's Scarman Lecture Delivered at the Citizens' Convention 11th December London: HMSO).

Home Office. (2004a) *Population in Custody England and Wales Monthly Tables* (London: Home Office http://www.homeoffice.gov.uk/rds/index.htm).

Home Office. (2004b) *Compensation and Support for Victims of Crime* (London: HMSO).

Home Office Communication Directorate. (2001) *A Review of the Victim's Charter* (London: HMSO).

Hooks, B. (1982) *Ain't I a Woman: Black Women and Feminism* (London: Pluto Press).

Hough, M. and Mayhew, P. (1983) *The British Crime Survey: First Report* (London: HMSO).

Howarth G. and Rock, P. (2000) 'Aftermath and the Construction of Victimisation: The Other Victims of Crime', *The Howard Journal of Criminal Justice*, Vol. 39 (1), pp. 58–78.

Hoyle, C. (1998) *Negotiating Domestic Violence* (Oxford: Clarendon Press).

Hoyle, C., Morgan, R. and Sanders, A. (1999) 'The Victim's Charter – An Evaluation of Pilot Projects', *Research Findings*, No. 107 (London: Home Office Research Development and Statistics Directorate).

Hume, M. (1998) *Televictims: Emotional Correctness in the Media AD (after Diana)* (London: InformInc LM Magazine).

Hunt, M. (2000) 'Status, Religion and the Belief in a Just World: Comparing African Americans, Latinos and Whites', *Social Science Quarterly*, Vol. 81, pp. 325–343.

Iganski, P. (2002) 'Introduction: The Problem of Hate Crimes and Hate Crime Laws', in P. Iganski (ed.) *The Hate Debate* (London: Profile Books Ltd), pp.1–14.

Indermaur, D. (1995) *Violent Property Crime* (Leichhardt NSW: The Federation Press).

Islamic Human Rights Commission. (2002) *The Hidden Victims of September 11th: The Backlash Against Muslims in the UK* (London: Islamic Human Rights Commission).

Jacobs, J. and Potter, K. (1998) *Hate Crimes: Criminal Law & Identity Politics* (New York: Oxford University Press).

James, O. (1997) *Britain on the Couch* (London: Century).

Janoff-Bulman, R. and Frieze, I. (1983) 'A Theoretical Perspective for Understanding Reactions to Victimisation' *Journal of Social Issues*, Vol. 39 (2), pp. 1–17.

Janoff-Bulman, R. (1985) 'Criminal Versus Non-criminal Victimisation: victims' Reactions', *Victimology: An International Journal*, Vol. 10 (1–4), pp. 498–511.

Jenness, V. (2002) 'Contours of Hate Crime Politics and Law in the US', in P. Iganski (ed.) *The Hate Debate* (London: Profile Books Ltd), pp. 15–35.

Johnstone, G. (2002) *Restorative Justice: Ideas, Values, Debates* (Cullompton: Willan).

Jones, T., MacLean, B. and Young, J. (1986) *The Islington Crime Survey* (Aldershot: Gower).

Jurgensen, G. (1999) *The Disappearance* (London: Flamingo).

Karmen, A. (1990) *Crime Victim: An Introduction to Victimology* (Belmont, CA: Wadsworth Publishing Company).

Karstedt, S. (2002) 'Emotions and Criminal Justice', *Theoretical Criminology*, Vol. 6 (3), pp. 29–317.

Katz, S. and Mazur, M. (1979) *Understanding the Rape Victim* (New York: John Wiley & Sons).

Kelly, L. (1988) *Surviving Sexual Violence* (Oxford: Polity Press).

Kelly, L., Burton, S. and Regan, L. (1994) 'Researching Women's Lives or Studying Women's Oppression? Reflections on What Constitutes Feminist Research', in M. Maynard and J. Purvis (eds) *Researching Women's Lives from a Feminist Perspective* (London: Taylor & Francis) pp. 27–48.

Kelly, D. and Erez, E. (1997) 'Victim Participation in the Criminal Justice System', in R. Davis, A. Lurigio and W. Skogan (eds) *Victims of Crime*, second edition (London: Sage), pp. 231–244.

Kennedy, J., Davis, R. and Taylor, B. (1998) 'Changes in Spirituality and Well-being Among Victims of Sexual Assault', *Journal of the Scientific Study of Religion*, Vol. 37 (2), pp. 322–328.

Kindermann, C., Lynch, J. and Cantor, D. (1997) 'Effects of the Redesign on Victimisation Estimates', *National Crime Victimization Survey* (Washington DC: US Department of Justice Bureau of Justice Statistics).

King, D. (1987) *The New Right: Politics, Markets and Citizenship* (London: Macmillan).

Kinsey, R. (1984) *Merseyside Crime and Policing Survey* (Merseyside: Merseyside County Council).

Kochan, N. and Whittington, B. (1991) *Bankrupt: The BCCI Fraud* (London: Gollancz).

Koffman, L. (1996) *Crime Surveys and Victims of Crime* (Cardiff: University of Wales Press, 1996).

Konradi, A. (1996) 'Preparing to Testify: Rape Survivors Negotiating the Criminal Justice Process' *Gender and Society*, Vol. 10 (1), pp. 404–452.

Kutash, I. (1978) 'Treating the Victim of Aggression', in I. Kutash and L. Schlesinger (eds) *Violence: Perspective on Murder and Aggression* (San Francisco: Jossey-Bass) pp. 50–68

Lamb, S. (ed) (1999) *New Versions of Victims* (New York: New York University Press).

Lasley, J. and Rosenbaum, J. (1988) 'Routine Activities and Multiple Personal Victimisation', *Sociology and Social Research*, Vol. 73 (1), pp. 47–16.

Laub, J. (1990) 'Patterns of Criminal Victimization in the United States', in A.J. Lurigio, W.G. Skogan, and R.C. Davis (eds) *Victims of Crime: Problems, Policies, and Programs* (London: Sage), pp. 23–49.

Lawrence, F. (2002) 'Racial Violence on a Small Island: Bias Crime in Multicultural Britain', in P.Iganski (ed.) *The Hate Debate* (London: Profile Books Ltd), pp. 36–53.

Lees, S. (1996) *Carnal Knowledge: Rape on Trial* (London: Penguin Books).

Lees, S. (1999) 'The Accused', *The Guardian*, Monday 1 March.

Lerner, M. (1980) *The Belief in a Just World: A Fundamental Delusion* (New York: Plenum).

Levi, M. (1987) *Regulating Fraud: White-Collar Crime and The Criminal Process* (London: Tavistock Publications).

Levi, M. and Pithouse, A. (1992) 'The Victims of Fraud', in D. Downes (ed.) *Unravelling Criminal Justice* (London: Macmillan Press Ltd), pp. 229–246.

Lewis, B. and Ramazanoglu, C. (1999) 'Not Guilty, Not Proud, Just White: Women's Accounts of Their Whiteness', in: H. Brown, M. Gilkes and A. Kaloski-Naylor (eds) *White? Women* (York: Raw Nerve Books), pp. 23–62.

Lewis, M. and Sarrell, P. (1969) 'Some Psychological Aspects of Seduction, Incest and Rape in Childhood', *Journal of the American Academy of Child Psychiatry*, Vol. 8, pp. 607–619.

Lurigio, A. and Resick, P. (1990) 'Healing the Psychological Wounds of Criminal Victimisation: Predicting Postcrime Distress and Recovery', in A. Lurigio, W. Skogan and R. Davis (eds) *Victims of Crime: Problems, Policies and Programs* (London: Sage), pp. 50–68.

MacDonald, J. (1971) *Rape Offenders and their Victims* (Springfield III: Thomas).

Macpherson, W. (1999) *The Stephen Lawrence Report* (London: HMSO).

Maguire, M. (1982) *Burglary in a Dwelling: The Offence, The Offender and The Victim* (London: Heinemann).

Maguire, M. and Pointing, J. (eds) (1988) *Victims of Crime: A New Deal?* (Milton Keynes: Open University Press).

Maguire, M. and Shapland, J. (1997) 'Provision for Victims in an International Context', in R. Davis, A. Lurigio and W. Skogan (eds) *Victims of Crime*, second edition (London: Sage) pp. 211–230.

Mama, A. (2000) 'Woman Abuse in London's Black Communities' in K. Owusu (ed.) *Black British Culture & Society* (London: Routledge), pp. 89–110.

Marshall, A. (1983) *Changing the Word: the Printing Industry in Transition* (London: Comedia Publishing Group).

Masters, G. (2002) 'Family Group Conferencing: A Victim Perspective', in B. Williams (ed.) *Reparation and Victim-focused Social Work* (London: Jessica Kingsley), pp. 45–65.

Mason, A. and Palmer, A. (1996) *A National Survey of Hate Crimes Against Lesbians and Gay Men* (London: Stonewall).

Matthews, R. and Young, J. (1992) 'Reflections on Realism', in J. Young and R. Matthews (eds) *Rethinking Criminology: The realist debate* (London: Sage), pp. 1–23.

Mawby, R. (2001) *Burglary* (Cullompton: Willan).

Mawby, R. and Colston, N. (1979) *Crime and the Elderly: A Report Prepared for Age Concern* (Bradford: Bradford University Press).

Mawby, R. and Walklate, S. (1994) *Critical Victimology* (London: Sage).

Mayhew, P. (2000) 'Researching the State of Crime: Local, National and International Victim Surveys', in R. King and E. Wincup (eds) *Doing Research on Crime and Justice* (Oxford: Oxford University Press), pp. 91–120.

Mayhew, P., Aye Maung, N. and Mirrlees-Black, C. (1993) *The 1992 British Crime Survey* (London: HMSO).

Mayhew, P., Elliott, D. and Dowds, L. (1989) *The 1988 British Crime Survey*, Home Office Research Study No.111 (London: HMSO).

Mayhew, P. and Hough, M. (1988) 'The British Crime Survey: Origins and Impact', in M.Maguire and J.Pointing (eds) *Victims of Crime: a new deal?* (Milton Keynes: Open University Press), pp. 156–163.

McCabe, S. and Sutcliffe, F. (1978) *Defining Crime* (Oxford: Blackwell).

McClaurin, I. (2001) 'Theorizing a Black Feminist Self in Anthropology: Toward an Auto Ethnographic Approach', in I. McClaurin (ed.) *Black Feminist Anthropology* (London: Rutgers University Press), pp. 49–76.

McManus, J. (2001) *Friends or Strangers? Faith Communities and Community Safety* (London: NACRO).

McNeill, S. (1987) 'Flashing: Its Effect on Women', in J. Hanmer and M. Mayner (eds) *Women, Violence and Social Control* (London: Macmillan), pp. 93–109.

McShane, M. and Williams, F. (1992) 'Radical Victimology: A Critique of the Concept of Victim in Traditional Victimology', *Crime & Delinquency*, Vol. 38 (2), pp. 258–271.

McVeigh, R., Welch, M. and Bjarnason, T. (2003) 'Hate Crime Reporting as a Successful Social Movement Outcome', *American Sociological Review*, Vol. 68 (December), pp. 843–867.

McVicar, J. (1982) 'Violence in Prisons', in P. Marsh and A. Campbell (eds) *Aggression and Violence* Oxford: (Basil Blackwell) pp. 200–214.

Mendelsohn, B. (1956) 'A New Branch of Bio-psychological Science: la victimology', *Revue Internationale de Criminologie et de Police Technique*, No. 2.

Mezey, G. (1988) 'Reactions to Rape: Effects, Counselling and The Role of Health Professionals', in M. Maguire and J. Pointing (eds) *Victims of Crime: A New Deal?* (Milton Keynes: Open University Press (1983)), pp. 66–73.

Miller, D. and Porter, C. (1983) 'Self-blame in Victims of Violence', *Journal of Social Issues*, Vol. 39 (2), pp. 139–152.

Miller, P. and Rose, N. (1993) 'Governing Economic Life', in M. Gane and T. Johnson (eds) *Foucault's New Domains* (London: Routledge), pp. 75–105.

Mirrlees-Black, C. and Budd, T. (1997) 'Findings from the 1996 British Crime Survey', *Research Findings*, No.60 (London: HMSO).

Mirrlees-Black, C. and Ross, E. (1995) 'Findings from the Commercial Victimisation Survey 1994', *Home Office Research Study*, 146 (London: Home Office).

Mirrlees-Black, C., Mayhew, P. and Percy, A. (1997) *The 1996 British Crime Survey* (London: HMSO).

Mirrlees-Black, C., Budd, T., Partridge, S. and Mayhew, P. (1998) *The 1998 British Crime Survey* (London: HMSO).

Miers, D. (1989) 'Positivist Victimology: A Critique', *International Review of Victimology* Vol.1 (1), pp. 3–22.

Mirza, H. (1997) 'Introduction: Mapping a Genealogy of Black British Feminism' in H.Mirza (ed.) *Black British Feminism: A Reader* (London: Routledge), pp.1–28.

Modood, T. (2003) 'Muslims and the politics of difference', *Political Quarterly*, 74 (1), pp. 100–115.

Mokhiber, R. (1998) *Corporate Crime & Violence* (San Francisco: Sierra Club Books).

Moore, E. and Mills, M. (1990) 'The Neglected Victims and Unexamined costs of White-collar Crime', *Crime & Delinquency*, Vol. 36, No. 3, pp. 408–418.

Morgan, J. (2002) 'US Hate Crime Legislation: A Legal Model to Avoid in Australia', *Journal of Sociology*, Vol. 38 (1), pp. 25–48.

Morell, C. (1996) 'Radicalising Recovery: Addiction, Spirituality and Politics', *Social Work*, vol. 41 (3), pp. 306–12.

Morrison, W. (1995) *Theoretical Criminology: From Modernity to Post-Modernism* (London: Cavendish Publishing Limited).

Moss, L. (2004) *Domestic Abuse and Homeopathy* (Birmingham: Birmingham School of Homeopathy).

Myhill, A. and Allen, J. (2002) 'Rape and Sexual Assault of Women: The Extent and Nature of the Problem. Findings from the British Crime Survey', *Home Office Research Study*, 237 (London: HMSO).

National Association of Victim Support Schemes. (2003) *Insult to Injury: How the Criminal Injuries Compensation System is Failing Victims of Crime* (London: NAVSS).

National Census (2001) 'Ethnicity and Religion' http://www.statistics.gov.uk/cci/nugget.asp?id=395

Nelken, D.(1994) *The Futures of Criminology* (London: Sage).

Neville, H., Oh, E., Spanierman, L., Heppner, M. and Clark, M. (2004) 'General and Culturally Specific Factors Influencing Black and White Rape Survivors' Self-esteem, *Psychology of Women Quarterly*, Vol. 28, pp. 83–94.

Newburn, T. and Merry, S. (1990) 'Keeping in Touch – Police–Victim Communication in Areas', *Home Office Research Study*, 116 (London: HMSO).

Newburn, T. and Stanko, E. (1994) 'When Men are Victims', in T. Newburn and E. Stanko (eds) *Just Boys Doing Business?* (London: Routledge), pp. 153–165.

Norris, J. and Feldman-Summers, S. (1981) 'Factors Related to the Psychological Impacts of Rape on the Victim' *Journal of Abnormal Psychology*, Vol. 90 (6) pp. 562–567.

Nuttall, M. (1997) *It Could Have Been You* (London: Virago).

Oakley, A. (1981)'Interviewing Women: A Contradiction in Terms', in H. Roberts (ed.) *Doing Feminist Research* (London: Routledge), pp. 30–61.

O'Beirne, M. (2004) *Religion in England and Wales: Findings from the 2001 Home Office Citizenship Survey* (London: Home Office).

O'Malley, P. (1992) 'Risk, Power and Crime Prevention', *Economy and Society*, Vol. 21 (3), pp. 253–275.

Palmer, C., McNulty, A., D'Este, C. and Donovan, B. (2004) 'Genital Injuries in Women Reporting Sexual Assault', *Sexual Health*, March, Vol. 1 (1), pp. 55–59.

Passas, N. (1996) 'The Genesis of the BCCI scandal', *Journal of Law and Society*, Vol. 23, pp. 57–72.

Pearce, F. and Tombs, S. (1992) 'Realism and Corporate Crime', in R. Matthews and J. Young (eds) *Issues in Realist Criminology* (London: Sage), pp. 70–101.

Pease, K., Lloyd, S. and Farrell, G. (1994) *Preventing Repeat Domestic Violence: A Demonstration Project on Merseyside*, Crime Prevention Unit Series, 49 (London: HMSO).

Pease, K. (1998) *Repeat Victimisation: Taking Stock* Crime Detection & Prevention Series, 90 (London: HMSO).

Penal Affairs Consortium. (1996) *Race and Criminal Justice* (London: NACRO).

Perloff, L. (1983) 'Perceptions of Vulnerability to Victimisation', *Journal of Social Issues*, Vol. 39 (2), pp. 41–61.

Peters, J. (1976) 'Children Who are Victims of Sexual Assault and the psychology of Offenders', *American Journal of Psychotherapy*, Vol. 30, pp. 398–421.

Phillips, C. and Bowling, B. (2003) 'Racism, Ethnicity and Criminology: Developing Minority Perspectives', *British Journal of Criminology*, Vol. 43, pp. 269–290.

Pickering, S. (2001) 'Undermining the Sanitised account; violence and emotionality in the field in Northern Ireland', *British Journal of Criminology*, Vol. 41, pp. 485–501.

President's Commission on Law Enforcement and Administration of Justice. (1967) *The Challenge of Crime in a Free Society* (Washington DC: United States Government Printing Office).

Prime, D., Zimmeck, M. and Zurawan, A. (2001) *Active Communities: Initial Findings from The 2001 Home Office Citizenship Survey* (London: HMSO).

Quinney, R. (1980) *Class, State & Crime: Second Edition* (New York: Longman).

Radford, J. (1992) 'Womanslaughter: A Licence to Kill? The Killing of Jane Asher', in J. Radford and D. Russell (eds) *The Politics of Killing* (Buckingham: Open University Press), pp. 253–266.

Reiman, J. (1979) *The Rich Get Richer and the Poor Get Prison* (New York: John Wiley).

Resick, P. (1990) 'Victims of Sexual Assault', in A. Lurigio, W. Skogan and R. Davis (eds) *Victims of Crime: Problems, Policies and Programs* (London: Sage), pp. 69–86.

Richie, B. (2003) 'Gender Entrapment and African–American Women: An Analysis of Race, Ethnicity, Gender and Intimate Violence', in D. Hawkins (ed.) *Violent Crime: Assessing Race and Ethnic Differences* (Cambridge: Cambridge University Press), pp. 198–210.

Riggs, D. and Kilpatrick, D. (1990) 'Families and Friends: Indirect Victimisation by Crime', in A. Lurigio, W. Skogan and R. Davis (eds) *Victims of Crime: Problems, Policies and Programs* (London: Sage), pp. 120–138.

Ringham, L. and Salisbury, H. (2004) *Support for Victims of Crime: Findings from the 2002/2003 British Crime Survey*, Home Office Online Report 31/04.

Roberts, B. (2002) *Biographical Research* (Buckingham: Open University Press).

Rock, P. (1998) 'Murderers, Victims and Survivors', *British Journal of Criminology*, Vol. 38 (2), pp.185–200.

Rock, P. (2002) 'On Becoming a Victim', in C. Hoyle and R. Young (eds) *New Visions of Crime Victims* (Oxford: Hart Publishing) pp. 1–22.

Russell, D. (1975) *The Politics of Rape* (New York: Stein and Day).

Russell, D. (1982) *Sexual Exploitation: Rape, Child Sexual Abuse, and Workplace Harassment* (London: Sage).

Russell, D. (1990) *Rape in Marriage* (Indiana: Indiana University Press).

Said, E. (1978) *Orientalism* (Harmondsworth: Pengiun Books).

Sales, E., Baum, M. and Shore, B. (1984) 'Victim Readjustment Following Assault', *Journal of Social Issues*, Vol. 40, No.1, pp. 117–136.

Scharff Smith, P. (2004) 'A Religious Technology of the Self', *Punishment & Society*, Vol. 6 (2), pp. 195–220.

Scheppele, K. and Bart, P. (1983) 'Through Women's Eyes: Defining Danger in the Wake of Sexual Assault', *Journal of Social Issues*, Vol. 39, No.2, pp. 63–81.

Schwendinger, H. and Schwendinger, J. (1975) 'Defenders of Order or Guardians of Human Rights?', in Ian Taylor, Paul Walton and, Jock Young (eds) *Critical Criminology* (London, Routledge) pp. 123–157.

Sebba, L. (2001) 'On the Relationship Between Criminological Research and Policy: The Case of Crime Victims', *Criminal Justice*, Vol. 1 (1), pp. 27–58.

Shapland, J., Willmore, J. and Duff, P. (1985) *Victims in the Criminal Justice System* (Aldershot: Gower Publishing Company).

Sharp, D. (2002) 'Policing after Macpherson: Some Experiences of Muslim Police Officers', in B. Spalek (ed.) *Islam, Crime & Criminal Justice* (Cullompton: Willan) pp. 76–93.

Sheridan, L., Gillett, R., Blaauw, E. and Winkel, F.W. (2003) *Effects of the Events of September 11th on Discrimination and Implicit Racism in Five Religious and Seven Ethnic Groups*, paper presented at the University of Leicester, School of Psychology.

Shichor, D. (1989) 'Corporate Deviance and Corporate Victimisation: A Review and some elaborations', *International Review of Victimology*, Vol. 1, pp. 67–88.

Shorter-Gooden, K. (2004) 'Multiple resistance strategies: how African–American women cope with racism and sexism', *Journal of Black Psychology*, Vol. 30 (3), pp. 406–425.

Shover, N., Fox, G. and Mills, M. (1994) 'Long-Term Consequences of Victimisation by White-collar Crime', *Justice Quarterly*, Vol. 11, pp. 213–240.

Silver, R., Boon, C. and Stones, M. (1983) 'Searching for Meaning in Misfortune: Making Sense of Incest', *Journal of Social Issues*, Vol. 39, No. 2, pp. 81–102.

Silver, R. and Wortman, C. (1980) 'Coping with Undesirable Life Events', in J. Garber and M. Seligman (eds) *Human Helplessness* (New York: Academic Press).

Sim, J., Scraton, P. and Gordon, P. (1987)'Introduction: Crime, the State and Critical Analysis', in Scraton, P. (ed.) *Law, Order and the Authoritarian State* (Milton Keynes: Open University Press) pp. 1–70.

Simon, J. (1988) 'The Ideological Effects of Actuarial Practices', *Law & Society Review*, Vol. 22 (4), pp. 771–800.

Singer, S. (1981) 'Homogeneous Victim-Offender Populations: A Review and Some Research Implications', *The Journal of Criminal Law & Criminology*, Vol. 72 (2), pp. 779–789.

Slater, S. (1995) *Beyond Fear* (London: Fourth Estate).

Smart, B. (1992) *Modern Conditions, Post-modern Controversies* (London: Routledge).

Smiljanic, N. (2002) 'Human Rights and Muslims in Britain', in: B. Spalek (ed.) *Islam, Crime and Criminal Justice* (Cullompton: Willan), pp. 118–132.

Smith, S. (1982) 'Victimisation in the Inner City', *The British Journal of Criminology*, Vol. 22 (1), pp. 386–402.

Smith, D. (1997) 'Ethnic Origins, Crime and Criminal Justice', in M. Maguire, R. Morgan and R. Reiner (eds) *The Oxford Handbook of Criminology*, Second Edition (Oxford: Oxford University Press), pp. 703–759.

Snider, L. (1991) 'The Regulatory Dance: Understanding Reform Process in Corporate Crime', International Journal of the *Sociology of Law*, Vol. 19, pp. 209–236.

Snider, L. (2002) 'The Sociology of Corporate Crime: An Obituary (Or: Whose Knowledge Claims Have Legs?), *Theoretical Criminology*, Vol. 4 (2) pp. 169–206.

Spalek, B. (1999) 'Exploring Victimisation: A Study Looking at the Impact of the Maxwell Scandal upon the Maxwell Pensioners', *International Review of Victimology*, Vol. 6, pp. 213–230.

Spalek, B. (2001) 'White Collar Crime and Secondary Victimisation, an analysis of the effects of the closure of BCCI', *The Howard Journal of Criminal Justice*, Vol. 40 (2), pp. 166–179.

Spalek, B. (2002) 'Muslim Women's Safety Talk and their Experiences of Victimisation: A Study Exploring Specificity and Difference', in B. Spalek (ed.) *Islam, Crime and Criminal Justice* (Cullompton: Willan), pp. 50–71.

Spalek, B. (2004) 'Victim Work in the Probation Service', in W. Chui and M. Nellis (eds) *Moving Probation Forward* (London: Pearson), pp. 214–225.

Spalek, B. (2004) 'Policing Financial Crime: the FSA and the Myth of the Duped Investor', in R. Hopkins-Burke (ed.) *Hard Cop/Soft Cop: Dilemmas and Debates in Contemporary Policing* (Cullompton: Willan) pp.163–174.

Spalek, B. (2005a) 'British Muslims and the Criminal Justice System', in T. Choudhury (ed.) *Muslims in the UK: Policies for Engaged Citizens* (Budapest: Open Society Institute), pp. 253–340.

Spalek, B. (2005b) 'A Critical Reflection on Researching Black Muslim Women's Lives Post September 11th', The *International Journal of Social Research Methodology*, Vol. 8 (5), pp. 1–14.

Sparks, R., Genn, H. and Dodd, D. (1977) *Surveying Victims* (Chichester: John Wiley).

Stanko, E. (1985) *Intimate Intrusions: Women's Experience of Male Violence* (London: Routledge).

Stanko, E. (1988) 'Hidden Violence Against Women', in J. Pointing and M. Maguire (eds) *Victims of Crime: A New Deal ?* (Milton Keynes: Open University Press), pp. 40–46.

Stanko, E. (1990) *Everyday Violence: Women's Mad Men's Experience of Personal Danger* (London: Pandora Press).

Stanko, E. and Hobdell, K. (1993) 'Assault on Men', *The British Journal Criminology*, Vol. 33 (3), pp.400–540.

Stark, E. (2003) 'Race, Gender and Woman Battering', in D. Hawkins (ed.) *Violent Crime: Assessing Race and Ethnic Differences* (Cambridge: Cambridge University Press) pp. 171–197.

Steinberg, S. H. (1996) *Five Hundred Years of Printing* (London: The British Library).

Sutherland, E. (1949) *White-Collar Crime* (New York: Holt, Rinehart & Winston).

Swanbrow, D. (1997) 'Worldwide rates of Religiosity and Church Attendance' (Michigan: University of Michigan News and Information Services). http://www.umich.edu/news/index.html? Releases/1997/Dec 97/chr 121097a

Sykes, C. (1992) *A Nation of Victims: The Decay of the American Character* (New York: St Martin's Press).

Tatchell, P. (2002) 'Some People are More Equal than Others', in P. Iganski (ed.) *The Hate Debate* (London: Profile Books Ltd), pp. 54–70.

Taylor, S. Wood, J. and Lichtman, R. (1983) 'It Could be Worse: Selective Evaluation as a Response to Victimisation', *Journal of Social Issues*, Vol. 39, pp. 19–40.

Titus, R., Heinzelmann, F. and Boyle, J. (1995) 'Victimisation of persons by fraud', *Crime & Delinquency*, Vol. 41 (1), pp. 54–72.

Tombs, S. (2000) 'Official Statistics and Hidden Crime: Researching Safety Crimes, in V. Jupp, P. Davies and P. Francis (eds) *Doing Criminological Research* (London: Sage), pp. 64–81.

1990 Trust Human Rights for Race Equality, Black information link website, http://www.blink.org.uk/pdescription.asp?key=4804&grp=55&cat=163, accessed on 23 November 2004.

Tudor, B. (2002) 'Probation Work with Victims of Crime', in B. Williams (ed.) *Reparation and Victim-Focused Social Work* (London: Jessica Kingsley), pp. 130–145.

Upson, A. (2004) *Violence At Work: Findings From the 2002/2003 British Crime Survey*, London: Home Office Online Report, 04/04.

US Department of Justice. (2000) *Attorney General Guidelines for Victim and Witness Assistance* (Washington DC: Office of the Attorney General).

US Department of Justice. (2001) *National Victim Assistance Academy Special Topics Hate and Bias Crime*, http://www.ojp.gov/ovc/assist/nvaa2001/chapter22_1.html (2001), accessed on 11/11/2004.

US Department of Justice Office for Victims of Crime. (2002) *Responding to Terrorism Victims: Oklahoma City and Beyond* (Washington DC: Office of the Attorney General).

Valenti, K. (2003) 'Others want in on Sept 11 fund', *The Journal News*, 9 September.

Victim Support. (1995) *The Rights of Victims of Crime: A Policy Paper by Victim Support* (London: National Association of Victim Support Schemes).

Victim Support. (2001) *New Rights for Victims of crime in Europe: Council Framework Decision on the Standing of Victims in Criminal Proceedings* (London: National Association of Victim Support Schemes).

Victim Support. (2002a) *Victim Support Annual Review 2002* (London: National Association of Victim Support Schemes).

Victim Support. (2002b) *Criminal Neglect: No Justice Beyond Criminal Justice* (London: National Association of Victim Support Schemes).

Victim Support. (2002c) *Criminal Neglect: No Justice Beyond Criminal Justice* (London: National Association of Victim Support Schemes).

Victim Support. (2003a) *Annual Report and Accounts for the year ended March 31 2003* (London: National Association of Victim Support Schemes).

Victim Support. (2003b) *Annual Review 2003* (London: National Association of Victim Support Schemes).

Victim Support. (2003c) *Insult to Injury: How the Criminal Injuries Compensation System is Failing Victims of Crime* (London: National Association of Victim Support Schemes).

The Virtual Chase (2005) What's New Archive for January 2005 http://www.Virtual chase.com/newjanos.html.

Walklate, S. (1989) *Victimology. The Victim and the Criminal Justice Process* (London: Unwin Hyman Ltd).

Walklate, S. (1992) 'Appreciating the Victim: Conventional, Realist or Critical Victimology ?', in J. Young and R. Matthews (eds) *Issues in Realist Criminology* (London: Sage), pp. 102–118.

Walklate, S. (2001) *Gender, Crime and Criminal Justice* (Cullompton: Willan).

Walklate, S. (2002)'So who are the victims now?', *British Journal of Community Justice*, Vol. 1 (1), pp. 47–63.

Watson, H. (1994) 'Women and the Veil: Personal Responses to Global Processes', in A. Ahmed and H. Donnan (eds) *Islam, Globalisation and Postmodernity* (London: Routledge) pp. 141–159.

Webster, C. (1995) 'Youth Crime, Victimisation and Racial Harassment', *Community Studies* No.7, revised edition (Ilkley: Centre for Research in Applied Community Studies, Bradford and Ilkley Community College).

Weller, P., Feldman, A. and Purdam, K. (2001) 'Religious Discrimination in England and Wales', *Home Office Research Study* 220 (London: HMSO).

Wertham, F. (1949) *The Show of Violence* (New York: Doubleday).

Wetherall, M. (1996) 'Life Histories/Social Histories', in M. Wetherell (ed.) *Identities Groups and Social Issues* (Milton Keynes: The Open University Press) pp. 299–361.

Williams, B. (1999a) *Working with Victims of Crime* (London: Jessica Kingsley).

Williams, B. (1999b) 'The Victim's Charter: Citizens as Consumers of Criminal Justice Services', *The Howard Journal of Criminal Justice*, Vol. 38 (4), pp. 384–396.

Williams, B. (2003) 'Community Justice, Victims and Social Justice', Inaugural Lecture 27 March, DeMontfort University.

Williams, P. (1997) 'Spirit-Murdering the Messenger: The Discourse of Finger Pointing as the Law's Response to Racism', in A. Wing (ed.) *Critical Race Feminism: A Reader* (New York: New York University Press), pp. 229–236.

Williams, S. and Bendelow, G. (1998) *The Lived Body: Sociological Themes, Embodied Issues* (London: Routledge).

Winter, J. (2002) 'The Trial of Rose West: Contesting Notions of Victimhood', in: C. Hoyle and R. Young (eds) *New Visions of Crime Victims* (Oxford: Hart Publishing) pp. 173–196.

Wolfgang, M. (1958) *Patterns in Criminal Homicide* (New York: New York University Press).

Woodward, K. (1997) 'Concepts of Identity and Difference', in K. Woodward (ed.) *Identity and Difference* (London: Sage), pp. 7–62.

Wortman, C., Battle, E. and Lemkau, J. (1997) 'Coming to Terms with the Sudden, Traumatic Death of a Spouse or Child', in R. Davis, A. Lurigio and W. Skogan (eds) *Victims of Crime* second edition (London: Sage), pp. 108–133.

Wortman, C. (1983) 'Coping with Victimisation: Conclusions and Implications for Future Research', *Journal of Social Issues*, Vol. 39 (2) pp. 195–221.

Yarrow, S. (2005) *The Experiences of Young Black Men as Victims of Crime* (London: Office for Criminal Justice Reform).

Young, J. (1986) 'The Failure of Criminology: The Need for a Radical Realism', in R. Matthews and J. Young (eds) *Confronting Crime* (London: Sage) pp. 4–30.

Young, J. (1994) 'Incessant Chatter: Recent Paradigms In Criminology', in M. Maguire, R. Morgan and R. Reiner (eds) *The Oxford Handbook of Criminology* (Oxford: Oxford University Press) pp. 69–124.

Young, J. (1999) *The Exclusive Society: Social Exclusion, Crime and Difference in Late Modernity* (London: Sage)

Young, J. and Matthews, R. (1992) 'Questioning Left Realism', in R. Matthews and J. Young (eds) *Issues in Realist Criminology* (London: Sage) pp. 1–18.

Young, R. (2000) 'Integrating a Multi-Victim Perspective into CJ Through Restorative Justice Conferences', in A.Crawford and J.Goodey (eds) *Integrating a Victim Perspective within Criminal Justice* (Aldershot: Ashgate), pp. 227–252.

Zedner, L. (1994) 'Victims', in M. Maguire, R. Morgan and R. Reiner (eds) *The Oxford Handbook of Criminology* (Oxford: Clarendon Press), pp. 1207–1246.

Zedner, L. (2002) 'Victims', in M. Maguire, R. Morgan and R. Reiner (eds) *The Oxford Handbook of Criminology* (Oxford: Clarendon Press, third edition), pp. 419–456.

Index